The Competent Leader

19 Critical Skills
Any Manager or Supervisor Must Know

Peter Stark
Jane Flaherty

HRD Press, Inc. ❖ Amherst ❖ Massachusetts

Published by: HRD Press, Inc.
                 22 Amherst Road
                 Amherst, MA 01002
                 800-822-2801 (U.S. and Canada)
                 413-253-3488
                 413-253-3490 (fax)
                 http://www.hrdpress.com

ISBN 978-1-59996-232-0

Production services by Jean Miller
Editorial services by Sally M. Farnham
Cover design by Eileen Klockars

Table of Contents

Shea Homes
Sony
St. Paul's Sr. Homes & Services
3 Rivers Federal Credit Union
Torrey Pines Bank
Toshiba America Information Systems
USE Credit Union
Vantage West Credit Union
Vessey & Company
WD-40
Websense
Wells Fargo Home Mortgage
Western Alliance Bancorp
Western Growers Association

Preface

No matter how you arrived at your position as a supervisor, you now need a whole additional set of skills in order to work successfully with your employees. Feeling positive about yourself, making decisions, and solving problems will still be a part of your daily life, but you will now also need to add the significant and challenging leadership skills of communicating, delegating, coaching, motivating, hiring, and leading.

In your supervisory role, one big difference is that your achievement will now be measured in terms of the performance of your staff. Knowing how to work well with your employees will increase your department's effectiveness. Your employees may turn out to be your most valuable support system as you grow increasingly stronger in your leadership role.

The Competent Leader outlines and describes the skills you will need to become an even stronger and more competent supervisor and manager. This book is for those of you who want to not only survive in today's competitive business environment, but thrive.

Introduction

For the past 30 years, we have had the opportunity to read hundreds of books on leadership, supervision, and management. Each book contained ideas that we were able to use to expand our knowledge, as well as share with our clients. With so many leadership books readily available, we debated about completing a revised edition of our previous work, *The Competent Leader.* After much thought, we arrived at the following three reasons that motivated us to complete the rewrite and update of our original work.

First, we keep on learning. Each year, between the two of us, we interact with thousands of managers and employees. Just when we think we've heard it all, we encounter a new situation. We wanted to continue to share with you what we are learning on a daily basis, not from textbooks, but in the real world of work.

Second, supervision has gotten harder, not easier. We not only have a more diverse workforce than ever before, but we have four distinctly different generations, complete with significantly different values and approaches to work in our workforce. More than ever, a successful leader needs to be continually refining his or her "people skills." Most supervisors or managers who worked their way up into a position of leadership were promoted due to their technical expertise. To continue to be successful, they now need to "fine tune" their relationship-building skills. This book focuses heavily on the skills, strategies, and techniques needed to build strong, effective working relationships with your employees.

A final reason for the decision to rewrite the book is that we wanted to write a book that supervisors would want to read and not see as just another textbook that they were forced to read. You will find each chapter light on theory and full of practical suggestions that work. Each of the chapters is a standalone "read," meaning, if you've got a challenging employee coming to your office in 15 minutes, and you plan to give some constructive feedback to that employee, you can quickly turn to the chapter on Coaching to Improve Performance. A quick review of the key concepts and a final look at the 10 tips at the end of the chapter will boost your confidence and enhance your coaching skill set. Although the reading is intended to be easy, building the skills and going through the associated growth process described in each chapter will be challenging. It will take commitment and hard work on your part.

As you begin reading, you will note that we use the terms *supervisor* and *manager* interchangeably. Our reasoning for doing so is two-fold. First, we have found little consistency in how organizations decide whether someone is a manager or a supervisor. In one organization, a person with certain responsibilities may be called a supervisor, but in another organization, a person with the same responsibilities may be called a manager, or even a vice president. Some vice presidents in some organizations don't even have employees reporting to them. The second reason we overlap the terms is that we believe that although the responsibilities may be significantly different, the people-related skills are the same.

As we share our ideas with you, it is important to see this book for what it is: insight from two consultants on the skills needed to be a great supervisor or manager. We are the first to agree that the information will not work in every situation. You will have to adapt the material to meet your unique needs and situations. At the same time, we are also convinced that if managers and supervisors apply the skills we have described, they will eliminate about 90 percent of the consulting work done in most organizations!

The skills presented here will work *if* you are willing to learn and then practice them. If you are willing to invest the time to read, as well as the skill-building practice on the job, we promise that you will be proud of the results. You and your employees will not only accomplish more, everyone will gain more enjoyment from working together. We wish you great success!

Chapter 1

Understanding the Changing Role of Supervision

"Predicting the future is easy. It's trying to figure out what's going on now that's hard."

— Fritz R. S. Dressler

Each year, the authors coach, train, and mentor hundreds of leaders involved with organizations as large and diverse as the Department of Defense and as small as entrepreneurial start-up companies. Ranging in age from their early 20s to their late 80s, these leaders provide insight into the methods used by a wide range of supervisors and managers.

Some supervisors have been truly inspirational; others admitted the need for improvement; and still others were in a state of denial, believing any and all problems were caused by someone else—namely, "the employees." A bewildered manager recently said in one of our seminars, "Did the whole world change and I didn't get it?" Simply put, yes, the whole world did change, and seasoned managers, those with 20 to 30 years of experience, unanimously agree on one issue: the role of the 21st-century manager and the skills required to get the job done today are significantly different from the role of the supervisor/manager as recently as 20 years ago.

Typically, people are promoted into supervisory roles based on their technical expertise. Some newly appointed supervisors make a smooth transition into leadership. Others stumble and experience multiple challenges with managing people. In addition to technical expertise, to be successful in a leadership role today, the manager or supervisor needs a whole new skill set based on being "people smart."

Why do leaders need to be "people smart"? No doubt you earned your leadership role by honing your technical expertise, working harder than most, and being loyal and committed to management and the success of your organization. Your organization recognized your talent and promoted you, giving you a supervisory title. However, when you were promoted, they forgot to tell you that supervisory title is not a guarantee for your success as a leader. With your title comes a degree of authority, but no assurance that your employees will get the job done. Effective leadership is all about a good working relationship between the employees and the

1

boss. Your title gives you authority, but it's the working relationship you've got with your employees that gives you the power. The test of leadership is whether you have followers—people who are willing to do whatever it takes to ensure you and your team's success.

In past decades, just having a supervisory title was enough to ensure that you had your employees' attention and respect, and the job would get done. Those days are over. Today, due to a wide range of environmental and economic changes, the role of supervisor has changed substantially, requiring a whole new leadership skill set. This chapter reviews some of the reasons that contribute to this changing role.

Workforce Composition Changes

The composition of the American workforce continues to change. Several major trends have contributed to this new workforce.

There are more women in the workforce. In the past 50 years, the most significant change in our workforce has been the number of women on the job. In 1960, less than 40 percent of women in the United States worked outside the home. Today, laws protecting women's rights in the workplace, coupled with genuine financial necessity, have allowed women to gain an increasing foothold in the business world. According to the *Population Bulletin*'s 2008 edition of U.S. labor trends,[1] nearly 60 percent of all American women hold a job. The majority of new workforce entrants will be women and minorities. At the time this book was published, women made up slightly more than half of the composition of the American workforce.

The average age of the workforce is increasing. Between 2010 and 2030, workers who are 55 and older are projected to make up 23 percent of the workforce, compared to only 13 percent in 2000. In 2008, the first of the Baby Boomers were eligible for retirement. Given their general good health and the recession of 2008–2010, less than expected numbers of Boomers left the workforce. Many Boomers have had to significantly alter their retirement plans and will continue working until the economy improves. Never before has such a large segment of our workforce been so near to retirement age, potentially posing a significant talent drain when they begin to retire in mass once the economy ramps up.

---

[1] Lee, M. A., & Mather, M. (June, 2008). U.S. labor force trends. *Population Bulletin, 63*(2).

The number of minorities in the workplace will continue to increase. By the year 2050, minority groups in the United States, especially Asians and Hispanics, will be less of a minority in the workforce than ever before. With the passage of each decade, immigration will continue to change the size and composition of the population and workforce. The rate of growth of the Hispanic population is expected to be greater than that of all other racial and ethnic groups. Hispanics constituted 12.9 percent of the civilian population in 2005 and are projected to increase their share to 23.2 percent by 2050. At that time, they will make up approximately 24 percent of the entire American workforce. (These statistics were obtained from the Bureau of Labor Statistics' long-term labor report[2] compiled in 2006.)

Entry-level workers are not prepared. A study of employers conducted by the Corporate Voices for Working Families in 2009[3] indicated that employees hired into entry-level jobs are not prepared to join the workforce. The study identified the three most important skills required for success in the 21st century as communication, professionalism, and problem solving. When asked how they would rate the preparation of recent students or graduates for entry level jobs, 37 percent of the employers said American workers are not very prepared; 34 percent said they were somewhat prepared; and 14 percent said they were very prepared.

These workforce trends make it even more difficult to be a successful supervisor. Aside from getting the job done, other issues arise: a worker who is older than the supervisor, a worker who does not understand English or does not read well, a worker who has more formal education than the manager, and coworkers who encounter cultural conflicts.

Changing Workforce Values

In addition to the composition of the American workforce changing significantly, the values of the workforce have undergone radical changes. One of the most striking ways to study how the role of the supervisor has changed over the past 50 years is to look at the values of the workers they supervise. A list of typical work values in the 1950s and 1960s is illustrated below, as well as some of the critical values of today's workforce. What a contrast!

---

[2] Lee, M. A., & Mather, M. (June, 2008). U.S. labor force trends. *Population Bulletin, 63*(2).

[3] Jewell, R. American workers and employers agree: new entry-level workers are not prepared for the 21st century workplace. *Corporate Voices.* (March 3rd, 2010).

Values of the Workforce: Past and Present

Values of the 1950s and 1960s Workforce	Values of Today's Workforce
Family	Benefits
Good craftsmanship	Concern for health
Happy to have a job	Education
Job stability	Flexible schedule/Need for time off
Loyalty to boss	Work/life balance
Loyalty to company	High concern for self
Patriotism	Desire meaningful work
Savings account	Input appreciated
Technical ability	Interesting work
	Open communication
	Opportunity to advance
	Personal growth
	Recognition

Even accounting for the 2008–2010 recession and its impact on unemployment, it is still clear that today's worker is no longer happy to have just any job. Today's workers want work to be meaningful and fun, and want to be recognized for their contributions. Occasionally, we hear frustrated managers say, "Workers today have no work ethic!" Typically, the manager, a Baby Boomer who worked long, hard hours to get where he or she is today, has difficulty understanding Gen X's and the Millennials' priorities, which include the need to be recognized, workplace flexibility, opportunity to move up, equality among team members, and an employer who recognizes the employee's need to have a balanced life.

This is the first time in American history that we have had four very different generations working side-by-side in the workplace. Although proportionately fewer in number, the Veterans, or "Silents" as they are sometimes called, born 1922–1945, make up the oldest component of our workforce. Following them are the Baby Boomers, born 1946–1964. Next to join the workforce was Generation X, born 1965–1976. Just arriving on the scene are Gen Y, or the Millennials, born 1977–1998.

Research abounds showing that people communicate with one another based on their generational backgrounds. Each generation joining the workforce brings with it distinct behaviors, attitudes, values, habits and different triggers that motivate them. For example, the topic of work/life balance is widely discussed these days. For the Veteran, it is a no brainer discussion. The job has always come first. For the

Boomer who lives to work, there is little empathy for workers demanding a life outside of work. For Gen X, the job serves a purpose: to ensure quality in one's life. Gen Xers work to live, not live to work. And, while the trends for the Millennials are still to be determined, this generation appears to also place a high value on achieving a work/life balance.

While there may be a tendency on the part of some Boomer or Veteran managers to discount Gen X's and the Millennials' values as being "soft," self-serving, or not loyal to the employer, taking a quick look at the facts will help us understand why today's workers are bringing with them a very different set of values.

First, we jokingly say employees today listen to radio station "W.I.I.F.M.," or "What's in it for me?" Workers are keenly interested in how much you pay and what benefits you offer. They see themselves as providing you, the employer, with a needed commodity and want to be fairly paid for what they offer. As we write this book, there are some harsh economic facts driving the financial concerns of Generation X and the Millennials:

- Unemployment among young male workers is the highest it has been in 61 years.

- U.S. workers spend an average of one month per year more working than they did 10 years ago, yet real wages have steadily declined since 1974.

- Home ownership may be unrealistic for many members of Generation X and the Millennials. The median price of a home (adjusted for inflation) has increased 78 percent in the past 30 years. Home ownership is at its lowest level in 50 years.

- About a third of American workers under age 35 live at home with their parents and are far less likely to have health-care insurance or job security than they were 10 years ago.

In addition to financial challenges, younger employees look to the future they will be inheriting and see an unsure economic future for organizations, global pollution, crime, immigration challenges, all leading to a sense of powerlessness. Experienced managers often see these skeptical employees as "negative" and "jaded," noting they don't share the same sense of optimism that the manager did when he or she started working.

Perhaps one of the most difficult aspects for today's manager, though, is this generation's lack of respect for authority and limited interest in titles. Gen Y was the first to grow up in an egalitarian home atmosphere. Both parent and child had rights and provided input into family affairs. Further, this was the first generation that spent long hours on their own, after school, waiting for parents to return home after

work. Divorce and single working moms created latchkey kids who were independent, resilient, and adaptable. The ability to fend for themselves has resulted in a
more self-reliant, autonomous employee. Gen Yers are being raised as the most
child-centric generation in the history of the United States. They've been showered
with attention and recognition for their achievements. They are technically the most
literate of all generations. They display deep-seated confidence in their abilities and
expect to be treated as an equal player from day one. Some display so much confidence that it is misread for arrogance or cockiness.

Based on historic workplace values, what skills did it take for supervisors prior
to the 1980s to effectively manage their workers? If the worker was loyal to the
boss, loyal to the company, and thankful to have a job, the skills needed to manage
might look like those outlined in the following chart.

Skills to Manage Employees: Past and Present

Supervisory Skills Needed: Historically	Supervisory Skills Needed: Today
Ability to control	Clarifying expectations
Delegation	Coaching and counseling
Directive	Communication
Problem solving	Confidence
Strong authority figure	Consulting
Technical expertise	Creativity
	Delegating
	Enabling
	Empowering
	Leadership
	Listening
	Mentoring
	Motivating
	Negotiation
	Organizing
	Problem solving
	Questioning
	Recognizing
	Team building

How is that for a list of what is required for supervisors to do their jobs effectively? One seminar participant stated, "You almost need to be a psychologist to get the job done." In many ways, he is right. Supervising today is much more difficult than it was even as recently as 20 years ago. Technical expertise is still required of supervisors, just as it has been historically. But today, being technically sound is no longer enough if one wants to be a successful supervisor.

Ten years ago we could look at the list of what today's workers want and agree that it would be nice if we could provide a work environment like that. We might even agree that it would be theoretically the right thing to do. Today, however, we are faced with a new reality, and that is, if you are managing a business where the majority of your front-line employees are members of Gen X and the Millenials, your business will not be successful and may not even survive unless you manage them well. Given the changing values younger employees bring with them to the workplace and the challenges associated with the downsizing of our teams resulting in fewer people doing more work, it makes sense that effectively managing the workers of today is not an option, it is mandatory.

The challenge for all supervisors today is to gain the attention, trust, enthusiasm, and commitment of their employees. It is no longer adequate to assemble, organize, and manage capital, raw materials, and a workforce within a tightly defined system of production. What is required is the leadership skills to create work environments of creativity, innovation, and enthusiasm so that once in, our employees are committed, loyal, and stay with us. In the following chapters, we will discuss the skills that help build relationships, encourage motivated employees, and foster a creative environment. The remaining chapters are devoted to enhancing your skills to become a confident, successful leader in today's environment.

Chapter 2

Building Your Confidence and Self-Esteem

"Our own attitudes have far more to do with how happy we are than do any external circumstances."

– *Dr. Nathaniel Branden*

Chances are good that one of the reasons you were selected for a leadership position is that you have great technical expertise. You perform your job really well, you possess a hard-working, positive attitude, and management wanted you to be a role model for other employees. One of the things that management didn't tell you, though, is that not every employee is as motivated as you to do a great job. In fact, some challenging employees just seem to be hanging around, doing as little work as possible to collect their paycheck. It's not the actual work that causes a supervisor stress; it is the people who are hired to do the work that can undermine a supervisor's leadership confidence.

Most managers and supervisors in the early stages of their supervisory career have not had much training or practice in "people skills." When people problems surface, and the problems are not easily solved, the supervisor often begins to question whether he or she has what it takes to lead others. When we begin to question our ability to be a good supervisor, our self-esteem, or how we feel about ourselves, begins to plummet. It's common for us in our role as leadership coaches to hear a supervisor say, "I can't do it. I just want to go back to being a worker. I don't even care about losing the extra pay for supervising. It's not worth the headaches and stress."

Being a great supervisor starts with *you*. The way you feel and see yourself affects every aspect of your role as a leader. You've most likely heard this bit of wisdom before: "We aren't what we think we are, but what we think we are," meaning that what we think about, comes about. What we're talking about here is self-talk, or the continual chatter that goes on inside your head about your ability to lead people. What you say to yourself has a profound effect on your ability to confidently lead people and feel good about yourself. The more positive the self-talk, the higher your self-esteem. The higher your self-esteem, the better your chances are of being a great supervisor and a great leader. This chapter discusses the importance of having a positive self-esteem and what you can do to raise your self-esteem to an even higher level.

As a first step to enhancing self-esteem, we begin with a self-assessment. This is an opportunity for you to take an honest look at yourself and assess how you feel about your abilities as a supervisor. In which aspects of supervision do you have a high degree of confidence? In which aspects are you unsure or feel a lack of confidence? The following Self-Esteem Assessment gives you a starting point to determine your strengths as a supervisor and leader, as well as provides a springboard for setting goals and improving skills.

Self-Esteem Assessment

On a scale of 1 to 10 (10 being the highest confidence score, 5 being an average confidence score, and 1 being the lowest or no confidence score), rate how you feel about yourself in each of the 16 areas. Use any number between 1 and 10 to accurately describe your feelings. For example, if you feel just slightly above average on your communication skills as a supervisor, you might rate them as a 6, but if you feel more confident, rate them as an 8.

As a supervisor, I feel the following levels of confidence in each category, ranging from 1 to 10, 10 being the highest level of confidence:

1. _____ My working relationship with people who report to me
2. _____ My relationship with my boss
3. _____ My verbal communication skills
4. _____ My written communication skills
5. _____ My technical skills to get the job done
6. _____ My ability to motivate others
7. _____ My ability to solve problems in my department as they arise
8. _____ My ability to coach and counsel people so that they improve their performance
9. _____ My relationships with coworkers
10. _____ My ability to effectively organize my tasks and my work area
11. _____ My ability to accomplish my organizational goals
12. _____ My ability as a leader
13. _____ Others' level of trust in me
14. _____ My level of trust in my employees
15. _____ My ability to interview and hire the right people
16. _____ My ability to effectively delegate tasks and responsibilities
17. _____ My ability to influence my manager or upper management
18. _____ My ability to lead organizational change
19. _____ My ability to prioritize and manage my time effectively
20. _____ My ability to hold difficult conversations with challenging people

Next, identify your top three areas of strength and your three areas for improvement.

Areas of Strength	Areas for Improvement
1.	1.
2.	2.
3.	3.

What Is Self-Esteem?

Self-esteem is quite simply how you *feel* about yourself. How we feel about our-selves critically influences virtually every aspect of our lives. Our self-esteem impacts everything from the way we function at work, to our personal relationships, to our role as parents, to what we accomplish in life. Every response we make in life—every goal we set—is shaped by whom and what we think we are. Thus, self-esteem is the major key to our success, our failure, and the level of our accomplish-ment as a supervisor or leader.

Self-esteem has two components: (1) a feeling of personal competence and (2) a feeling of personal worth. In other words, self-esteem is the sum of our self-confi-dence and self-respect. Self-esteem, on whatever level, is a personal, intimate experience; it resides in the core of our being. It is what you think and feel about yourself, not how someone else thinks or judges you. The tragedy is that so many people look for self-confidence and self-respect everywhere *except* within them-selves, and so they fail in their search. Unless you perceive your own true worth as a person or supervisor, you cannot come close to achieving high self-esteem.

As a leader, to have high self-esteem is to feel confidently appropriate to life, that is, competent and worthy in the sense that you can master what you set out to accomplish. As a supervisor, this means you are competent at getting the job done and are worthy of having the position of increased leadership responsibility. With these feelings, you cannot only effectively lead your team, but face life with greater confidence and optimism.

What Contributes to Self-Esteem?

Self-esteem is your overall feeling or opinion about yourself: how you honestly feel about your total self with all of your successes, limitations, abilities, and flaws. How is self-esteem shaped? Some of the common contributors to our collective self-esteem are listed below:

- **Our parents.** The most dynamic of the contributors are the ideas, beliefs, and values that we have accepted from our parents. Until recently, many adults raising children were not overly concerned with the importance of having high self-esteem. Today's Generation Y, however, has grown up in schools and homes that placed a significant focus on children having high self-esteem and feeling overwhelmingly positive about themselves. Gen Y is entering the workforce with an "I can do anything I set my mind to" attitude. They are working alongside Boomers who want Gen Y to pay their dues, display a work ethic, and play the corporate game by the traditional rules. As different as both groups are, both have been profoundly influenced by their parents and the messages they received during their formative years.

- **Significant others in our lives.** Relationships with people who are close to you have the potential to powerfully impact your self-esteem, either positively or negatively. Whether they are teachers, bosses, spouses, partners, children, peers, or people we hold in high regard, our self-esteem is molded by how these people act and react toward us. We can all think of a teacher, boss, coach, parent, or friend whose actions or behaviors had an impact on how we felt about ourselves. Whether it was our ability to play the piano or a sport or how well we did in school, feedback from others, whether it be positive or negative, helped shape our self-esteem.

- **Comparison of ourselves to others.** The media has a profound impact on shaping our thoughts about how much we should weigh, what we should wear, where we should live, what we should drive, and in general, what success looks like. If we don't measure up to what the media says is "in" or "cool," our self-esteem can be negatively impacted. In our quest to fit in, our prime competitive motivator is to be or do better than the next person. People with high self-esteem, on the other hand, do not feel the need to compete. They do not need to look and see what others are doing or have the need to be better than the next person. Recognizing their capabilities for what they are, they strive for excellence in their own lives. Their only competition is with themselves. Leaders with high self-esteem set their own standards and measure their success personally, not competitively.

- **Religious or spiritual upbringing.** Depending on the household you were brought up in, religion can be a very positive influence or may cause you feelings of guilt, worry, and shame. People with high self-esteem use their spiritual and religious teachings to serve them in a positive way.

- **Unrealistic goals.** In our work coaching troubled leaders with low self-esteem, we find that they have a tendency to set very high, unrealistic goals. When your goals are set unrealistically high and you do not achieve them, it reinforces negative self-esteem. On the other hand, our work with leaders who have high self-esteem shows us that these leaders set only moderate goals, just out of their reach. When they achieve them, it reinforces their positive self-esteem. A subsidiary effect of unrealistic goals is that people with low self-esteem will eventually stop setting goals. When they stop setting goals, they slowly begin to lose the feeling of mastery over their environment, and this once again reinforces a negative "I failed" attitude. People with high self-esteem set realistic and attainable goals.

- **What we say to ourselves.** The five factors we've discussed previously all impact our inner voice, or self-talk. The continual chatter that goes on in our head about how good we are, or are not, is hugely influenced by our environment. Unfortunately, we live in a society where most people are quicker to tell you what you cannot do, rather than encouraging you to take your success to even greater heights. People will tell you about your faults and weaknesses before they will expound upon your strengths. For example, when entrepreneurs start their own business, they are almost always told that eight out of ten new businesses fail and the chances of making it past the three-year mark are slim. While the statistics for startups are accurate, successful entrepreneurs choose to focus on success stories like Microsoft, eBay, Apple, Google, Dell Computer, and Starbucks Coffee. Those with high self-esteem associate themselves with other positive people. People with high self-esteem look at the positive side of life and do not have a need to put others down. Their self-talk is generally positive, and even though they may encounter challenges, they know that they will ultimately succeed.

What Are the Benefits of High Self-Esteem?

If you have ever been in a relationship with someone who has poor self-esteem, you know that life can be very difficult for you and the other person. Whether it is your boss, friend, or significant other, the effect of low self-esteem has deep roots. With poor self-esteem, life can be difficult at its best. Fortunately, we can improve our self-esteem. If you are willing to take the time to work at developing your self-esteem, there are many benefits:

- **You will feel happier about life.** When you feel more positive about yourself, it is only natural that you will be able to better cope with life and its interesting twists and turns. When you have high self-esteem, you can maintain an "I can do it" or "I can get through it" type of attitude. These are the people who live by Reverend Robert Schuller's words: "Tough times never last, but tough people do."

- **You are more motivated and ambitious.** People with high self-esteem tend to set more goals and seem to accomplish more with their lives. These same people have a goal of contributing positively to make a difference in their world. Whether it be their work environment, their families, or their civic accomplishments, people with high self-esteem know they make a positive difference.

- **You will have better relationships.** When you have high self-esteem, you tend to treat others better. You can do this easily because you feel good about yourself. When you treat others better, they will treat you better in return. When you have high self-esteem, it dictates what relationships you will even enter into. If you are treated poorly by someone, your self-esteem thermostat will tell you that you deserve to be treated better and you will look elsewhere for your rewards.

- **You will live life more humorously.** Have you ever had an incident in your life that devastated you? Maybe it was a relationship that soured, an embarrassing situation, or a project that you did not complete as well as you would have liked. Usually, when one of these situations occurs, we feel terrible. We feel like we failed! Then, as time passes by, we slowly start to see the situation as humorous. In fact, years later, we can sit around the dinner table and share the entire incident in the form of a joke. The benefit of having high self-esteem is that you have the ability to see the humor sooner.

- **You will be more open to change and risk taking.** Whether it is new ideas, situations, opportunities, or challenges, when you have high self-esteem, you are more willing to experience new things. Anything new requires learning. Along with learning comes mistakes. People with high self-esteem look at mistakes as learning and use this learning to grow. Colin Powell says, "There are no secrets to success. It is the result of preparation, hard work, and learning from failure."

- **You will be more comfortable giving and receiving compliments.** When paying someone a compliment, how many times have you heard the reply, "Oh, it was nothing" or "It's just an old thing I threw on"? When someone downplays a compliment, the person who gave the compliment is not rewarded. By belittling the response, the person receiving the compliment has invalidated the complimenter. People with high self-esteem find it easy to say either a simple "Thank you" to compliments or a sentence of "Thank you, I appreciate your compliment." With this type of response, the complimenter will feel comfortable giving compliments again. People with high self-esteem find it very easy to give compliments. By giving others compliments, others like them better, and this reinforces the attitude of having high self-esteem.

- **You will be more open to feedback.** Supervisors with low self-esteem do not have the ability to listen to or accept feedback from their employees. When you have high self-esteem, you will find it easier to accept feedback from others. You recognize their responses as a learning experience and incorporate what you can learn to make yourself a better person. People with low self-esteem spend their time defending their actions, blaming others, and making excuses about why things have to be the way they are.

- **You will be better able to think for yourself.** Supervisors with high self-esteem are able to incorporate the opinions of others, assimilate the information, and form their own definite feelings, opinions, and positions. With high self-esteem, you have a strong sense of what is right and wrong, and that makes your decision making an easier process. With strong self-esteem, you will find it easier to be more assertive and stick up for what you believe is right.

- **You will not need constant approval and recognition from others.** People with low self-esteem feel a stronger need to do and say things that will win the approval of others. Some people spend their entire life trying to win the approval and support of others. Others stay in bad relationships far too long, afraid to take the bold step and be on their own for fear of what the change may bring.

- **You will have the ability to accept people, including yourself, as they are, not as you would like them to be.** When you have high self-esteem, you have the ability to walk in the other person's shoes. With high self-esteem, you will not feel a strong need to change your life for another person's approval. You will also be less inclined to try to change others.

15 Steps to Higher Self-Esteem

In the preceding pages, we learned about self-esteem: what it is, how we develop it, and the benefits of obtaining high self-esteem. Now let's look at what we can do to raise our self-esteem. There are hundreds of little things you can do on a daily basis that will enhance your self-esteem.

Here are 15 of the things we feel are most important for supervisors. Do not attempt to try all 15 at the same time. We recommend that you determine which one or two areas you would like to work on and concentrate only on those one or two areas. After you have concentrated on those points for a period of four to six weeks, that specific point will begin to become a part of your life. In other words, you will have replaced self-defeating habits of your past with these good habits. The result is a higher degree of self-esteem that will permeate and penetrate your entire life.

1. **Live for today.** One phrase we'd like to cut from the English language is "if only." "If only" I would get one more promotion, could make a six-figure income, or would close a certain sale. "If only" I could afford a bigger house or a new car. "If only" my boss would get off my back. "If only" I could motivate this one employee...*then* I would really be happy.

   It is important to have a purpose, to set goals, and to strive for future success. But it is equally important to be happy with your life right now. Do not put your self-worth and self-confidence out of reach until some future date. Most people learn only too late that if the quest is irrational, the longing will always be for "something more." Focus on what is good right now. Each day ask yourself, "What am I thankful for?" and "What can I do *today* for myself?"

2. **Set goals.** To gain mastery over your environment, it is important that you be able to accomplish the things in life that you feel are important. Setting and achieving predetermined goals are the most important roads to travel if you are going to increase your self-esteem. Setting goals is intimately associated with living actively. It is through actions that an attitude of self-responsibility is developed. Ask yourself, "What actions can I take to increase my self-esteem or advance my career, investments, and relationships?" "What actions will bring me closer to my goals?" When you set goals, you will realize you do have control in your life, you will be more motivated, and you will be proud of your accomplishments. Don't let being afraid of failure hold you back.

3. **Dress and look your best always.** You can tell a lot about how a person feels by looking at the way he or she dresses. The workplace has become increasingly casual. Options for what we wear to work have expanded considerably in the past decade. With all the choices, we are suggesting that you

take the time to dress and groom appropriately so that you feel good about how you look. People respond to us, in part, by our appearance. By feeling good about your appearance, you send a message to others that you care about and like yourself. How you look on the outside deeply affects how you feel on the inside.

4. **Be honest with yourself.** Unfortunately, the appropriate use of self-honesty is not automatic; rather, it is an active choice. The way we use our consciousness, the honesty of our relationship to reality, and the level of our personal integrity will influence our self-esteem. If you choose to fake the reality of who you are, you will mislead others, as well as yourself. You may do so because you feel or believe that who you are is not acceptable. You value a delusion in someone else's mind above your own knowledge of the truth. The penalty is that you go through life with the frustrated sense of being an impostor. This means, among other things, that you sentence yourself to the anxiety of wondering when you will be found out. The lies most devastating to our self-esteem are not so much the lies we tell, as the lies we live. Good self-esteem demands congruence, which means that the self within and the self projected to the world must be in accord.

   Remember that self-esteem is not determined solely by worldly success, physical appearance, popularity, or any other value not directly under our control. Rather, it is a function of our rationality, honesty, and integrity—all operations of the mind for which we are responsible. Be honest with yourself. Acknowledge your special talents and gifts. Be aware of your faults or weaknesses and decide what and how you want to improve.

5. **Look people in the eye.** Before you can look others in the eye, you need to be able to look yourself in the eye. When you look into a mirror, you need to feel good about *you*. Most people will tell you that they like people better who are able to look them eyeball-to-eyeball. Research has shown that people who look others in the eye are perceived as more honest, trustworthy, and credible. Those three adjectives are valuable to anyone.

6. **Volunteer your name first.** Whether you are introducing yourself or answering the telephone, you tell a lot about yourself by volunteering your name first in a conversation. You are telling others you have self-confidence, and self-respect and are proud of who you are. Others, in turn, will respond to you with a higher level of respect.

7. **Take full responsibility for your life.** Men and women who enjoy high self-esteem have an active orientation to life rather than a passive one. They take full responsibility for the attainment of their goals. They ask the questions,

"Where do I want to be?" and "How do I get there?" They do not wait for others to fulfill their wants and dreams. Self-responsibility is indispensable to good self-esteem. Avoiding self-responsibility victimizes us in our own lives. It leaves us helpless. We give power to everyone except ourselves. When we are frustrated, we look for someone to blame; we find others at fault for our unhappiness. In contrast, the appreciation of self-responsibility can be an exhilarating and empowering experience. It places our lives back into our own hands. In short, people with high self-esteem take responsibility for their own existence.

8. **Treat everyone you meet with dignity and respect.** From the president of your corporation to the janitor who cleans your office, from your significant other to the person who waits on your table when you eat out, treat everyone with dignity and respect. With this attitude, people will go out of their way to help you. Friendships are easier to attain and you will find most people will like you better. As a side benefit, you will never have to worry about offending the wrong person. Being liked by others once again enhances our self-esteem.

9. **Think for yourself.** Often what people call "thinking" is merely recycling the opinions of others, not true thinking. Thinking independently—about our work, our relationships, the values that will guide our lives—is part of what is meant by living consciously. Often, you will find yourself bowing to the wishes of others. It takes a conscious effort on your part to think through the situation, form an opinion, and then steadfastly execute your opinion.

10. **Improve your communication skills.** Communication is the tool that connects us to others. Clearly expressing your ideas allows you to be understood. Listening allows you to grow, learn, and open up to other people and ideas. Communication is the glue that binds friendships, marriages, and successful relationships at work. There are hundreds of ways available to improve your communication skills: books, tapes, seminars, Toastmasters, etc. Find one and take some time to improve your ability to connect with others. You will see that as your confidence in your communication skills improves, so will your self-esteem.

11. **Take a self-esteem inventory.** Change always starts with awareness. To increase your own self-awareness, take a self-inventory. Make a list of all your positive attributes. Most people undervalue their assets. Each year, it is important to acknowledge your strengths, your areas for improvement, and your significant accomplishments for the past year. With your attributes on paper, you will find it easier to value yourself, feel proud of strengths, and set new goals for areas of improvement.

12. **Think and act positively.** Your self-esteem is shaped by the way you communicate with yourself. The sooner you can change the way you communicate with yourself, the sooner your communication with others will change as well. When you change your communication with others, it changes the way others respond to you, and this reinforces your positive self-talk. As your self-talk is enhanced and becomes more positive, your self-esteem will follow in a positive manner. Assess your self-talk. Are you being kind to yourself? If you don't like what you hear, change your negative self-talk into positive self-talk. Focus on positive belief in yourself. Then hang out with others who think positively. Choose not to be in the company of negative people who look at the downside of any situation and want you to share in their misery. When you associate with other individuals who have high self-esteem, you will reap the benefits they have to offer. They tend to be happier with life, deal easier with change and adversity, and will offer you support and unequaled encouragement. Choose your friends and associates wisely.

13. **Be a volunteer or a mentor.** Give back. Help others as you have been helped. Give some of your time to those who could benefit from your friendship or expertise. Whether it is a person or an organization, you will feel good after you have touched another in a positive way. It usually costs you very little and you have a lot to gain knowing you have helped someone.

14. **Accept change.** The one thing we can most certainly count on in this world is change. It's the one constant. Be aware that change is inevitable. You can choose to resist change and view it as negative. If you take this perspective, you set yourself up for constant disappointment. Or you can view change as an opportunity. With any change, you can look for the good—for an opportunity to grow. Remember, if you always do what you've always done, you'll always get what you've always gotten.

15. **Focus on what you want, not what you do not want.** People with high self-esteem focus on what they want in life, not what they do not want or what they want to avoid. If you want a new job, an improved relationship, or a slimmer you, do not focus on being stuck where you are, the negative aspects of the relationship, or your current weight. Put your sights on the new job: What will it be? Where will it be? What will you be doing? Focus on how the relationship will be better: Is there better communication? Do we have greater mutual respect? Are we having more fun? And, the slimmer you: How will you feel? What will you look like? How will others react to you? Remember, you will get what you expect. So expect the best.

☞ Tips for Success

Confidence and Self-Esteem

1. Recognize that your self-esteem and self-image impact every aspect of your role as a supervisor.

2. Stop valuing your self-worth by comparing yourself to others. Set your own standards and then strive to achieve those standards.

3. Set realistic and obtainable goals. This is the fastest way to raise your self-esteem. When you set a goal and achieve it, you feel you have mastery over your environment.

4. Associate with high self-esteemers. You do have a choice as to whom you associate with. Individuals with high self-esteem have the capacity to help build your self-esteem.

5. Laugh sooner. If you have ever experienced a crisis or a failure, you know at some point you are able to laugh about it. The goal is to laugh sooner.

6. Give and accept compliments. When you give sincere compliments, people like you better. When you accept compliments, it demonstrates high self-esteem.

7. Ask for and accept feedback from others. When people care about you enough to offer feedback, either positive or negative, you have the opportunity to grow.

8. Take full responsibility for your actions. Empowered people with high self-esteem know they are responsible for their decisions and actions.

9. Use positive self-talk, because what you think about comes about. Remember, if you think you can, or you think you can't, you're probably right.

10. Successful people have experienced failure. Successful people with high self-esteem do not view failure as failure, but rather as an opportunity to learn how to do things differently.

Chapter 3

Leading Organizational Change

"The trouble with the future is that it usually arrives before we're ready for it."

– Arnold H. Glasgow

Being a leader during the turbulent past decade has been a wild ride! You've seen the best of business and the worst of times. During the past ten years, every organization has felt the impact of change. Some organizations experienced rapid growth; many others felt the effects of downsizing. Expenses have gone up and profits declined. Customers increased their demand for quality products. Their expectations and standards for service escalated. Many markets have expanded, and just as many have crumbled. Organizations experienced greater competition and advanced technological demands. All indicators are that organizations will continue facing challenges created by sharp economic swings, keen competitive pressures, globalization of the marketplace, and reshaping of businesses worldwide. Constant change is the new reality today, and those organizations and people who will not change will not survive what some have called "The Age of Instability."

For a multitude of reasons, changes in our economy or environment have forced leaders and organizations to respond with a fundamental change in the way they do business. Whether we like it or not, organizational changes result in supervisors having to implement those changes. In addition to the other more traditional skills we possess as supervisors, it is critical that we understand our role as leaders or change agents during these rapidly changing times. Having an understanding of the way change affects our organization and recognizing the resulting impact of the change on the individuals within our organization are critical. Our ability to deal positively with change, in a large part, determines our effectiveness as leaders during these rapidly changing times.

Unfortunately for managers and supervisors, it is a given fact that employees do not all respond to change with the attitude "Fantastic, another organizational change. I'm excited to be a part of it!" We have found that when change is introduced to an organization, or better yet, rumored, employees will respond in one of three ways:

23

- ***This is stupid.*** First, some of the strongest-willed employees will fight organizational change, even when deep down inside they recognize that the change is in the best interests of the organization. Strong-willed employees are like dinosaurs. They may be well on the way to extinction, but they will fight change each step of the way.

- ***Let's wait this one out.*** The second type of employee takes a "let's wait and watch" approach to change. These employees don't fight change because they don't think that the change will have any direct impact on them. They quietly hunker down with hope that the change will eventually pass them by. These employees are like rabbits on the highways at night. They sit and are mesmerized by the lights. Unfortunately, some rabbits get hit. Employees who ignore change can become victims of the process as they sit on the sidelines and watch the passing parade.

- ***To survive, we gotta do this.*** Last, the third type of employee can accurately see the future and has the flexibility to adapt accordingly. These employees are like dolphins. Dolphins are one of the brightest mammals in the ocean. They possess the skills needed to adapt to any environment. They are comfortable swimming in a pool of carp. They are equally confident swimming in a sea of sharks. They successfully adapt to a constantly changing environment. Dolphins are always thinking ahead, planning their next strategy. They learn from and respond appropriately to their rapidly changing environment. These employees expect and welcome change as the key to their survival.

Reasons People Resist Change

Given that change is here to stay and has a direct impact on the way we do business within our organization, why do some people seem to dig in their heels and need to be dragged along, resisting making changes in their behavior and attitude at all costs? The following reasons best describe why some people have a tough time changing their mindsets and behavior:

- **Fear of failure or success.** Some employee resistance to change is rooted in fear. During periods of change, an employee may feel the need to cling to the past because it was a more secure, predictable time. Employees may be afraid to commit to a change in the way they do things out of fear of not being successful. If what they did in the past worked well for them, they may resist changing their behavior out of fear that they will not achieve as much in the future.

- **Creatures of habit.** Doing things in the same routine, predictable manner is comfortable. Asking people to change the way they operate or think requires them to move outside their comfort zone. "We've always done it this way, so why do we need to change?" becomes the rallying cry for people who have difficulty changing their routines. In some cases, employees may ignore or deny the change simply because it requires them to experience something beyond their normal method of operation. Their minds are already made up. They already know that this change is going to be bad.

- **No obvious need.** "If it has been working good all this time, why do we need to change?" Like the old expression "If it ain't broke, why fix it?" employees within an organization may only see a change from the perspective of the impact it has on them and their particular jobs. Not seeing the big picture, they may resist the change because they fail to recognize the positive impact of the change on the organization as a whole. They find the talk about change disruptive and totally unnecessary.

- **Loss of control.** Employees working in familiar routines develop a sense of control over their work environment. They fear the unknown. They know what works and what doesn't. Therefore, they are confident about their contribution to the organization. For some employees, asking them to change the way they operate creates a feeling of being powerless and confused during the transition. Some may even doubt their ability to learn new processes and technology.

Typical Employee Responses Regarding Change

During times of organization change, you will notice employees reacting to change with a variety of responses. As a leader tasked with implementing organization change, it is important for a supervisor to be able to understand employee reactions when change is implemented and recognize that these are normal reactions and part of the process employees go through during periods of organizational change. The following reactions are some typical responses to organizational change:

- *Not me!* Typically, when employees are asked to do a different job, or change the way they currently do a particular job, they may initially respond, "Not me!" They might begin to tell their supervisor about someone else better suited for the job or deny that they are capable of making the proposed change. This initial reaction is a result of the employees' satisfaction with the current status quo and fear of what unknowns the change may create for them personally.

- ***What will this do to my job security?*** "What's in it for me?" is often an employee's first response upon learning about a proposed organizational change. It is natural for employees to see change in perspective to their own job security. Employees wonder what will happen to their job if technological advances are introduced or the organization is restructured. Employees are also concerned about what financial impact the changes will have on them personally. Will the change result in less work for them or even do away with their job altogether? It is normal for employees to view organizational change first from the perspective of their own job security and second from the needs of the organization.

- ***I'm mad.*** Some employees are so resistant to change that they become frustrated and angry. Their anger may be repressed, causing an increased stress level, or overt, resulting in emotional outbursts. Whether repressed or overt, anger is a typical reaction to change. Anger results from employees feeling their job security is being threatened, or they are feeling a sense of loss of control over their work environment.

- ***Guess what I just heard?*** Gossip, always an organizational challenge, often escalates during periods of organizational change. Employees who respond to organizational change with frustration, anger, and disbelief often resort to vicious gossip or "back-stabbing" activities. Feeling a sense of loss of information, power, and control, people often respond by gossiping to others in the organization. The gossip typically is a far stretch from the truth.

- ***Who's in charge here?*** During times when organizations are experiencing rapid change, it is natural for employees to question leadership. Suddenly, everyone seems to be an expert and management is clueless, from the employees' perspectives. When employees have not been communicated to adequately, and when they do not see the positive results of the changes, it is normal for them to question the wisdom of their leadership.

- ***I'm so stressed out!*** Some employees, finding comfort in a predictable routine, panic at the mere mention of change. For them, upsetting the routine and making changes in the way they normally complete their jobs can cause panic. People with a low tolerance for navigating uncharted waters and ambiguity may have such a difficult time with change that they may actually become physically ill. They may resist change at all costs, not out of stubbornness, but out of sheer panic at the thought of how the change will impact them personally. They may be so plagued with the feeling of panic that they are not able to rationally deal with the change.

- *I quit!* Some employees may actually be so resistant to accepting organizational changes that they elect to quit rather than make the needed changes. Unfortunately, changes going on in one organization are typical of changes going on in other organizations. Electing to stand on one's principles and fight change by quitting often makes the point, but usually at cost to the employee making the point, *not* to the organization.

Don't get discouraged. Not all employee responses to change are negative! The following positive responses to change typically come from employees who feel a high degree of self-esteem, personal competence, and self-confidence. They see change in an entirely different perspective and, when in alignment with the supervisor, help support and sell organizational change to other employees. These employees typically have the ability to remain open-minded in response to change and see change as having a positive influence on both them personally and the organization. Here are some of their responses:

- *I can do it!* Employees viewing change as a challenge feel they can rise to the occasion. They feel that they have what it takes to be a contributing team player when the change affects their work world. They remain open to new ideas, ask questions, and feel confident in their ability to acquire the knowledge needed to complete the task. They exhibit a "can do" attitude in their approach to change. They may admit to the task being difficult, the procedure being a bit cloudy, and the outcome unknown or questionable, but they are committed in their quest for rising to the challenge!

- *I'm excited!* Some employees naturally approach life and challenges more enthusiastically than others. These employees have the gift of embracing change enthusiastically. Instead of trying to pick apart proposed changes and find all the ways they won't work, enthusiastic employees see change as a natural part of an organization's evolution. These are employees who understand the bigger picture. They understand the value in making change. They visualize what could be and have a positive vision about the company's future. Enthusiastic employees can infect others with their enthusiasm. Supervisors lucky enough to have enthusiastic employees need to support and nurture these employees as they can help make the implementation of change much more palatable for other employees.

- *Maybe I could adjust to this change.* Some employees don't embrace change enthusiastically or jump out of their seats ready to accept a challenge resulting from organizational change. Instead, they may watch from the sidelines, but they remain open-minded. They may not commit initially but, after a period of observation, agree to give the change a chance. They remain open-

27

minded enough to entertain the thought that they could adjust to the change. While they may not be eager participants in the change process, they give the new ideas and processes a chance. They express a willingness to learn new techniques and procedures and do not sabotage change activities.

We've explored why people resist change and typical reactions to change, many of which are challenging for a manager. You may be tempted, at this point, to be discouraged regarding your ability to drive organizational change. Don't give up. Fortunately, there are several specific actions and straightforward approaches managers and supervisors can take to help guide their employees successfully through organizational change. These guidelines can make times of change some of the most rewarding and productive times in your leadership history!

Guidelines for Leading Organizational Change

Involve employees in the change process. We are firm believers that employees are not so much against change as they are against being changed. Anytime managers are going to implement organizational change, there is always a lag between the time the change has been discussed at the management level and the time the change is going to be implemented. During the lag time, managers often naively believe that no one else knows about the change. The reality is, though, employees are guessing how the change will impact them. Our experience has been that the rumors and gossip surrounding proposed changes are often exaggerated and seem to get richer in faulty detail each time they are passed from one employee to another! The sooner you involve employees in the change process, the better off you will be implementing the change. A formal communication channel will be more effective at implementing change than a negative informal one.

Ask questions, don't tell. It is critical that managers and supervisors understand what employees are feeling regarding the change. It is only when you accurately understand their feelings that you know what issues need to be addressed. We are fond of the statement "You can tell tough employees, but you can't tell them much." People who do not deal well with change generally are the same employees who cannot be "told" anything. For this reason, we recommend asking them questions rather than telling them why the changes are taking place.

Recently, we worked with two financial organizations that were merging. Although the merger was referred to as a "merger of equals," employees in both organizations were openly resentful of the loss of their individual organization. Management repeatedly told employees why the merger and resulting changes were needed. Employees remained adamantly opposed to the merger, and it was evident that "sides" were being drawn. As a last resort, senior management switched strategies and asked the following question: "If we didn't merge our organizations and assets, what would happen?" At that point, the majority of employees stated that not changing would lead to the demise of one if not both organizations. With this new data, management involved all the employees in helping to design the specific change strategy that would be implemented to help unite the previously divided team.

Get both negative and positive informal leaders involved. It is easy to get the positive informal leaders involved in helping implement changes. They have a reputation for supporting management, regardless of the change. The mistake many managers make is not getting the negative informal leaders involved in the beginning stages of the change process. Several things happen by involving them early in the process. Usually, they are left out of any change efforts. Since they are ignored, they have a lack of commitment and may even try to sabotage the change. By involving them, their behaviors will change. Second, if you know what their objections and concerns are regarding the change, it will help you design your change strategy. Third, if you can meet their concerns, they will help in selling the change to the rest of the organization.

Raise expectations. Now, more than ever, you should ask more from your employees. It is expected that more work needs to be done during the change process. While it may be more practical to expect less in terms of performance, this is the time to raise your levels of performance for both yourself and your employees. During change, employees are more likely to change their work habits. Reach for the opportunity and push them to try harder and work smarter. Require performance improvements and make the process challenging, but remember to keep goals realistic so that you eliminate frustration and failure.

Over-communicate. The change process usually means that normal communication channels will not be working as well as they usually do. During this time, your employees will be hungrier than ever for information and answers. You can "beef up" communication in two ways. First, give employees an opportunity to give you input. Start by becoming more available and asking more questions. Get employee opinions and reactions to the changes. Maintain your visibility and make it clear that you are an accessible boss. Just letting your employees know that you do not have any new information is meaningful information to them. Second, strive to be specific. Clear up rumors and misinformation that clutter the communication regarding changes. Remember, it is almost impossible to over-communicate.

Be firm, but flexible. As you introduce a change, it is important that you see the change through to completion. Abandoning it halfway through the change process accomplishes two things. First, it destroys your credibility. Second, it tells every employee that if you take the stance of a dinosaur, the change will pass by, even if you lose your job and become extinct in the process. Remain flexible because you may have to adapt to a myriad of situations to successfully implement your change.

Keep positive. Your attitude as a manager or supervisor will be a major factor in determining what type of climate is exhibited by your employees. Your attitude is the one thing that keeps you in control. Change can be stressful and confusing. Try to remain upbeat, positive, and enthusiastic. Foster motivation in others. During times of transition and change, try to compensate your employees for their extra effort. Hand write a note of encouragement and leave it on an employee's desk. Leave a nice message on their voice mail. E-mail a word of thanks or encouragement. Take them aside and tell them what a great job they are doing. Listen to their comments and suggestions. Last, try to instill organizational change as a personal challenge.

Finally, the best way to predict the future is to invent it. Consider what changes are coming, what needs to happen, and how you can contribute. Instead of changing with the times, make it a habit to change just a little ahead of the times.

☞ Tips for Success

Organizational Change

1. Be a role model for leading the new change. Gain a reputation for leading your team forward, not defending the past.

2. Hold yourself accountable for successful implementation of change. Maintain high personal standards and hold others accountable to agreed-upon team standards.

3. Develop a compelling positive vision of the future. While you may not have all the details, the more positive your vision, the greater the chance for your success. Also, the clearer your vision, the easier it is for your employees to follow your lead.

4. Set clear, specific goals and communicate the goals to each member on your team so that they know the target and understand how their individual effort contributes to the team's success.

5. Double your communication efforts during periods of rapid organizational change. Over-communicate to make sure that employees feel they are getting enough communication regarding the change.

6. During times of change, focus on ensuring customer satisfaction, both internally and externally. This focus reminds all members of the team what your real purpose for existence is.

7. Show unwavering commitment to the success of your team and your organization. Expect the waters to get choppy during times of fast change. Hang on. Ride the waves. Your tenacity will be a source of inspiration for your team.

8. Get in the habit of rewarding the messenger, even if the news is not good. During times of change, you want to know, firsthand, what your employees are thinking and feeling. Their insights will help make you a more informed, better decision maker.

9. Expect resistance. Robert F. Kennedy said, "Twenty percent of the people are against any change!"

10. Don't drag your heels and resist change. Move fast! All the research shows that fast change is easier to deal with than slow change.

Chapter 4

Setting Goals and Planning Actions

"If you don't know where you're going, you'll end up someplace else."

— *Yogi Berra*

In working with thousands of supervisors in diverse settings, we have noted that great leaders, among other positive characteristics, always have a set of clearly defined goals. We have also noted the reverse. Supervisors who struggle in their relationships with employees and have difficulty getting their team motivated often have only one goal: "Just let me survive one more day!" It's a known fact that individuals and teams that set and achieve goals accomplish more, feel better about themselves, and are more confident in their abilities. Goals can be powerfully motivating.

The accomplishment of anything great begins with clear goals. While most people would readily agree with this statement, it is amazing how many lack goals in both their personal and professional lives. Some studies have found that up to 90 percent of the population do not set goals. Often, these people do not really know how to go about setting a goal. Well-defined goals are part fantasy and part pragmatism. If you can dream, conceive, and believe, then you can achieve your goals.

There is a procedure for setting and reaching your goals. The following pages describe the goal-setting process. You will learn what it takes to be a great goal setter and goal achiever. Whether your goals are financial, business, educational, family, physical, social, spiritual, or recreational, you will be successful if you follow this process.

It is important to realize that achieving any goal will take persistence, commitment, and a willingness to forego temporary pleasures for the pursuit of your goal. Goals will give you a well-defined purpose, a sense of accomplishment, and a feeling of mastery over your environment. This, in turn, will lead to a high self-confidence that will penetrate your entire life. Without goals, you are like a ship without sails or a rudder. You are truly at the mercy of the wind. You will drift, but you will not drive. Without goals, you spend the majority of your time reacting to, instead of creating, your environment.

Whether you choose to be a great goal setter or a ship floundering at sea, it is important for you to realize that whatever you do with your life, you write your own ticket!

Defining Success

Success is a very personal journey. *You* are a success in life if *you* are able to realize what *you* deem as an important and worthwhile accomplishment. Success is different things to different people. Success is about doing, participating, learning, and progressing. These processes are all personal achievements. What are *you* after? What is important to *you*?

Unfortunately, the vast majority of people look at success as a comparison: "Am I doing better than my parents, my neighbors, my associates, or myself compared to last year?" Your success cannot be a comparison of you to others, your environment, or your past. To truly be a success, you must accomplish pre-set goals that are meaningful to you. As Zig Ziglar notes, "Success means doing the best we can with what we have. Success is the doing, not the getting; in the trying, not the triumph. Success is a personal standard, reaching for the highest that is in us, becoming all that we can be."

When you set and accomplish goals, you gain a sense of mastery over your environment. With the feeling that you can accomplish what you set out to do, you will become successful. If you *must* compare, look at your success as a comparison of yourself to your potential. Most people never realize that success has to do more with an internal mental environment than with external physical surroundings.

One of the differences between successful supervisors and unsuccessful supervisors is their purpose in life. If you do not know where you are going, then you will probably end up "somewhere." But if you do have specific goals and a clear-cut plan for your life, then your chances for achieving your objectives within or near the time frame you have set for yourself are extremely high. So set meaningful goals, achieve your goals, and breathe the feeling of success.

Why People Don't Set Goals

Fear of failure. Many people have a fear of setting goals—a fear that they may not accomplish what they set out to do. Because of this fear, they do not set concrete goals. If you do not set goals, then you are truly not living up to your potential.

Not sure what they want. In the great Lewis Carroll novel, *Alice's Adventures in Wonderland*, Alice turns to the Cheshire Cat and asks, "Which way do I go from here?" The cat replies, "Where do you want to end up?" When Alice states that she's not quite sure where she wants to end up, the cat rightfully replies, "Then it does not really matter which way you go."

Don't know how. Numerous studies have shown that people who consistently set goals achieve more in life than those who do not. Researchers generally agree that less than 3 percent of Americans have written goals; of those that do, less than 1 percent review their goals on an annual basis. Most people simply don't know how to write out their goals for clarity and direction.

Negative attitude. If you have a negative attitude toward life, you are not likely to be a goal setter. People who are successful goal setters have a great positive mental attitude. Your ability to control your attitude on a daily basis is proof of your success. Those who achieve significant results in their careers and in their lives recognize the importance of viewing the glass as *half full* instead of as *half empty*.

Poor self-image. Your self-image is the *picture* you have of yourself, or how you *see* yourself. This picture contributes to your self-esteem or how you *feel* about yourself. If you see yourself as a failure or as someone who cannot achieve what you really want, you will feel unempowered and unmotivated to even try to accomplish a goal. So the easy way out is to avoid setting goals in the first place.

Limited thinking. Another reason why people do not set goals is because of limited thinking—that is, they can see only a narrow perspective on what they could achieve. Some people box themselves into a narrow thought process. This imaging box does not allow them to see beyond the box or expand their thinking to new horizons. Limited thinking perpetuates the status quo of no growth.

Procrastination. People who avoid setting goals are often victims of their own procrastination. How long have you been promising yourself that you would take a course, learn a new language, start an exercise program, stop drinking or smoking, write or call someone, or start a certain project? If you are like most people, you probably never get around to doing a lot of things you would like to do. You really mean to, but you find yourself making excuses like "I am too busy this week" or "I will get to it as soon as I finish this project."

The Goal-Setting Process

Step One: Create a Vision

We will discuss the power of a vision in Chapter 19. Successful leaders know the practical value of the visioning process. They also know that creating a vision is the first step in goal setting. Before you begin to set a goal, you need a clear mental *picture* of what it is you want to achieve. This picture is your vision of success. Creating a vision is the ability to see beyond *what is* to the picture of *what could be*.

To start the visioning process, you must get in touch with your true desire. What is important to you? What matters? What do you care about? What do you really want? A vision comes from the heart. It must be truly meaningful to you.

Once you are clear on what you want, begin to form the picture. Create a mental picture of what you want. Make the picture clear, specific, and detailed. See yourself in the picture. What are you doing? What are you saying? What are you wearing? Who else is with you? How are people treating one another? How do you feel about yourself? About the others around you?

The visioning process requires quiet reflection. Step back from your busy, fast-paced environment and relax. Visioning requires imagery and creativity. The more relaxed you are and the farther away you are from day-to-day tensions, the easier it is to create, the easier it is to visualize. Many people have a difficult time creating a vision because that vision may be so far removed from reality. Yet it is that very distance or gap between the vision and current reality that propels you toward achieving the vision.

In summary, to achieve your vision, first crystallize the vision. Make it real, in your mind and in your heart. Then acknowledge current reality. Feel the tension between the two. Allow yourself to be propelled toward your vision. As author Dennis Waitley notes, "Failures do what is tension relieving, while winners do what is goal achieving."

Step Two: Decide on Actions

Now that your vision is clear, you can begin to determine the actions that must be taken to achieve the vision. These actions become the specific goals that are to be accomplished. A goal is a target, an end, or an objective. It is the accomplishment of these targets, or goals, that brings you closer to your vision.

For example, if your vision is to achieve a more prominent position in your organization or to move higher on your career path, you would first go through the visioning process and become crystal clear on what it is you actually want. You would know exactly what it would look like and how it would feel. Then ask yourself, "What do I need to accomplish to get to my vision?" One action may be to go back to school to complete a degree program. If you need the degree to achieve the vision, it becomes one of your key goals.

At this point in the goal-setting process, simply list the various actions you must take to achieve the vision. As we move through the next steps, we will discuss how to write effective goal statements.

Step Three: Identify Roadblocks

Now that you know what it will take to achieve your vision by outlining key actions or goals, you can begin to identify the barriers or roadblocks that may get in your way. It may sound negative to spend your time and energy thinking about barriers or problems, but there are two good reasons for this. First, if you are able to think about what problems could stop you, you can also begin to generate plans to get around the problems if they should arise. And second, when problems do come up, they do not paralyze you. Many people have had their goals undermined when problems surfaced. Sometimes people will even tell you they thought the problems would arise.

For example, a supervisor sets a goal to reorganize his or her department. The full reorganization never takes place because as soon as the supervisor introduces the changes, the employees start to roadblock the process. When asked if he or she had thought that the employees may make the process difficult, the supervisor responds affirmatively. If you know that it is going to be a problem, you should create a plan to effectively deal with and eliminate that roadblock. If we think through what problems may stop us, we are seldom blind-sided by major roadblocks.

Back to our example of going back to school to get your degree. Some of the roadblocks you could anticipate in this goal might include (1) not enough time, (2) fear of going back to being a student, and/or (3) financial constraints. For each of the roadblocks you identify, develop some strategies to get around the problem. It may include (1) changing your own thinking, (2) getting help from others, and (3) committing to specific time blocks to do what you need to do. Keep the vision in mind and then overcoming the roadblocks will not be so tough.

Step Four: List the Benefits

If you spend time listing the problems or roadblocks you could encounter, you will find it much easier to generate a list of benefits you would receive when you achieve the goal. The question that then needs to be answered is, "Do the benefits make the goal worth achieving?" If the answer is *yes*, you know that it is worth tackling the problems to achieve the benefits of goal attainment.

Continuing with our example, some of the benefits of going back to school and obtaining a degree might be (1) improved chances for promotion, (2) increased salary, (3) enhanced self-esteem, and (4) the feeling of accomplishing something you have wanted for many years.

As you list the benefits, you will want to make sure the benefits outweigh the problems you will encounter. If the benefits do not outweigh the problems, the problems will stop you. Focus on the benefits. They will help you get through the tough times.

Step Five: Write the Goal

The research on high achievers shows that successful goal setters write out their goals. There is something almost magical about writing down goals. Without writing down the goal, it is merely an idea or a wish. Writing it down helps bring it to life.

Here is a classic, yet effective guideline for writing good goals. It is called the **S-M-A-R-T** model. Each letter of the S-M-A-R-T model refers to a characteristic of effective goals:

Specific. Good goals are specific. They detail exactly what is to be accomplished. Don't be vague or general. Write out specifically what is to be accomplished.

Measurable. You must be able to measure the success of your goal. Whether the goal is broken down into number of units produced, salary earned, days worked, pounds lost, chapters completed, or number of classes attended, you need a way to quantify your results. Measuring your results motivates you to keep moving toward your goal.

Attainable. Research shows us that high achievers set goals that challenge their abilities, but that are not unrealistically out of reach. Be realistic about your goals. It is not unrealistic to go back to school for a degree. It is unrealistic to expect to get a doctorate in only one year. Make your goals a stretch, but make them a more guaranteed stretch.

Relevant. Do not forget that your vision is the driver for your goals. Make sure that your goals are relevant to the vision. The accomplishment of each goal should move you closer to realizing your vision. Keep your goals moving on the track to your desired future.

Time bound. Good goals have a time frame. When you set a specific time frame to get something done, it will always take you that amount of time or even less time to complete the task than if you had no time frame at all. For example, when you are leaving on a trip, you have all sorts of tasks that must be accomplished before you leave. You may be rushed, but you will always get the tasks done. You have to because you are leaving. If you were not leaving, those same tasks may take you two or three times as long to accomplish. Life is short! Set a time frame, because you will always accomplish more.

Step Six: Design an Action Plan

Now that you have your goals and they are S-M-A-R-T goals, you know exactly what you want to achieve and by when. The last step in the goal-setting process is to design a specific action plan to achieve the goals. This is a step-by-step breakdown of the small actions you will take to achieve each goal and when you will take them.

Back to the degree example. Let's say your goal is stated like this:

I will complete my M.S. degree in two years.

Your specific action plan might look like the example below. Each time you complete an action, check it off or scratch it out and then celebrate. You are on your way to achieving your ultimate goal!

Remember, the secret to achieving goals is your willingness to do whatever it takes to get there. It means that you are willing to sacrifice to accomplish your goal. It means that you are willing to confront problems and roadblocks and work around them. It means that you will write out your goals and ensure that they are S-M-A-R-T. It takes work. And it also means that you will reap the benefits, bringing your vision to life.

Specific Action Plan

GOAL: To complete my M.S. degree in two years	
Specific Actions	**By What Deadline**
1. E-mail the university for an application	May, this year
2. Arrange for former college transcripts to be sent	June, this year
3. Complete application and send it in	July 15, this year
4. Set up meeting with university counselor	August 1, this year
5. Register for classes	August 22, this year

Setting Goals with Employees

If you are setting goals that involve your employees, here are some suggestions that will help you create successful goals that employees will feel motivated to achieve:

- **Involve employees in the goal-setting process.** One of the classic pitfalls supervisors stumble into is setting goals *for* their employees versus *with* their employees. People want to contribute to the goals for which they will be held accountable. Dumping your goals on employees without their input is a de-motivator. Have your employees create their goals with you. You will be surprised at the level of commitment and personal ownership you will see.

- **Ask how the employee can accomplish the goal before you tell how.** Ask your employees for their ideas on how to accomplish the goal before you give your input. Even if you take the risk of asking the employee if a certain goal is possible, and the employee tells you it is not possible, you are still better off. If you had dictated the goal to the employee without allowing any input, the employee is still going to harbor the feelings that the goal cannot be accomplished. If you get their input on how the goal can be accomplished, you may get some new, creative, and better approaches. The key here, as with all good communication, is to listen.

- **Ensure the goal's feasibility.** If you set a goal with your employees to have the departmental budget completed by the end of the month, you must make sure the employees have access to the tools and information they need to complete the task. Set your employees up for success by ensuring they have what they require to do the job. This goes back to making sure that the goal is realistic and attainable.

- **Make the goal challenging.** Tasks that are not challenging are not motivating. One of the most fundamental motivations for any employee, especially one who is basically competent at his or her work, is challenge. Challenge creates motivation to achieve goals. If you allow mediocrity to continue in your department, you are undermining your own success.

- **Ensure that the goal is relevant.** Most people do not want to accomplish a goal just for the sake of accomplishing a goal. They want to understand the purpose or why they are doing a particular task. Employees need to understand how the tasks they are doing are connected to the larger purpose of the organization. Most jobs do have significance. Make sure you take the time to explain the importance or relevance of the goal. People will extend themselves for work they see as important. Remember, good goals are relevant.

- **Recognize success.** Make sure to recognize your employee's success. We all want to know that our work is acknowledged and recognized. This does not take much time but will buy you a great deal. Most employees want to please supervisors. Take the time to acknowledge them with a written note, a pat on the back, or a simple "good job," and you will have a cadre of loyal, hard-working employees.

To help you visualize what a goal-setting action plan looks like, the following template is provided.

Goal-Setting Action Plan

1. Is my/our vision crystallized? ❏ Yes ❏ No
   (Can I clearly see myself or us achieving this goal?)

2. Describe the goal:

   _____

   _____

   _____

3. What problems could stop me/us?

   _____

   _____

   _____

4. What are the benefits of achieving this goal?

   _____

   _____

   _____

5. What is my/our plan to overcome the problems I/we listed?

   _____

   _____

   _____

   _____

   _____

   _____

   _____

6. When will I/we complete this goal? (specify date) _____

7. What are the milestone markers?
   (What will be evidence that I/we am/are getting closer to achieving the goal?)

WHAT	BY WHEN
_____	_____
_____	_____
_____	_____
_____	_____

8. How will I/we measure this goal?

_____

_____

_____

_____

9. Is the goal realistic and obtainable?   ❏ Yes   ❏ No

10. If others are responsible for accomplishing this goal, have I/we involved them in setting the goal?   ❏ Yes   ❏ No

11. What can I/we do to help others feel ownership of this goal?

_____

_____

_____

_____

12. What is my/our action plan to achieve this goal?

WHAT	BY WHEN
_____	_____
_____	_____
_____	_____
_____	_____

☛ Tips for Success

Goals and Actions

1. Set goals. Most people do not set goals. Those who do are far more likely to accomplish what they want in life.

2. Adopt a positive attitude. People who achieve significant results and a sense of fulfillment in their lives view the glass as half full instead of half empty.

3. Do it now. Successful goal setters take action *now*. Remember, the most important step in overcoming procrastination is the first step, no matter how small.

4. Clarify your vision. What do you truly want? Create a clear and specific mental picture. Use this vision to guide you in the goal-setting process.

5. Write S-M-A-R-T goals (Specific, Measurable, Attainable, Relevant, and Time bound).

6. Design a specific action plan with target dates for completion.

7. Get your employees involved in the goal-setting process. Their involvement will foster significant personal motivation.

8. Be sure the goal is possible. Does the person have the tools and information necessary for successful completion of the goal?

9. Discuss the significance of the goal. Believe it is a goal that should be accomplished.

10. Recognize success. Any achievement deserves recognition. Whether it is a personal, team, or employee accomplishment, take time to acknowledge and recognize success.

Chapter 5

Managing Time to Accomplish Your Goals

"The only way there is true equality in this world is we all have the same amount of time. Some people just accomplish more."

– Peter B. Stark

How many times have you heard the comment "I just don't have enough time to get it all done"? How many times have you used it yourself? Every time we do not accomplish something we should have, or intended to, this line seems to surface.

Picture this: you have spent your entire morning in a meeting—an unproductive meeting at that. You get out of the meeting, answer e-mails, return phone calls, and then eat lunch. After lunch, you attend another two-hour meeting. At the conclusion of the meeting, you answer more e-mails and return more phone calls. At 3:30 p.m., an employee comes into your office and needs to review a project she is working on. At 4:30 p.m., you realize you have to leave to go pick up the kids from preschool. All of a sudden, panic strikes. You realize that you have a report due by tomorrow afternoon. You have two choices. You can take it home with you and complete it tonight after the kids go to bed (significant others do not endorse this alternative). Or you can delegate it by dumping it on one of your employees. Either choice is not ideal.

What happened? Although you were busy all day, you literally ran out of time—time needed to complete a very important project in an effective manner. The reasons? Lack of priorities, unclear goals, interruptions, unproductive meetings, disorganization, inability to say "no," and possibly ineffective delegation.

The 168-Hour Limit

Another great cliché in time management is "If there were only more hours in the day." Wishing there were more hours in the day is just that: a wish. There are two facts we know about time. First, there are exactly 24 hours or 1,440 minutes in every day. That amounts to 168 hours in a week and 8,760 hours in a year. Second, we all have the same amount of time. Rich people cannot buy more. Forgetful people cannot lose it. Scientists cannot invent more. Powerful people cannot yield influence and gain more. When it comes to time, it is the only aspect of life where there is true equality. So the question is not one of where do you find more time. You cannot do it. The real question we need to be asking is how do we manage the things that we do in the 168 hours that are available in a week.

The following is a typical breakdown of how activities may consume our time:

Time at work (9 hours per day)	45
Travel to work (1 hour per day)	5
Eating meals (2 hours per day)	14
Sleeping (7 hours per day)	49
Bathing and dressing (1 hour per day)	7
Total	**120**

What this means is that we have 48 hours to spend on other activities. Things such as:

Family time

Leisure activities

Religious/spiritual worship

Paying bills

Personal growth

Activities for children

Grocery shopping

Yard work

Cleaning the house

Maintaining the car

Watching television

Surfing the Internet

Free time

If the typical breakdown of activities is fairly accurate for you, then you have approximately 48 hours to spend on other activities. If you have a career that takes more time, say 55 hours in a week, then you only have 38 hours to divide up on other activities. If you have a new baby or very young children in your family, you may have even fewer hours for other activities.

Conducting a Time Management Audit

If you are going to be successful managing your time, it is critical that you know how you spend your time. If we are focusing on accomplishment, then it is important you realize when you are productive and when you are not. The best way to conduct a time audit is to record your time, activity by activity, as you progress throughout the day. To conduct a time audit, follow the seven steps listed below:

1. List boundary times. For example, list what time you get up in the morning and what time you go to bed at night.

2. Then write down/fill in activities that are conducted on a ritual basis: taking a shower, checking personal e-mails, reading the paper, driving to work and back, or eating meals are things that you do on a consistent daily basis.

3. Shade in meetings and other large blocks of time where you spent your day.

4. Outline all other activities that made up your day.

5. Compute the length of time you spent in that activity.

6. Circle anything you accomplished or completed.

7. Summarize the areas where you did not make the best possible use of your time.

One problem with this method of a time audit is that when you forget to record your activities as you complete them, you may find you have blank spots during your day. If someone asked you what you did at that time slot, you may find it necessary to reply, "I worked... I think."

A sample time audit might look something like this:

Time		Activity	Duration
5:00	am	Get up and fix the coffee	10 minutes
5:10	am	Take a shower, get dressed	30 minutes
5:40	am	Check news on the computer	15 minutes
5:55	am	Organize day (home office)	30 minutes
6:25	am	Fix breakfast for family	35 minutes
7:00	am	Help get children ready for school	30 minutes
7:30	am	Take children to school	20 minutes
7:50	am	Drive to office	10 minutes
8:00	am	Staff meeting	1 hour
9:00	am	Return e-mails & phone calls	15 minutes
9:15	am	Write article for company newsletter	30 minutes
9:45	am	Listen to John whine about the policy change	30 minutes
10:15	am	Solve a problem for an angry customer	10 minutes
10:25	am	Leave for a 10:30 meeting	5 minutes
10:30	am	Attend meeting on the XYZ project	2 hours
12:30	pm	Working lunch; answer e-mails	45 minutes
1:15	pm	Return phone calls	15 minutes
1:30	pm	Update boss (unexpected)	1 hour
2:30	pm	Handle a customer problem	10 minutes
2:40	pm	Write a proposal for the ABC Company	1 hour
3:40	pm	Answer e-mails	15 minutes
3:55	pm	John back for clarification... more whining	10 minutes
4:05	pm	Work on Mary's performance review (overdue)	25 minutes
4:30	pm	Walk to Andy's desk to update the ABC project	15 minutes
4:45	pm	Return two phone calls	10 minutes
4:55	pm	Talk with Larry about football game	15 minutes
5:10	pm	Organize desk	10 minutes
5:20	pm	Leave to pick up children from day care	30 minutes
5:50	pm	Get home, decide what to fix for dinner	15 minutes
6:05	pm	Prepare and eat dinner	55 minutes
7:00	pm	Clean up kitchen after dinner	15 minutes
7:15	pm	Help children with homework	45 minutes
8:00	pm	Watch television with family	30 minutes
8:30	pm	Get children ready for bed	30 minutes
9:00	pm	Decide to watch TV but fall asleep	2 hours
11:00	pm	Wake up and go to bed	6 hours
5:00	am	Get up and start the routine all over again	

What are the benefits of conducting a time audit? It lets you see how you really do spend your time. Some of the learning points from this audit are:

- I spent 3 hours in meetings in the day.

- I spent 40 minutes of my day listening to John whine.

- I wasted 15 minutes walking to Andy's desk when an e-mail would have worked just fine.

- Mary's review was the most important task I had to complete and I still did not get it done.

- The ABC proposal could have been easily delegated if I had planned ahead.

In this exercise, I just estimated that I probably missed two hours of my time. What's scary is this was a typical day for me. So what's two hours a day? When you think about the big picture, minutes turn into hours and hours quickly turn into days. For example, let's say you find that you waste just 15 minutes each day. At the end of the year, that adds up to 11 full eight-hour days of productivity. Thirty minutes wasted equals 22 full eight-hour days. One hour a day equals 44 full eight-hour days, and last, if you find two hours, like I did, that equals 88 full eight-hour days of productivity.

A blank template is provided so that you can complete a time audit. For ease, though, we recommend using an electronic version. At the time we published this work, several were available on the Internet at no cost. We recommend that you conduct a time audit at least four times a year.

Time audits identify where time is currently being spent and give you ideas about how to better utilize those 1,440 minutes you have been allotted each day.

Daily Time Log

Note: Do not try to account for each minute of the day. Account for 15-minute blocks of time.

Day of Week: M T W T F		Date:	
Time	**Activity**	**Time**	**Activity**
6:00		1:00	
6:15		1:15	
6:30		1:30	
6:45		1:45	
7:00		2:00	
7:15		2:15	
7:30		2:30	
7:45		2:45	
8:00		3:00	
8:15		3:15	
8:30		3:30	
8:45		3:45	
9:00		4:00	
9:15		4:15	
9:30		4:30	
9:45		4:45	
10:00		5:00	
10:15		5:15	
10:30		5:30	
10:45		5:45	
11:00		6:00	
11:15		6:15	
11:30		6:30	
11:45		6:45	
12:00		7:00	
12:15		7:15	
12:30		7:30	
12:45		7:45	

Was this day: ❑ Typical?   ❑ More busy?   ❑ Less busy?

Successful Time Management and Task Accomplishment

Now that you have completed your time audit, you will find the following four steps helpful in managing your time.

Step One: Create a Master "To Do" List

This is a critical step. Many managers and supervisors try to keep track of all their tasks by leaving reminder notes for themselves. Yes, 3M Post-it® Notes and little slips of paper work great for reminders. The problem with this method is that little pieces of paper get lost. It can also be confusing. We recommend using an electronic "to do" list, such as the Tasks feature in Outlook. Using an electronic "to do" list saves time and ensures that required actions don't get lost. This first step is critical in helping you get organized.

Step Two: Prioritize Your Tasks

One thing is certain: despite what many managers think, you can only do one task at a time. And we need to do the most important task first. The following five categories may be helpful in breaking down your priorities:

- **Category 1: Highest priority** *(critical to my success and urgent)*. Do Category 1 tasks first. If you do not get them done, bad things will happen. Whether it is your boss, an employee, or a client, if you do not get these tasks completed, the person who expected you to complete the task will make their dissatisfaction known. If you were supposed to solve a customer's problem and did not, the chances are good that the customer would tell someone else in your organization about the problem. If your boss found out, he or she would feel you were not doing your job. Many supervisors and managers have lost their jobs or customers because they did not recognize a task as Category 1. Category 1 tasks are high priority and urgent. Do them now.

- **Category 2: Proactive** *(helpful to my success but not urgent)*. A great example of a Category 2 task would be going to a time management seminar. It is not critical that you go right at this moment. But by going, you may find better ways to manage your time. By managing your time better, you accomplish more. By using some time each day for Category 2 tasks, you will eliminate some of the fires that come up on a daily basis. Thus, you will have more time for your Category 1 tasks.

- **Category 3: Repetitive, routine tasks** *(time discretionary and time bound).* Category 3 tasks need to be completed on a routine basis. A report is a great example. It has a specific date and time when it is due. You could work on the report at night after dinner. You could do it first thing in the morning. It is your discretion when you complete the report. The only time the report becomes a Category 1 task is 15 minutes before it is due.

- **Category 4: "I'll get to it later" spare time tasks** *(not time bound).* These are the tasks and projects that you would like to complete, but there are no penalties or time constraints if you do not. A great example is that many of us have a stack of papers or other documents on our desk. Sometimes it is a big stack; other times it is a small stack. What we know is that most items in the stack fall into Category 4. With 4s, you can almost always delegate or dump. Give the project to someone else or throw it out. If it has been in your 4 pile for a month, it will not make much difference who does it or if it gets done at all.

- **Category 5: Leisure time.** Everyone needs to spend some time each day or week doing something that is pleasurable to you. Leisure is different things to different people. For some people, going to the beach and enjoying the sunshine is a leisurely pastime. For others, this same activity is stressful. Pick what works best for you and spend some time each week or each day in an activity that you find relaxing.

Step Three: Reprioritize throughout the Day

The best of plans can be sabotaged by a crisis, unplanned interruptions, or a sick child needing to be picked up at school. It is important, throughout the day, to periodically check your master "to do" list and reprioritize, as needed. Great leaders have a plan, work their plan, and rework the plan, as needed, to ensure they remain productive and time efficient, despite surprises to their schedule.

Four Tips to Help You Focus on the Right Priorities

Do your 1s (highest priority) first. Many supervisors find it a lot easier to do 3s. The classic line is, "I will get these 3s off the list first and then I will get to the 1s." The problem is you run out of time before you get to complete your 1s. The 3s will not cost you your job. Failure to complete 1s will, so do them first.

Proactively work on your 2s each day. The easiest thing to do is to say you never have any time to move your 2s up to a higher priority on your list. An example of a 2 might be to create a model or template for one of the types of projects you are required to complete. If you had the model or template, others in the department could complete the task for you. You never seem to find the time to do this task, but if you would make the time, it would free up hours every time this type of task surfaces in the future. Although you do not think you have the time to complete the template, you always have to find the time to complete the actual task. Make time each day to work on a 2.

Place less emphasis on 3s. These are your repetitive daily aspects of your job. Unfortunately, 3s are usually easier to complete than 1s. For this reason, the natural tendency is to do 3s first. This is an error that many supervisors and managers make. We say to ourselves, "I will just get these few things out of the way, then I'll tackle the tough task." Each day, it is important to consciously prioritize each task. For example, returning an angry customer's phone call needs to take precedence over reviewing your monthly budget. Once tasks are prioritized, do the highest priority, most urgent item first.

Use the GUTS Theory on 4s. Everyone has a few 4s. The best example is the pile of things you have stacked up in places like your desk, credenza, or some other slightly out-of-the-way location. With 4s, you can practice the GUTS Theory. GUTS stands for:

> **G** = Give it away to someone else
> **U** = Use it
> **T** = Throw it away
> **S** = Save and file it

If you practice the GUTS Theory, you will eliminate a lot of clutter from your life. The problem with unattended 4s is that they eventually multiply and will psychologically overwhelm you. Every time you walk into your office and see your stack of 4s or a cluttered drawer or shelf, it bothers you because you are reminded of what you have not done. Use GUTS, and you will keep your 4s to a manageable level.

Step Four: Identify Your Time Wasters

What wastes your time? The following are a list of typical time wasters. Place a checkmark (✓) by those you feel have the biggest impact in wasting your time.

❏ Misplacing something	❏ Surfing the web	❏ Socializing
❏ Unclear directions from boss	❏ Watching television	❏ Procrastination
❏ Correcting others' mistakes	❏ Tough employees	❏ Paperwork
❏ Unproductive meetings	❏ Fighting fires	❏ Interruptions
❏ Traffic to/from work	❏ Multitasking	❏ Other _____

At the time we published this work, studies were beginning to surface citing multitasking as a hindrance to effective time management. Multitasking is handling more than one task at the same time, or performing multiple functions on a variety of projects. Society's expectations for responsiveness and the never-ending array of faster, more complex gadgets to keep us connected 24/7 lead to an ever-faster pace of life and work. Multitasking was thought to be the way to stay informed and on top of everything, and would lead to self-satisfaction and happiness. Yet recent studies have found quite the opposite. Their findings note that multitaskers actually have increased stress levels, feel dissatisfied with what they have accomplished (as well as what they still have to accomplish), and have reduced ability to efficiently perform tasks. Their stress and frustration can all be attributed to their scattered, ineffective approach to task completion. The following recommendations will help you focus on the right priorities:

- Take a moment when you are feeling stressed to ask yourself, "Is what I'm doing right now the most effective use of my time?"

- Focus. You are not at your personal best when you are scattered. Turn off your e-mail. Complete your work, uninterrupted, for a specific period of time. Check your e-mail at the top of each hour, responding to urgent messages and prioritizing other messages on your task list for a later response.

- Ask yourself, "What could I postpone for a later date or not do at all?"

- Set time limits. Tell yourself that this task should be completed in one hour, then focus on efficiently completing the task. You'll be amazed at how effectively this approach works. Most often, you will finish the task in less time than you have estimated and gain the satisfaction of checking the task off your list.

Once you know where you waste your time, following the suggestions in this chapter will help you overcome these time wasters and make the best possible use of your time.

Are You a Procrastinator?

Recently an employee told us that her supervisor suffered from a severe case of "T.N.T." Not being familiar with that condition, we inquired and learned that "T.N.T." translates to "I'll do it **T**omorrow, **N**ot **T**oday." The supervisor was a noted procrastinator!

What's one task that you should accomplish now but, for whatever reason, you have been putting it off for tomorrow or some other distant time in the future? All of us, from time to time, have procrastinated doing something that we know should be accomplished. By definition, procrastination is the intentional and habitual postponement of a task in order to do a task of less importance. If we have a legitimate reason for postponing a task, then by this definition, it is not procrastination. For example, if you decide not to work on the department budget today because the corporate budget is not going to be finalized until tomorrow, you may have a legitimate reason for postponement. You do not want to do the work twice. But if you choose to not work on the budget because it is tedious and you would rather reorganize your files, the chances are good you are falling into the pit of procrastination.

According to data we have collected in seminars, the following are some of the most common excuses why people procrastinate. Place a checkmark (✓) by the excuses you have used in postponing your procrastinated tasks.

❏ It's not due yet.

❏ I work better under pressure.

❏ The task is boring.

❏ I hope it will take care of itself.

❏ The task is tedious.

❏ The task is too complicated.

❏ I do not feel motivated to do it right now.

❏ I think I will have a drink first.

❏ I think I will eat first.

❏ I think I will watch a little TV first.

❏ I think I will take a short nap.

❏ I'm too busy.

❏ I really do mean to do it, but I keep forgetting.

❏ It needs further study.

❏ It's too nice a day to be spending it doing that.

❏ I will wait until Friday.

❏ It's too late now.

❏ I'm not sure where to begin the task.

❏ I do not want to spend more money.

❏ Before I start, I need to…

❏ I am waiting for someone else to get something back to me.

❏ They might tell me no.

❏ It's too early/late in the day to start that now.

Characteristics of Procrastinators

Procrastinators know they have a problem and know they need to take action. Procrastinators generally feel guilty every time they look at the task that needs to be completed. Procrastinators often have a good idea of exactly what needs to be done. However, great procrastinators continually postpone the very action that will relieve their guilt.

Great procrastinators always promise to take action at some indeterminate time in the future. The hallmark of procrastinators is that they do not ever take immediate action unless there is a crisis concerning the task. The self-talk of a procrastinator generally utilizes the phrase "I need to" rather than "I will." For example, a procrastinator feels comfortable saying, "I need to clean out the garage." A more goal-directed individual might say, "I will clean out the garage by noon tomorrow."

Great procrastinators like to make the performance of the procrastinated task contingent on something else. This makes the delay seem rational and justifiable. For example, a procrastinator might say, "I will take a vacation as soon as the pace slows down." Unfortunately, for the true procrastinator, the pace never slows down. In this scenario, the delay tactic is a convenient excuse rather than a legitimate reason for the delay.

Everyone, from time to time, falls victim to procrastination. The following tips will help you take action to overcome procrastination, the great thief of time.

Eight Steps to Overcoming Procrastination

1. **Identify what is causing the delay.** To win the battle with procrastination, it is critical that you figure out what is causing you to delay the task. Look back over the list of excuses and see which ones apply to you. Once you pinpoint the cause, it is easier to generate a solution.

2. **Change your attitude.** If you are telling yourself, "I don't even know where to start" or "This is so boring," those messages will undoubtedly encourage procrastination. Who wants to do overwhelming or boring tasks? You are much better off focusing on the benefits of completing the task rather than the negative aspects of getting started on the task.

3. **Conquer your fears.** Sometimes we procrastinate a task because we fear the outcome. An individual puts off going back to school because he is much older than most students and is not sure how well he will do. A good way to overcome your fears and get on with life is to analyze what is the worst possible thing that could happen. After you recognize the worst possible outcome, then ask yourself, "Can I live with the worst possible scenario?" Most times, we can live with the worst possible outcome.

4. **Make a master procrastination list.** To know what really needs to be done, analyze the different areas of your life and make a list of all the things you are presently procrastinating. Then, next to each procrastinated task, estimate how much time it will take to complete. Some tasks will take only minutes, others will take hours and days, and still others may take years. After you analyze the amount of time needed to complete the tasks, prioritize an order for completion.

5. **Organize a plan for completion.** After you have prioritized your tasks, the next step is to organize a plan to complete each project. Break down each project into smaller tasks. For example, if you presently have a large pile of magazines you need to read, it may be easier to accomplish the task by taking the following steps. First, separate them into piles by the different magazines you subscribe to. Second, work on only one type of magazine at a time. Third, flip open each magazine to the table of contents and highlight the articles you want to read. Fourth, tear out the articles that are important to you and throw out the rest of the magazines. Fifth, set a goal to read or review articles for 15 minutes at a time (at least once or twice a day) until you have completed the task.

6. **Act now.** There is only one real solution to winning the battle with procrastination. Like Nike says, "Just Do It." Let's say you have to write an article for your corporation's newsletter. The article will take approximately one hour to write. At this moment, you only have 15 minutes before you need to be at a meeting. You can still act now. In 15 minutes, you could put together an outline of the article.

7. **Do the toughest part first.** A young boy was sitting at the dinner table staring at some broccoli he hated. The problem was that his mother had said, "You cannot leave the table until you finish all your dinner, and that includes your broccoli." After looking at the cold broccoli for over an hour, the boy's father shared with him this pearl of wisdom: "Son, if you have to swallow a frog, don't sit there and look at it." And so is the case with procrastinated tasks. They normally don't get better with time.

8. **Reward yourself.** When you accomplish a task you have been procrastinating, reward yourself. Rewards differ from person to person. For one person, the reward might be drinking beer; for another person, it might be walking on the beach. Do something to celebrate when you have successfully completed a previously procrastinated task.

☞ Tips for Success

Time Management

1. Organize your work environment. Does the environment you work in work for you or against you? The more your environment is organized, the more productive you will be.

2. Establish place habits. It is estimated that the average American spends six months of his or her life looking for items that are lost, misplaced, or just plain missing. Think how much time you could save if everything you needed had a specific place, just like your screwdriver or flashlight.

3. Create a master daily "to do" list. Each day you need to create a *new* "to do" list. The tasks may take longer than you like, but if each task is on your list, it will eventually be done. (There are several types of computer-generated organizers people utilize that do an excellent job.)

4. Prioritize your tasks. Once you have prioritized your tasks, then do your highest rated, most urgent items first.

5. Set goals. Without a specific set of goals, it really does not matter how you spend your time. (For more information on the specifics of goal setting, refer to Chapter 4.)

6. Cluster common tasks. When you return to your office after a meeting, there will be several phone messages on your voice-mail. You can quickly cluster the messages and return them within five minutes. Clustering common tasks saves time.

7. Delineate time blocks. Block off a portion of time and work on only that task during the specific time frame. This technique works great on tasks where you have been procrastinating.

8. Eliminate distractions. Focus. Check your e-mails and respond to them once an hour, not as they arrive.

9. Delegate where appropriate. It is often more appropriate and efficient for someone else to accomplish the task. (For more information on effective delegation, refer to Chapter 7.)

10. Routinely ask yourself, "Is what I am doing right now the best possible and most important use of my time?" Also ask, "Five years from now, what will be the most important to have completed?" These questions also help you put things in perspective.

Chapter

Communicating Effectively

> "I'm a great believer that any tool that enhances communication has profound effects in terms of how people can learn from each other, and how they can achieve the kind of freedoms that they're interested in."
>
> — *Bill Gates*

We've never lived in a more connected society. Daily we are witness to faster, smarter, cheaper technology, all designed to enhance our ability to communicate with one another. The following technological advances enhance our communication experience:

- Phones bounce messages off satellites, instantly relaying our messages across town or around the world.

- E-mail delivers critical (or not so critical) messages to hundreds of people simultaneously.

- Webinars and teleconferencing connect people virtually around the world.

- Social media allows us to keep up with one another in real time.

- The Internet provides instant access to education, games, music, videos, and much, much more.

All these incredible high-tech advancements in communication, and yet, two people standing right in front of each other, speaking the same language, cannot seem to understand one another!

As many advancements as have been made in communication technology, human communication continues to be the most challenging. National and international crises point to the problems of communication among cultures and nations of the world. Government misunderstands the people and the people cannot seem to get their message across to their elected leaders. Managers say that their employees do not follow instructions, and employees say that their bosses do not listen.

Communication is blamed as the root of relationship problems and acknowledged as the key to successful relationships. Divorced couples cite "poor communication" as the greatest contributor to their marital problems; and when successful couples are asked the reason for their success, the most frequent comment is "We communicate."

The same concept applies to the business environment. When employees are asked to describe their best and worst bosses, guess what item is at the top of both lists? You guessed it: communication!

The most common characteristics that describe both the best bosses and the worst bosses are listed below.

Description of Bosses

Worst Boss	Best Boss
Doesn't care about others	Gives feedback
Poor communicator	Good communicator
Doesn't listen	Listens
Gives mixed messages	Speaks clearly
Tells instead of asks	Solicits input
Self-focused	Other-focused

Research has consistently shown that communication ability is the characteristic judged by supervisors and managers to be most critical in determining promotability. In one study of 88 profit and nonprofit organizations, of the 31 skills assessed, interpersonal communication and listening skills were rated as the most important. A manager's number one challenge can be summed up in one word: communication.

What We Know About Communication

The following known aspects of communication impact our day-to-day lives:

- **No matter how hard one tries, one cannot avoid communicating**. Said another way, you cannot *not* communicate. Often, we think we are not communicating because we are not speaking. That is simply not the case. We are always communicating, whether we want to or not. We communicate nonverbally: with our eyes, facial expressions, gestures, and even by the color of our skin. During 30 minutes of discussion, people can exchange approximately 800 different nonverbal messages. The messages we send without words have a greater impact than when we speak. Peter F. Drucker, a noted scholar on management, reminds us, "The most important thing in communication is to hear what isn't being said."

- **Communicating does not necessarily mean understanding.** Can you think of a time when you were convinced that you got your message across but later found out quite the opposite? We enjoyed this sign on an executive's desk: "I know you believe you understood what you think I said, but I'm not sure you realize that what you heard is not what I meant to say."

- **Communication is irreversible.** Once you have communicated a message and it has been received, either verbally or nonverbally, it is irreversible. Have you ever said something that you have regretted? When dealing with employees, it is critical to choose words and messages carefully because they will have a lasting impact. Unlike writing, where we can delete what does not sound right, our verbal and nonverbal communication is forever. Dr. Laurence J. Peter, best known for his Peter Principle concept of leadership, reminds us, "Speak when you are angry and you'll make the best speech you'll ever regret."

- **Communication is affected by physical and social settings.** When we interact with someone, it is not in isolation but within a specific physical and social surrounding. For example, when our boss talks to us seated behind his or her desk, the conversation will probably be quite different than when we are having lunch at the corner deli.

- **Communication is dynamic.** Communication is an ongoing and ever-changing process. As participants in communication, we are constantly affected by other people's messages and, as a consequence, we undergo continual change. Every time we interact with someone, we leave that moment with new information and a changed relationship.

Making Communication Work

Effective communication skills form the foundation for successful management and supervision. Our communication skills are so fundamental that it is easy to sometimes forget their significance. Because we communicate a lot, we often assume that it means we communicate well. You cannot lead without being able to communicate your ideas or without being able to understand those you are trying to lead.

All critical management skills require effective communication. Whether you are leading, coaching, delegating, building a team, making decisions, counseling, hiring, or just about any management activity you can think of, you will need to communicate. Effective communication involves (1) speaking clearly, (2) listening for understanding, and (3) fostering an open communication climate. In this chapter, we will look at each of these communication factors and offer valuable tips that you can use to improve your communication ability.

Speaking Clearly

As a manager, one of your primary responsibilities is to get the right message to the right person in order to get the results you expect. Because the communication process is so complex, getting your message across is not an easy task.

Think of all the things that can get in the way of your getting your message across to another person and ensuring that you get the results you expect. Here are some of the barriers or roadblocks that can get in the way: lack of understanding (on your part or theirs), interruptions, noise, emotional state (yours or theirs), bias, prejudice, boredom, resentment, language problems, culture, physical environment, lack of trust, poor listening habits, mixed messages, and unclear priorities.

To work your way around these barriers, consider the following ideas:

- **Think through what you want to say before you say it.** Begin by focusing on your intention or goal. Be clear about what you expect as a result of your communication. Do you want an employee to do a certain job? Do you want a coworker to support you on a particular project? Do you want your boss to give you more information? In your mind, clearly define what you want to accomplish. Once you are clear about what your communication goal is, you can focus on the message you need to get across.

- **Match your message to your audience.** Your message must be tailored to the needs of the receivers or listeners. Consider the receivers' point of view. What information will they need? What will their opinions be? How are they likely to respond? Once you have thought through some of these issues, you can formulate a clear statement that is more likely to be well-received by the listeners.

- **Once you have made your point, ask for feedback.** Make sure that each listener has understood your intention and specifically what it is you want. You can get this feedback by observing and asking. Observe the listener's behavior. Is it in agreement? Does he or she appear to have questions or to disagree? Ask the listeners what questions they have. Ask for their opinion or for their input. Also pay attention to the nonverbal cues you are receiving.

- **Speak clearly and concisely.** Some people believe that wordiness is a sign of knowledge or power, but it actually gets in the way of effective communication. Being overly verbose is a distraction. Many people will simply tune out a speaker who is too wordy. Keep your words and sentences short and to the point. Pay attention to how others are responding to you. If you notice signs of restlessness (loss of eye contact, fidgeting, or daydreaming), you have lost your listeners and may be rambling, from their perspective. Move on to your next point and summarize the discussion. Keep your responses to questions short and direct. A good rule of thumb: keep answers less than one minute.

- **Speak with enthusiasm and expressiveness.** If you are trying to convince others or to motivate a team or individual, your ability to be enthusiastic is critical. Be aware of your tone of voice. Are you speaking in a monotone? If so, this is one of the quickest ways to lose the listener. Add variety to your voice by varying the speed, rate, and tone of your voice. Be conscious of emphasizing key words and phrases to get your message across better. Make sure that your level of enthusiasm is appropriate for the topic and the listener. Too much enthusiasm at an inappropriate time can come across as phony or insincere. Adding examples, personal stories or experiences, and analogies or metaphors always makes a speaker more interesting.

- **Develop a natural and informal style.** People are more likely to listen if you appear natural and informal in your discussions. Many employees complain that their bosses are stiff or formal when communicating with them. If you want to open up communication, be yourself. Let others get to know you by being yourself. Speak with your employees as you would to a friend. This informal approach will help you build trust and credibility with others.

- **Be sincere.** Your employees, your coworkers, and your boss can see right through you! It is important to always be sincere in your communication. This includes letting others know when you are unsure or do not understand. It also includes telling the truth and being as direct and honest as you can be. When others truly believe that you speak from the heart, you are beginning to create a trusting relationship. Others will be honest with you in return. When two people or a team of people are open and honest with one another, the chances of getting and receiving clear communication will increase tenfold.

Listening for Understanding

Communication is a two-way street. In addition to speaking clearly, the effective communicator is a good listener. Listening involves not only hearing the speaker's words, but also understanding the message and its importance to the speaker, and then communicating that understanding to the speaker.

Most of us are not good listeners. There are many reasons for this. To begin with, we are not taught to be good listeners. Think of your formal education. Did you ever have a course in listening? You had plenty of courses in the other communication skills such as reading and writing. You may have even had a class in speaking. But very few of us have had lessons in how to listen.

In addition, we think many times faster than we speak. An average speaker will vocalize approximately 135 to 150 words per minute, but the receiver can comprehend as many as 500 to 600 words per minute. This time differential makes it easy for the mind to wander and take side trips away from the topic at hand.

Another reason why listening is so difficult includes our tendency to only "half listen" while we are working on a reply. How often have you caught yourself busy formulating a reply and even starting to speak before the speaker has even finished his or her sentence?

Other factors that get in the way of effective listening include (1) noise or other disturbances, (2) mental or emotional distractions, (3) finding the individual or topic boring or uninteresting, (4) prejudice or bias, or (5) simply an unwillingness to truly understand another point of view.

To overcome these barriers, try some of the following tips for improving your listening ability:

- **Develop an attitude of wanting to listen.** Being a good listener starts with a positive attitude toward listening. Even if you do not feel like listening, remember that you can always learn something from everyone and that listening is a critical component to establishing trusting relationships. Good leaders always want to listen because they know the value of continuous learning. They also know that you cannot continue to learn if you do not listen.

- **Reschedule a conversation if you cannot give it your undivided attention.** If you are unable to devote yourself to listening, for whatever reason, tell the individual that you are unable to fully listen to him or her at this time. However, because you want to give your undivided attention, tell him or her that you would like to reschedule the conversation. Most people are more than willing to reschedule. In addition, many people will be impressed with your honesty and with the fact that you care enough to set aside time for them. When you do actually meet, make sure to eliminate all distractions and give your full attention.

- **Focus your attention on understanding the other person's meaning, not on formulating your response.** A good listener is "other-focused" rather than "self-focused." Your goal is to understand the other person. To do this, give your undivided attention, ask questions for clarification, and check your perceptions for understanding. Focusing your attention on the speaker will also help you listen without interrupting.

- **Show that you are listening by using "attending skills."** A critical part of the listening process is letting the person know that you are interested and that you are attending to his or her message. These are some of the attending skills you could use:

  - Maintain eye contact to show interest, and be observant.
  - Lean forward slightly to communicate concern and to better comprehend the message.
  - Come out from behind a desk or any other physical barrier.
  - Nod your head to indicate understanding.
  - Smile when the person uses humor.
  - Allow for pauses—don't feel you have to fill the space with your words while the other person needs time to collect his or her thoughts.

- **Use open-ended questions to open up communication.** Open-ended questions facilitate the conversation and provide an invitation to respond back and forth. They also let the other person know that his or her thinking is important to you. Open-ended questions cannot be answered with a simple "yes" or "no." These kind of questions begin with words like "Tell me," "What," "How," "Explain," and "Describe."

- **Use paraphrasing to ensure understanding.** A paraphrase is a brief re-phrasing of the person's words. Paraphrase by restating the information in your own words. Paraphrasing shows that you are listening and that you understand what he or she has said. It also ensures that your interpretation of the message is correct.

  Examples:

  "You think the XYZ program is not a good idea because..."

  "It sounds like your major concerns about this project are..."

- **Use reflective statements to ensure your understanding of the person's feelings.** Reflective statements are short declarative statements that reflect the person's feelings or emotions without indicating agreement or disagreement. The purpose of reflecting is to let the person know that you understand how they *feel* about a particular topic or issue. Reflecting helps establish rapport as well as provides an opportunity for the person to simply vent or "let off steam."

Examples:

"You're excited about this opportunity."

"You seem worried about not being able to make the schedule."

- **Summarize conversations to ensure understanding and provide closure.** A summary statement is a concise restatement of the key points discussed during a lengthy conversation. The summary brings the conversation to a close. It may also include a recap of specific actions or agreements made.

Examples:

"We agree that the project has gotten off track and that we will take the following steps to correct the situation..."

"As I understand it, you feel that we should bring the marketing people in on this proposal. As we discussed, I will contact them and set up a meeting for next week to discuss their involvement."

Fostering an Open Communication Climate

Speaking clearly and listening for understanding are the first steps to being a more effective communicator. In addition, good managers, supervisors, and leaders take specific actions to create a climate that is conducive to open and honest communication. In this open communication climate, people feel free to give their input and ideas, information is shared freely, conflicts are openly discussed and worked through, and people are more willing to express innovative ideas and to take risks.

The basis of open communication is trust. The leader establishes an environment of trust within and among all the people in the group. To begin to build or expand trust in your organization and to foster an open communication climate, try some of the following tips:

- **Keep your employees informed.** We all want to be "in the know." Take time to keep your employees informed about what is happening within the organization. Let employees in on the "big picture" and the reasons for management decisions. The more people feel informed about their organization, the better they feel about their participation in that organization. Managers who tend to hide information from their employees will soon lose credibility and will certainly not be included in important informal information loops. When you do not have the answer or are unsure of the reason for a particular decision, be honest with your employees and do whatever you can to get more information to them as soon as possible.

- **Use a "real" open door policy.** Most managers say they have an open door policy. However, employees often quickly find out that although the door may be open, the mind is closed! If you have an open door policy, it means you welcome people to come to your office with their ideas, comments, complaints, and suggestions. It also means that you are open to actively listen to and honestly respond to those who come to see you.

- **Encourage others to express contrary viewpoints.** Let people know that you expect them to challenge and disagree with you. When they do, let them state their case. Do not interrupt. Ask questions to ensure that you understand their point of view. Look for areas of agreement and be willing to see others' perspectives. Once you have a clear understanding of others' views, clarify the points that you support and those you cannot support. Provide a thorough explanation as to "why" you disagree. Help other people understand your perspective by speaking clearly and providing examples and illustrations to clarify your points.

- **Don't "shoot the messenger."** Nothing destroys trust and credibility more than this one. And, unfortunately, this is a common problem in many organizations. A good leader understands that in today's complex organizations people are required to relay messages. These messages may be from other groups within the organization, members of management, special groups or task teams, or employee or labor groups. All messages should be received calmly and no blame must be placed on the messenger. If you shoot the messenger one too many times, not only will the messenger not come back again, but everyone else will do whatever it takes to keep information from you.

- **Encourage employees to share information.** If your employees rely solely on you to keep them informed, you will quickly become overwhelmed and the employees will not get all that they need to do a quality job. Let your staff know that you expect them to share information on a regular basis. Set aside time in staff meetings simply for information sharing. Actively involve others in giving updates and sharing other relevant information. When employees come to you for information that someone else can handle, redirect the employee to go to one of their colleagues for that information.

- **Promptly respond to communication from others.** With advances in technology, people continue to expect response times to phone calls and e-mails to get shorter and shorter. When someone sends you an e-mail, letter, or phone message, get back as soon as you can to let that person know what you are doing about the concern. Even if you cannot respond with a complete answer or solution right away, you can let him or her know that you are working on it. Provide a realistic timeline for when you think that you will respond with the answer. Then do what you said you would do!

- **Keep your manager informed.** Managers differ in the amount of information they wish to receive from the people they manage. Take the time to discover what your boss expects from you. How often does he or she expect to hear from you? Does he or she prefer written information (reports or status updates), quick e-mail updates, or a weekly face-to-face meeting? What types of decisions does he or she expect to be consulted on? When can you make decisions on your own? How much detail does he or she like? These and many other questions must be answered so that you can respond appropriately to your boss. If you cannot readily find the answers to these questions, set up a meeting with your boss to go over these kinds of issues. Remember, just as you would expect from your employees, no boss likes surprises. Find out what your boss needs and keep him or her informed and up to date.

☛ Tips for Success

Communication

1. Think through what you want to say before you say it. Remember, you cannot *not* communicate.

2. Speak clearly and concisely. Also speak with enthusiasm and expressiveness.

3. Be sincere. Most people have a very fine insincerity detector.

4. Develop an attitude of wanting to listen. Demonstrate this by focusing on the sender's message, not on formulating your response.

5. Use a "real" open door policy with your employees.

6. Show that you are listening. Demonstrate this by using attending skills, such as eye contact and leaning forward.

7. Use open-ended questions to open up communication, but use reflective statements to ensure your understanding of the person's feelings.

8. Summarize conversations to ensure understanding and provide closure.

9. Don't shoot the messenger. Encourage or reward people who have contrary viewpoints or who bring you bad news.

10. Keep your boss informed.

Chapter 7

Delegating to Succeed Through Others

"Never tell a person how to do things. Tell them what to do and they will surprise you with their ingenuity."

– *General George Patton*

Most managers and supervisors have heard about delegation. We have read about it. We know that it is important for supervisors to practice. But like many of the skills presented in this book, very few managers or supervisors take the time to study and practice how to be an effective delegator. The most frightening thought about delegation is that when you delegate something, you are putting your reputation and your career path in the hands of other people. And they could damage you if they are not the right people, if you have not trained them properly, or if you fail to delegate properly. The concept of delegation is vitally important to supervisors and managers if they are going to be effective in their jobs. It is difficult to be an effective supervisor without being an effective delegator and vice versa.

There are many benefits to effective delegation:

- **Delegation extends the results from what one person can accomplish to what many people can accomplish.** By involving other people through effective delegation, we have the potential to get more things accomplished in our area of influence. In addition, we are likely to get new ideas and approaches to solve problems by tapping the input and brain power from others.

- **Delegation frees up our time to get the most important things accomplished.** Many of the tasks that supervisors and managers do can be completed by their employees. By delegating routine and ongoing tasks, managers will have more time for more critical tasks, for leadership activities, and for innovation and problem prevention.

- **Delegation develops our employees.** Many times we do not delegate tasks because we feel our employees are not capable of doing the task. And until

73

we delegate the task to them and develop their skills, knowledge, and competence, we will continue to feel that our employees lack the capability. When we delegate tasks to employees, we in effect say, "You've got what it takes to do this job." This will enhance levels of trust between the employee and supervisor. Delegation is a critical employee development tool.

- **Delegation helps empower our employees by taking the decision-making process to the appropriate level.** Historically, many managers have felt that the quality of a decision improved the higher up the organizational chart it was made. Now, we know that decisions involving problems at different levels of the organization are often better if they are made by the people who are actually doing the work. Making decisions at levels where employees are making the product or dealing with customers fosters motivation and a sense of ownership for the task at hand.

Operating Versus Managing Tasks

When we asked supervisors why they were promoted to supervision, most said it was because of their operational skill or ability to do the job they were doing well. They were good at "doing" tasks that got the job done. Most organizations do promote the person who is the best at getting the job done. Examples of this are numerous. The best salesperson is promoted to become the sales manager. The best teacher is promoted to become the principal. The best cook tries to open his or her own restaurant. The best worker, engineer, or computer specialist is made the supervisor. If the worker in the new position does not learn new supervisory and management skills, the tragedy is often double. This means, the company loses its best worker and, at the same time, sets up a supervisor for failure.

As we rise further up the ladder in organizations, our responsibilities change from less emphasis on the operational or doing tasks and more emphasis on the leadership tasks (managing, planning, leading). Getting bogged down in the doing functions rather than the planning, managing, and leading functions is one of the primary downfalls of many supervisors. It is common for supervisors, when called upon to perform both management work and technical, or "doing," work during the same time period, to give priority to the technical work. Most supervisors prefer the operational functions because (1) they are more familiar with them, (2) they are usually easier for the supervisor, (3) they have immediate results, and most importantly of all, (4) the supervisor has been rewarded with a promotion for successfully performing the operational tasks. The past experience and success actually hinders the current effectiveness as a supervisor.

The ideal ratio between *managing or leadership time* and *operating time* will vary, depending on your management level and your particular organization. One reality remains constant: the higher you progress in management, the more time you should spend in managing, planning, problem-solving, and leading tasks and the less time on operating tasks.

Take a moment to complete the following delegation assessment. It will help you rate yourself as a delegator in your current work structure.

How Good Are You at Delegating?

How well do you delegate? As a supervisor, answer each question according to your current work structure by placing a checkmark (✓) in either "Yes" or "No".

❑ Yes   ❑ No   1. I give my employees new tasks, even though they might make a mistake.

❑ Yes   ❑ No   2. My employees get promotions at least as frequently as other people with equivalent responsibility in our organization.

❑ Yes   ❑ No   3. I very seldom take work home or work late at the office.

❑ Yes   ❑ No   4. My operation functions smoothly when I am absent.

❑ Yes   ❑ No   5. I spend more time on planning and supervision than working on details.

❑ Yes   ❑ No   6. My employees feel they have sufficient authority over personnel, finances, facilities, and other resources.

❑ Yes   ❑ No   7. My follow-up procedures are adequate.

❑ Yes   ❑ No   8. I do not overrule or reverse decisions made by my employees.

❑ Yes   ❑ No   9. I never bypass my employees by making decisions that are part of their jobs.

❑ Yes   ❑ No   10. I do not do several things that my employees could—and should—be doing.

❑ Yes   ❑ No   11. If I were incapacitated for six months, there is someone who could take my place.

❑ Yes   ❑ No   12. My key employees delegate well to their own employees.

❑ Yes   ❑ No   13. When I return from an absence, there is not a pile of paperwork requiring my action.

❑ Yes   ❑ No   14. My employees take initiative in expanding their authority with delegated projects without waiting for me to initiate all assignments.

❑ Yes   ❑ No   15. When I delegate, I specify the expected results, not how the tasks are to be done.

Scoring Key: Give yourself one point for each **Yes** answer. A good score is anything above 12.

Why We Don't Delegate

Most supervisors and managers know that delegation is important to their success. So why don't they delegate more? Over the years, we have compiled a list of the most common responses to why people do not delegate.

Reasons for Not Delegating

Common Responses to Why People Do Not Delegate
1. It takes too much time to explain the task.
2. I can do the task faster myself.
3. I can do the task better myself.
4. My staff is already overworked.
5. I am not sure how to do the task myself.
6. If I delegate the task to an employee, I won't get the credit.
7. I don't think my employees can do a good job.
8. I need it done right.
9. I don't have anyone with the proper expertise.
10. I don't trust anyone else to do the job.
11. I like doing the job.
12. It looks better if I do it.
13. I can't delegate the whole task.
14. I'll have to double-check the work anyway.

Common Mistakes in Delegation and How to Avoid Them

When managers do decide to delegate, there are often mistakes made that can negatively impact the employee's ability to do the job. After reviewing the following common mistakes, determine how you can avoid making these errors:

- **An attitude to the workforce of "I can do it better myself."** Particularly because most supervisors started out by doing the job, there is often the feeling that they are still the best person to "do the job"—even though they have been promoted out of the job into supervision. Even if the supervisor could do a better job, the choice is not between the quality of his or her work and the quality of the employee's. The choice is between the benefits of the employee learning to perform that single task and the supervisor spending that time on planning, delegating, coaching, supervising, and developing an employee. Believe in your employees' abilities. They just might surprise you!

- **Failure to keep employees informed about plans the supervisor has for the operation.** Some supervisors delegate tasks without providing all the necessary information to do the task successfully. Many supervisors leave out the big picture. They omit the information about future goals, plans, and important organizational decisions. Employees must be fully informed to make the best possible decisions for the organization.

- **Failure to require, receive, and/or utilize progress reports.** When you do not have a method to check on the employee's progress, two things happen. First, you communicate to the employee that the task delegated to him or her is not important. Second, you may set yourself and the employee up for failure. Agree with the employee on specific times to check progress at certain intervals from the beginning of delegation through completion. Remember, these checkpoints are designed to help the delegation process, not to hinder its success.

- **Unwillingness to let employees supply their own ideas.** When you do not ask for your employee's ideas and opinions, you are communicating that you do not value the employee. You are also limiting your opportunity to gain new information. Remember, if you always do what you've always done, you'll always get what you've always got! Encourage employees to be creative and give their ideas about ways to complete the task.

- **Tendency to "dump projects."** Dumping projects usually occurs because the supervisor has not taken the time to properly plan the delegation. So, at a moment's notice, the supervisor assigns the project to the employee. There are two negative outcomes: (1) the chances for the project being done incorrectly increase immensely and (2) the employee loses motivation because the supervisor did not take into consideration the employee's strengths or ability to get the job done. To ensure that the delegation is successful, take time to plan the delegation, pick the right person for the job, and discuss the task and its expected outcomes.

- **Failure to give the employee credit for shouldering responsibility.** Typically, supervisors who do not delegate like to take all the credit in their area of influence. When an employee does take responsibility, no praise or recognition is passed to the supervisor. Acknowledging an employee's success may be viewed as threatening to the supervisor. With feelings of insecurity, this same supervisor will usually fail to back up an employee when he or she does make decisions. Give credit where credit is due. You will not only gain an enthusiastic employee, but also a loyal one!

- **Inattention to project completion.** Not recognizing a project's completion will practically guarantee that the next project delegated will be completed late, if at all. This then reinforces the supervisor's negative feelings about delegating in the first place. Take a moment to acknowledge task completion. You can also use this opportunity to praise a job well done or to refine or train new skills.

- **Lack of respect for the employee's ambitions.** Supervisors who do not delegate usually do not have an interest in developing their employees. This leads the employee to feel that the supervisor does not care about him or her. When we feel that the boss does not care about us, we lose our motivation and respect for the supervisor. So get to know your employees. Find out their strengths, weaknesses, and ambitions. If possible, support those ambitions. Help them grow.

Deciding What to Delegate

There are four basic steps in deciding what tasks you presently do that could be delegated:

1. Analyze your job.
2. Categorize your activities.
3. Estimate the percentage of time you spend in each category.
4. Decide what to delegate and to whom you will delegate the task.

Step One: Analyze Your Job

The easiest way to analyze your job is to make a list of at least ten tasks that you perform on a daily basis. The more complete the list is, the better understanding you will have of the tasks you may want to delegate. *(A worksheet is provided later in this chapter to help you determine what could be delegated).*

Step Two: Categorize Your Activities

Categorize each of your activities into one of the following four categories: RO for routine or ongoing activities, FF for fire-fighting or problem-solving activities, PR for proactive or initiative-taking activities, and ED for employee development or "helping-people-to-grow" activities.

Step Three: Estimate the Percentage of Time in Each Category

List your estimates by the percentage of time you spend on each activity listed. Then transfer those amounts into this section, remembering that the total should add up to 100 percent.

RO ACTIVITIES	_____
FF ACTIVITIES	_____
PR ACTIVITIES	_____
ED ACTIVITIES	_____
TOTAL:	100 percent

The typical supervisor spends 50 percent of his or her time on routine activities, another 30 to 40 percent on fire-fighting activities, and only 10 to 20 percent on proactive initiative-taking and employee-developing activities. To gain more time for problem prevention and employee development, you have to decide which routine activities you can delegate and to whom.

Step Four: Decide What to Delegate and to Whom

Study the information you have gathered so far, especially concentrating on the RO tasks. Which of these, as well as any of the others, could you delegate? The worksheet in this chapter will help you plan your delegation.

The reason we ask you to list the approximate number of minutes you will save each day if you delegate the task is because most people do not realize how a few minutes each day begins to add up quickly. The worksheet displays how minutes each day add up quickly into full eight-hour days when considered on a yearly basis.

If you were able to delegate just one task that takes 60 minutes each day, at the end of the year you would have 44 full eight-hour days to be spent another way. That is almost a full month of extra productivity to do more important leadership tasks. The worksheet below will help you analyze your job and effectively plan the delegation to ensure success.

Preparing for Delegation

First, list ten of the activities you do on your job. Second, decide which category each activity falls into: **RO** for routine, **FF** for fire-fighting, **PR** for proactive, or **ED** for employee development. Finally, estimate the percentage of time spent on each activity.

Activity	Category	Percentage
1.		
2.		
3.		
4.		
5.		
6.		
7.		
8.		
9.		
10.		

Planning Your Delegation

List the tasks you could delegate, to whom, by when, and the average number of minutes each day you will save if you delegate the task. In determining who to delegate the task to, consider employee development and learning. Are you selecting the appropriate person for the task?

	Task	To Whom	By When	Minutes Saved
1.				
2.				
3.				
4.				
5.				

Time Value of Delegation

Minutes each Day the Task Takes	Number of 8-Hour Days per Year
15	11
30	22
60	44

Another way to look at this is to ask, "How much is my time or my employees' time worth?" To find out what that means to you, use the following chart. Locate your approximate yearly income on the left side of the chart and then see what saving an extra hour a day could mean to your success and your organization's profits. When we look at the value of our time, it usually adds up much faster than we think.

Delegation Savings

Yearly Income	Per Hour	Hour a Day All Month	Hour a Day All Year
$20,000	$ 9.62	$202.02	$2,501
$25,000	$12.02	$252.42	$3,125
$30,000	$14.42	$302.82	$3,749
$35,000	$16.83	$353.43	$4,376
$40,000	$19.23	$403.83	$5,000
$45,000	$21.63	$454.23	$5,624
$50,000	$24.04	$504.84	$6,250
$60,000	$28.85	$605.85	$7,501

Income divided by 2,080 (52 weeks x 40 hours) for per hour rate; month as 21 days; year as 260 days

Planning for the Delegation

Now that you have determined what tasks to delegate to whom, take a few moments to plan for the delegation. To do this, you need to answer the following questions:

1. What is the overall goal or purpose of the task?
2. What specific results do I expect?
3. What does the task entail? What specific elements or skills are needed to successfully complete the task?
4. What resources are available to the employee to get the task accomplished?
5. What checkpoints or follow-up agreements need to be made?

Presenting the Delegation

After you have planned for the delegation, you should be clear on your expectations for getting the job done. These expectations must now be made clear to your employee. Keep in mind that your employee is likely to have some good ideas to offer, so plan on soliciting ideas from him or her as well. Below is a fail-safe process for ensuring delegation success. Be sure to follow each of the seven steps listed below to ensure a successful delegation.

Step One: Explain Overall Goal and Purpose

This critical first step lets the employee know the importance and value or relevancy of the task. Many supervisors make the mistake of skipping this step and start by explaining the task. Specifically, they explain the how-to's of the task. You will find you get better results if you begin by explaining the big picture—the overall purpose of the task—prior to explaining any of the small details. When employees understand the overall goal, they make better decisions.

Step Two: Outline Expected Results

Once the employee understands the overall goal and importance of the task, he or she needs to know exactly what is expected. Do not get this important step confused with the next step, describing the task. The purpose here is to ensure that you and your employee see the same end result and agree when that result will be in place.

Step Three: Describe Task (optional)

This step is usually for inexperienced employees who have never done the task. You may need to provide some training here. If the task is a large or complex one, break it down into smaller, more manageable pieces for easier explanation. The purpose of this step is to ensure that the employee knows how to do the job. For experienced employees, let them decide. As long as they know the expected results, they can decide how to do the job. And guess what? Maybe they'll have a better way to do it!

Step Four: Discuss Resources

To do the job effectively, employees need to know what resources are available to them to get the task accomplished. Are they able to purchase equipment or supplies? Are they able to involve other employees? Are they able to enlist the help of other departments? If it takes working overtime, is overtime authorized? Be specific so that the employee is clear on what resources are and are not available.

Step Five: Confirm Understanding; Get Commitment

Here is where you make sure that you made yourself clear. Ask your employee to restate in his or her own words what is expected. You want to do this for two reasons: (1) it involves the employee and (2) you have confirmed whether the employee understands the task at hand. If you have ever delegated a task to an employee and then had the task completed incorrectly, you will understand the value of this point. Encourage the employee to ask any questions to confirm understanding. Last, ask the employee for his or her commitment in completing the task within the agreed-upon time frame. Without commitment, the task may not be done.

Step Six: Ask for Ideas

One of the best ways to empower and motivate your employees is to ask for their ideas. If you tell the employee how you have done the task in the past, make sure you ask him or her for ideas and suggestions on how to complete the task this time. When employees are given the opportunity to provide their own ideas, they take more responsibility for the completion of the task. When you ask for their ideas, be quiet and really listen. Very often, a fresh perspective can provide great new ideas, especially if you have "always done it this way."

Step Seven: Establish Follow-Up Plan

Once the task has been clarified and confirmed, and the employee's contributions have been solicited and valued, the next step is to establish some guidelines for working together. The supervisor always bears ultimate accountability for any delegated task. Remember, upper management assigns tasks to the supervisor, not to his or her employees. If the supervisor chooses to delegate, it is still ultimately the supervisor's responsibility.

Additionally, the supervisor is responsible for the quality standards and deadlines of any work coming through the unit. No supervisor can afford to turn an employee completely loose on a project. To ensure the fulfillment of supervisory responsibilities, a supervisor has to give adequate and proportionate attention to the people delegated the assignments. One method is to schedule follow-ups at certain completion steps throughout the task. Another more hands-off method is to check with the employee midway from the time you delegate the task to the task's completion. To be effective with this technique, you must make notes on your calendar so that you do not forget. Be cautious not to micromanage. Give the employee room to grow. When you think about it, that is why you can do these tasks so well. Someone gave you room to grow, you made some mistakes, and hopefully, you learned from the mistakes you made. The same process will prove equally valuable to your employees.

Why Delegation Works to Empower Employees

Delegating tasks to our employees shows that we trust them. One of the fastest ways to build trust in a relationship is to take a risk with someone. Delegation is certainly a risk. As a supervisor, your reputation is on the line.

Most employees have a desire to work on their own. When employees work on their own without constant over-the-shoulder supervision, they feel more pride and a greater sense of accomplishment.

By giving our employees more challenging tasks, they feel they play a significant role in the organization. Delegation develops a sense of purpose, responsibility, belonging, and ownership within employees.

These three benefits alone are reason enough to delegate. Add to these the benefits stated at the beginning of the chapter and it is clear to see the value of delegation. Begin the delegation process now. Don't wait. Delegate!

☞ Tips for Success

Delegation

1. To be successful as a supervisor or manager, you have to delegate.

2. Remember that effective delegation will not only expand productivity but will also serve as an employee development tool.

3. List your typical daily activities and determine what percentage are routine, fire-fighting, proactive, or employee development. To be successful, spend more time in the proactive and employee development categories.

4. Calculate the value of your time. Remember, if you delegate a task that only takes you 15 minutes a day, at the end of the year you will have gained 11 full eight-hour days.

5. Plan the delegation. The better your preparation, the better your employees will accomplish the delegated task.

6. When you delegate, present the overall goal and outline the results expected. Do not tell the employee *how* to do the task, unless he or she is learning for the first time.

7. Discuss what resources are available to get the delegated task completed.

8. Confirm understanding, ask for the employee's ideas, and ask for his or her commitment to get the task accomplished.

9. Establish methods of working together and following up.

10. After you have delegated the task, ensure that the employee maintains ownership of the task.

Chapter 8

Coaching to Improve Performance

"Some supervisors spend way too much time running around putting out spot fires, rather than coaching and counseling the pyromaniacs that keep igniting the fires."

– Jane Flaherty

Being a supervisor would be so easy if people just did what they were supposed to do! When we ask supervisors in our seminars this question, "Why don't employees do what they are supposed to do?" we receive these types of responses:

- The employee does not know how to do the task.
- The employee thinks the supervisor's way to do it will not work.
- The employee is not motivated to do the task right.
- The employee does not know what he or she is supposed to do.
- The employee thinks his or her way is better.
- The employee thinks something else is more important.
- There are no positive consequences for correct behavior.
- There are no negative consequences for continuing wrong behavior.
- The employee is not capable of doing the task.
- The employee does not see the value in completing the task.
- There are obstacles that prevent the employee from completing the task.
- The employee has personal problems.

Now that we have a fairly complete list of reasons why employees do not do what they are supposed to do, the important question is this: "If you, as the supervisor, allow poor performance to continue because of these reasons, who is ultimately responsible for the poor performance?" Unfortunately, or fortunately, as the supervisor, *you are responsible.*

It is important to realize that almost all of these reasons for nonperformance are controlled by the supervisor or manager. Poor performance occurs because of poor supervision. If supervisors and managers took appropriate actions to make sure these reasons for poor performance are prevented or removed, the result would be satisfactory performance.

In this chapter, we will discuss how supervisors can effectively coach and counsel their employees for improved performance. We will also share a proven interactive management process that supervisors can utilize to prevent most of the reasons why people do not do what they are supposed to do.

Why Should Supervisors Coach?

In Chapter 7, Delegating to Succeed Through Others, we made reference to the fact that a manager or supervisor, by nature of the job, gives people things to do. Before you became a supervisor, your success was based solely on what you accomplished. Now that you are a supervisor, the rules have changed. Your success as a supervisor is no longer determined by what you accomplish, but rather, by what your employees accomplish.

As a supervisor, your raises, promotions, demotions, and nonpromotions are now based on the results your employees can generate. When your employees are successful, you will be viewed as a successful supervisor. In contrast, when your employees are failing, you will be recognized as an unsuccessful supervisor, no matter what you personally are accomplishing. The results of your staff are what determine your score.

To underscore the importance of what employees do, ask yourself this question: "Who needs whom more? Does the supervisor need the employees more or vice versa?" Another way to put meaning to this question is to ask this: "If you did not show up for work tomorrow, what percentage of your department's workload would still be completed?" Usually, supervisors will answer anywhere from 85 percent to 100 percent of the total workload. Now let's reverse the question and ask: "If all your employees did not show up for work tomorrow, what percentage of the workload would be completed by you?" If you answered any higher than 15 percent of the total workload, you may be kidding yourself.

The bottom line is that you get paid for what your employees do, not for what you do. For this very reason, you need to do everything in your power to help your staff be as successful as possible. The more successful your staff is, the more successful you will be as a supervisor. We can even look at this point from the opposite direction—when your employees fail, you have failed also.

Why Supervisors Fail As Coaches

Supervisors complain that the employees who do not do what they are supposed to do are their biggest headaches. This headache is usually the source of built-up frustration from unsuccessful attempts to get the employee to change his or her behavior. Some supervisors have said they have tried for years to motivate an employee to change his or her behavior without achieving any significant results. And there are several reasons why supervisors have difficulty in coaching.

The supervisor has had no formal training in coaching. Getting employees to change their behavior is not an easy task. Instead of getting each employee to understand that a problem exists and asking the employee for solutions, most supervisors do what they are comfortable doing: tell... Tell... TELL!

The problem with *telling* someone they have to change is two-fold. First, you have no guarantee that the employee agrees there is a problem. And second, most employees become defensive when being told they are doing something wrong. In the coaching process explained in this chapter, we will learn that the best coaches *ask* questions, rather than *tell* answers.

In frustration, the supervisor ceases to treat his or her employees with dignity and respect. "I am only human," I heard one supervisor say as he yelled at one of his employees for making a mistake. When we have an employee who is not doing what he or she is supposed to do, we tend to respond in ways that aggravate, not help, the situation. Some supervisors will attack an employee's personality, saying, "You are not motivated," "You are not ambitious," or "You are careless." Some supervisors will bang doors, slam down phones, or even throw things.

These same supervisors would never walk into the company president's office and exhibit these same aggressive behaviors. The reason why they do not exhibit these behaviors up the organizational ladder is because it would be self-destructive. They would be fired. Unfortunately, supervisors do not see that these behaviors are also self-destructive when used going down the organizational ladder. These behaviors usually achieve the exact opposite goal that the supervisor desires. They de-motivate, frustrate, and cause employees to increase undesirable behaviors.

Supervisors fail to see employees as "true resources." When supervisors encounter problems with machines, materials, facilities, or budgets, most figure out ways to make the most of what they have. For example, if you were the supervisor at a plant where a machine had stopped working, you would do everything in your power to get it up and running again. Most organizations do not have the luxury of replacing a machine every time it breaks down.

In contrast, when a human resource fails, supervisors are quick to explain the problem as "the employee's problem." By placing the blame on the employee, the supervisor absolves himself or herself of all responsibility to correct the "problem." The typical response to a human resource problem is to replace the person. It would almost sound funny to say, "It's the machine's fault. It's old. There's nothing I can do about it." In almost every area, *except human resources*, supervisors are great at taking the responsibility to solve problems.

Most supervisors never calculate the cost of replacing one of their human resources. We recently heard an example of what it cost to replace an employee. A manager told us that it cost her nearly $50,000 to replace a $60,000-a-year employee. When you add up severance pay, advertising, interview time and expenses, agency fees, relocation expenses, reorientation, and training time, it is easy to see how these costs can quickly add up. For a highly specialized or technical employee, replacement costs can easily add twice the employee's annual salary.

To manage all of your resources *except your human resources* is going directly against what you are paid to do as a supervisor. As a coach, your responsibility is to help develop *each* of your employees. As a supervisor, you must accept full responsibility for all your human resources, just as you always have with all of your non-human resources.

Attitude and the Coaching Process

"That employee has a rotten attitude" is a classic response supervisors use when they have problems getting an employee to do what he or she is supposed to do. What most supervisors assume is that any employee who does what he or she is supposed to do has a good attitude, and if the employee does not do what he or she is supposed to do, there's a bad attitude. But, there are two problems with relying on attitudes to determine your course of action.

First, it is difficult to truly know what an employee's attitude is. Attitudes are something internal and unique to every individual. If you think you know what an employee's attitude is, it is usually based on what your attitude is or would be in a similar situation. We can even go so far as to say we know what the employee's attitude is based on his or her actions. The problem with this line of thought is that people at times do things in direct opposition to their true feelings. Haven't you ever communicated with good manners and even possibly kindness with someone you did not like? We really do not know for certain what people's attitudes are. We only guess at what they are and then become trapped into believing our guesses are correct. As a rule, supervisors should stay clear of the mind-reading business.

Second, by placing blame on the employee's attitude, we absolve ourselves of responsibility for the problem. The real problem you need to deal with is not the employee's attitude, but the employee's behavior. If the employee is behaving in appropriate and productive ways, then it really does not matter what his or her attitude is.

For example, let's say a waiter hates his job. Normally, a waiter who hates his job is associated with providing poor service. But, if the waiter is exhibiting appropriate behaviors and the customers are happy, then you do not have a problem. If the waiter is giving poor service, then poor service is the problem you need to deal with, not the employee's bad attitude.

Attitude is not the issue when you are coaching an employee. Behavior is the only thing you can legitimately deal with. You can see it when it is bad, you can measure it, you can talk about it unemotionally, and you can acknowledge it when there is improvement. If you start trying to change behavior rather than trying to change people, you will no longer be faced with the resistance people naturally present because *they* do not want to be changed.

Ask Instead of *Tell*

Just because you are speaking to someone does not guarantee you are communicating with someone. Hearing is seldom the receiver's problem. The problem is usually related to the receiver's lack of concentration on the information the sender is sending. Part of this problem is that the mind can think up to four times faster than we can speak. This means that while we are listening, we are also usually using the extra time to think of other things. The mind is typically reacting even before the message has been completed.

What does this mean to supervisors who are coaching employees? It means that as long as you are telling employees what they are doing wrong, the employees will be thinking of something else—usually the reasons why what you are saying is not correct. An example could work like this:

> **Supervisor:** Bill, you have been late three times this week. What can you do so you arrive to work on time?
>
> **Bill:** Mary has been late also. Have you talked to her yet?

For supervisors, one of the biggest mistakes they can make is telling a problem employee what they are doing wrong. As soon as you say the words, the employee will hear them, but think of something else, like "Look at Mary, she's late also."

Because the mind is primarily a reactive instrument, successful communication is a function of thought transmission, rather than information transmission. In coaching employees, thought transmission takes place by asking questions. In the previous example, the supervisor could have asked any one of the following questions:

Supervisor: Bill, what happens when I need you first thing in the morning and you are not here?

Bill, when you are not here and your phone rings, other employees have to answer it for you. What impact does that have on their schedules?

Bill, if I allowed you to be late, what impact do you feel that might have on the other employees in our department?

Bill, when a customer needs you and you are unavailable because you are late, what impact might that have on our customers?

What is so interesting about this concept of thought transmission is that when the supervisor does not use it, the employee will. Think about a time when you ran into problems providing feedback to an employee. The chances are you felt frustrated because the more you told the employee, the more he or she seemed to find fault in what you were saying. The only way you can guarantee that the employee understands there is a problem is to get the words to come out of his or her mouth through thought transmission. And the way a supervisor facilitates thought transmission is by asking the appropriate questions.

Preparing for Coaching Discussion

Coaching is, in many ways, a negotiation. And, just like a negotiation session, the better you prepare, the better your chances of obtaining a favorable outcome. Consider the following questions before you begin a coaching discussion. Your answers will provide a framework for conducting a win/win interaction.

- **What is the problem?** Identify the specific problem. Exactly what is happening that shouldn't be or what should be happening that isn't? Some typical problems may include (a) coming in late, (b) excessive absences, (c) sales down, (d) customer complaints, or (e) incomplete reports. Make sure you define the problem in specific "behavioral" terms. Remember, a bad attitude is *not* a specific behavioral problem. However, ignoring customers or not providing follow-up within 24 hours is.

- **What is the cause of the problem?** You may not know for sure what the cause of the problem is until you have the coaching discussion. However, you can begin to identify possible causes. For example, sales may be down because (a) the salesperson is no longer calling on new accounts or (b) maybe existing accounts are not being asked about additional services that may be needed. Why are the reports incomplete? Is it because (a) the employee is not doing a thorough analysis or could it be that (b) the employee is not getting the information he or she needs from someone else to complete the report? A clear understanding of the cause of the problem will speed up the problem-solving process and will allow for realistic and practical solutions.

- **Does the problem warrant coaching?** If the problem is only an isolated incident or an issue that is not really important, it may not be worth your time or effort for an actual coaching discussion. In addition, it could be harmful to the employee's motivation. An example would be the employee who stays late each night until the job is done and then comes in late one morning. If the supervisor were to talk to the employee about the one late arrival, resentment could easily happen. The result of this kind of discussion could be two-fold: the loss of self-motivation and the loss of respect for the supervisor. Make sure the problem is in fact a problem before you enter into a coaching discussion.

- **Is the employee capable?** Is the employee physically and mentally able to do the job? Does he or she have the skills, knowledge, and abilities to successfully complete the job or task? If the answer is "no," then education or training may be needed to properly prepare the employee.

- **Does the employee have the right resources?** Does the employee have what he or she needs to complete the task? In other words, are the necessary resources available to the employee? Resources may include finances, other people, raw materials, equipment, and/or facilities. If the necessary resources are not available to the employee, they must be provided or the job expectations must change. Good managers set their employees up for success by ensuring that they can do the job and they have what they need to do a good job!

- **Does the employee know right or wrong?** The most common reason employees do not know that they are doing something wrong is because they think they are doing it right. Some supervisors have a bad habit of only providing feedback in severe instances when the employee has demonstrated inappropriate behavior. The other times, when the employee is plodding along on the path of mediocrity, the supervisor says nothing. Many employees think that mediocre performance is good enough because no one has ever told them differently. If workers in any job believe they are doing what they are expected to do, why should it occur to them to do anything different? As a supervisor, your obligation is to have good communication with your employees so that they know what is appropriate and inappropriate behavior.

- **Are there rewards for non-performance or punishments for performance?** A classic example of how an employee could be punished for performance is when a worker in a production facility works faster than the rest of the employees, and as a consequence, is given more work to do. The employees who take their time and work slowly are rewarded by having more work taken away from them. Supervisors experience this phenomenon every day. If you have problem employees, you seldom ask them to take on new tasks because you know it will be difficult to get them to agree to do the tasks. So, instead, you give the assignments to the employees you give all your tasks to because they are more willing to get things done. This is how supervisors can reward negative behavior.

Suggestions for Dealing with Performance Problems

Take immediate action. The longer you wait to confront a negative behavior, the harder it will be to change. It does not take long before the inappropriate behavior becomes a habit, and habits are very hard to break. Once you have determined that a negative pattern of behavior exists, take action.

Give feedback privately. Prior to beginning the discussion, you should make sure that you have a private location to meet. Take steps to ward off any interruptions. If at all possible, hold the meeting one-on-one. Only in rare instances is a third party necessary. (If the employee is to be terminated or is unwilling to cooperate, you may need a third party, such as a union representative or a human resources representative.)

Remain calm. If you have ever driven home from work saying, "Now why did I say that?" chances are you may have regretted giving feedback to an employee when you were mad. If you are angry or emotional, postpone the discussion until you are feeling more in control. Remember, communication is permanent. Do not lose control of the discussion or say something that may later come back to haunt you.

Be consistent. Do what you say you are going to do. If you tell employees you are going to do something if their inappropriate behavior does not change, do what you say you are going to do. If employees do not feel you are going to take action, they may see no need to change.

Correct behaviors selectively. Do not use a correcting session to point out all the negative things that you have seen over time. If you coach properly, you should only be dealing with one or two inappropriate behaviors at a time. If you do not have ongoing communication with your employees, you may start to generate a laundry list of behaviors you want to discuss. The laundry list will have little impact and will likely get thrown out in the wash! Our general rule of thumb is, "If it's more than two, they think it's you!" Meaning, if you do bring out your long list of inappropriate behaviors, after about point five or six, the employee begins to think, "Why bother to even come to work? I must not be doing anything right. I never thought my boss liked me anyway. She's always picking on me!"

Remain positive. Keep your thoughts positive. Help the employee identify what is causing the problem and what the employee will do to help resolve the problem. Remember, the goal of this discussion is to make the employee more successful. Only in rare instances is an employee not willing to grow by changing negative behaviors.

Coaching Discussion Model

The purpose of the coaching discussion is to redirect the employee's behavior. You want the employee to stop inappropriate behavior and start demonstrating appropriate behavior. It is a two-way process, a *discussion*. The intended purpose is for the employee to be engaged in a discussion as well. In fact, the employee should be talking more than the supervisor or the manager. Using the following six steps of the Coaching Discussion Model will make your coaching discussions effective.

Step One: Help the Employee See the Existing Problem

This is the most important step of the entire coaching discussion. If the employee does not agree there is a problem, then the supervisor actually has two problems to deal with: (1) the inappropriate behavior and (2) the employee not thinking the inappropriate behavior is a problem.

Step One is a difficult area for supervisors. Many lack a feeling of competence in this area. Without preparation, this beginning can be difficult; therefore, many supervisors want to just skip over this step. But, if the employee does not agree there is a problem, he or she will probably lack the motivation to improve behavior. The types of questions we could ask to gain agreement in this area include:

"What is/are the result(s) of this behavior (non-performance)?"

"What impact does this behavior have on other employees/departments?"

"What would happen if all employees did this behavior?"

"What would happen if I (the supervisor/manager) ignored this behavior indefinitely?"

"Do you know how many times you have done this behavior in the last _____?"

"What impact does this behavior have on our customers?"

"What credibility do you feel I have with my boss when I allow this behavior to continue?"

"I am puzzled why you don't perceive this as a problem. Can you elaborate?"

If the employee is still unwilling to admit there is a problem by answering any of the above questions, you may need to move to the second stage of questioning.

"What will happen if you continue with this behavior?"

When the employee responds with, "You could write me up or suspend me," you can then respond with, "You are right. And if you continued with this behavior after I documented this problem or suspended you, what else could I do?"

A second question you may try is, "Do you think I can decide to let you continue this behavior?"

If the employee states that allowing the negative behavior to continue is not your choice, you can respond with, "You are right! What do you think you can do differently so we no longer have this problem?"

If the employee states that you can decide to allow the behavior to continue indefinitely, you can respond with, "You are incorrect. As a supervisor, I am responsible for seeing that (the area of concern you are discussing) is not a problem in our department/company."

The employee's comments could activate some of the following responses:

"You could suspend, demote, inhibit my promotion, put something in my personnel file, fire me..."

Your response could be,

"You are right, because I need someone in that position who will do (describe the behavior) what needs to be done."

The employee might say,

"You could do anything you want, because you are the boss."

Your response could be,

"No, I cannot. Your choice of behavior limits my behavior."

You might think some of these questions and responses in this second round sound threatening. Well, you are right. If the consequences are realistic (that the employee could be suspended or fired) and if he or she is unwilling to change his or her behavior, it is important that the employee understand the consequences of his or her own behavior.

It may be difficult to get agreement that a problem exists. The following possibilities will help you evaluate the situation more thoroughly.

- You are not dealing with a behavior related to performance.

- It is important, but you have not correctly identified all of the negative consequences.

- You are not using thought transmission, but you are verbalizing the consequences instead of the consequences being verbalized by the employee.

- In the past relationship, you have never done what you said you were going to do and have limited credibility with the employee.

- There is a positive consequence for the employee to continue the negative behavior.

- The employee has psychological problems too severe to manage.

Step Two: Clarify the Cause of the Problem

Once the employee clearly sees that there is a problem, you can begin to ask, "Why?" The employee may have an idea why the problem is occurring; the employee may know something you don't know. Do not assume that you already know the cause of the problem. Make sure you ask for input and ideas. It is more likely that the person doing the job will have an understanding of why the job is not being done right. This person is also more likely to have good solutions to the problem. As a supervisor, you just need to ask—and then listen.

Step Three: Mutually Discuss Alternative Solutions

Once you have gained agreement that a problem exists and you have clarified the cause of the problem, you are ready to move to solutions. You can say to the employee, "Now that we agree there is a problem, what do you think you can do differently to solve the problem?" Make sure to focus on the word *differently*, because if the employee keeps on doing the same behaviors, he or she will keep getting the same results. It is important that the supervisor let the employee generate solutions. For example, if the inappropriate behavior resulted in errors in a document, then we would want to ask the employee what he or she thought could be done *differently* to produce fewer typos. The employee might reply

- "I could proofread each page" or
- "I could have someone else proofread each page."

With each response, acknowledge the good ideas. Ask, "What else could you do?" Remember, you are trying to generate viable alternatives. If the employee cannot think of any ideas, you need to be prepared to ask questions to help steer him or her down the right path. For example, you could ask

- "Would it be beneficial to spend time proofreading each page?" or
- "Would it help you to have someone else proofread each page?"

Step Four: Mutually Select an Alternative(s)

Do not waste time in Step Three debating which alternative is feasible. If you criticize an alternative an employee shares, the employee will stop sharing. In Step Four, you are now ready to pick an alternative. Once again, the best method to select an alternative is to ask questions. Ask the employee which alternative he or she thinks will work best—and why. Let the employee think it through and let the employee pick the solution.

Step Five: Follow Up

Make sure to follow up with employees to see how they are doing. Many supervisors make the mistake of not following up to ensure that the agreed-upon action has been taken. The supervisor may be too busy to check or may trust that the employee is going to change his or her behavior. The employee will often change the behavior immediately after the performance improvement discussion. But, because there is no recognition for the improved performance, the employee will often slip back to inappropriate behaviors. Two months later, the supervisor sees the negative behavior again and assumes that there has been no change. If the employee has not modified his or her behavior, the new problem becomes that the employee did not do what he or she agreed to do.

Step Six: Recognize Achievement When It Occurs

This step can be a tough one. Let's say your employee has been performing at the 50 percent level, but satisfactory performance is at 90 percent. You provide coaching, and during the next week, the employee raises his or her performance to 60 percent. You think to yourself, "It is a little better, but he or she still has a long way to go," therefore, you do not want to say anything about the improvement for fear that the employee will feel the little improvement is good enough.

If you want the improvement to continue, the key is to recognize it, no matter how small! Recognize the employee's progress. Then ask the employee what can be done to bring the next round of improvement to an even higher level.

This model is successful in handling the majority of employee-related problems. If you adequately plan for the discussion, you will have positive results. In the rare instances where an employee is still not willing to improve the behavior—even after the discussion—the Corrective Action Feedback Model then becomes appropriate.

Corrective Action Feedback Model

Unlike the Coaching Discussion Model, the Corrective Action Feedback Model is *not* a two-way discussion. It is the style most supervisors feel very comfortable with. In fact, in this model, you actually ask employees to hold their comments and questions until you have finished presenting your information.

Step One: Specifically Describe the Problem Behavior

Example: "John, in the last month, you have been late to work 15 minutes or more at least five times."

Step Two: Express Feelings about the Behavior's Impact

Example: "John, I am disappointed that you continue to come to work late. We have discussed this matter several times. As your supervisor, I feel this is unfair to the other employees who get here on time. I also feel it wastes my time and the other employees' time. When we need you and you are not here, we have to come back again to look for you."

Step Three: Value the Employee

Example: "John, you have been in our department for two years. You know the operation well and I value the job that you do."

Step Four: Specify Desired Future Behavior

Example: "In the next three months, I am holding you responsible for getting to work on time every day."

Step Five: Project Positive and Negative Outcomes

Example: "John, if you are able to be at work on time each day for the next three months, here are the *positive* things that could happen:

- First, I won't be talking to you about being late.
- Second, I will put a letter in your employee file saying that you have improved.
- Third, you will be eligible for a favorable performance review.
- Fourth, you will once again be eligible for raises and promotions.
- Fifth, you will keep your job."

Example: "John, if you continue to be late, here are the *negative* courses of action:

- First, we will have this discussion once again, we will document it, and we will place a copy in your employee file.

- The second time it happens, I will suspend you for two days without pay.

- The third time you are late, you need to understand that I will fire you."

At this point, you must ask the employee if he (John) understands the consequences. If he says "Yes," ask him to tell you what he understands. Take this step to make sure that he understands the major points.

There is no arguing that coaching is a tough supervisory skill. However, it is a skill that is critical to your success as a supervisor. No matter how accomplished your team, there will be times when you need to talk to a team member about changing some aspect of his or her performance. So take time to prepare, envision yourself being successful, and confidently deal with the occasional coaching challenges that come your way. Remember, your ability to lead a great team and progress in your supervisory career will be in direct proportion to your ability to coach your team members.

☛ Tips for Success

Coaching

1. Focus on behaviors, not on the employee's attitude.

2. *Ask* great questions; beware of *tell.*

3. Clearly define performance problems and understand consequences before you go into the performance improvement discussion.

4. Correct immediately. The longer you wait, the harder it gets to change negative behaviors.

5. Correct privately. One-on-one helps maintain the employee's dignity and respect.

6. Help the employee understand that a problem exists by asking questions.

7. Ask the employee for his or her suggestions about how to correct the problem.

8. If possible, allow the employee to select the solution.

9. If you choose to use the non-discussion model, make sure that you clarify both the positive and negative outcomes for the employee.

10. Do what you say you are going to do.

Chapter 9

Conducting Valuable Performance Reviews

"Top performers in any field are developed, not born."

– Joe Griffith

We were recently contacted by a small manufacturing firm that was interested in having us help them with their performance appraisal system. Prior to our meeting with senior management, we assumed they were interested in learning more about various performance review systems. Thinking this was the reason they had called us, we came to the meeting prepared with a number of samples of different types of employee appraisal/review programs. Imagine our surprise when half way through the meeting the CEO said, "We are not so much interested in changing the system we use, but in having someone from the outside conduct our performance reviews."

Collectively, the senior management in this organization had decided that having an outsider conduct reviews would be a better use of their supervisors' time and help keep the performance review and salary adjustment more objective. We quickly explained that we did not think that conducting performance reviews from the outside would result in a positive outcome for anyone involved in the process: the employee, supervisor, or us, the consulting firm. We left the meeting, more convinced than ever that the challenging process of conducting employee performance reviews is the least preferred supervisory activity, or the job nobody wants!

Despite the fact that supervisors typically look for every opportunity to move the task of conducting performance reviews to the bottom of their daily "to do" list, effective performance review systems are a vital part of increasing employee effectiveness. Systems that incorporate a combination of on-the-job coaching, performance appraisals, counseling sessions, interviews, and performance improvement plans developed jointly by supervisor and subordinate can be extremely effective in raising employee performance. Many organizations that we work with have well-developed and clearly defined performance review systems in place. Yet, on the whole, supervisors in these organizations still shy away from the process, and the system is feared and disliked by supervisor and employee alike.

In this chapter, our first goal is to help you become more familiar with the different aspects of a typical performance review system. Our second goal is to help raise your degree of confidence in your ability to conduct employee performance reviews that lead to greater rapport between you and the employees you supervise as well as increased employee effectiveness.

Overview of the Performance Review Cycle

It is important to understand that the performance review does not just consist of going over the items listed on the review form with the employee on a yearly basis. The intent of any performance review process is to improve employee performance. In order to get improved employee performance, a continuous process is necessary. While it is true that the review interview is an extremely important part of the process, it alone cannot effect change in employee performance.

The review process begins when the supervisor clarifies what is expected of the employee. Typically, this is done by identifying significant job elements, or segments, and then developing standards of acceptable performance for each element. After a set period of time, allowing the supervisor opportunities to observe the employee's performance, a performance review interview is conducted between the supervisor and the employee. At the conclusion of the interview, a performance improvement plan can be developed jointly by the supervisor and the employee. This plan details what the employee will be working on during the next review period.

The next step in the process is on-the-job coaching. The supervisor works closely with the employee to help raise the employee's level of performance. The first step in the process is then repeated at the end of the designated review cycle. To better understand the process, consider the following diagram.

Employee Performance Review Cycle

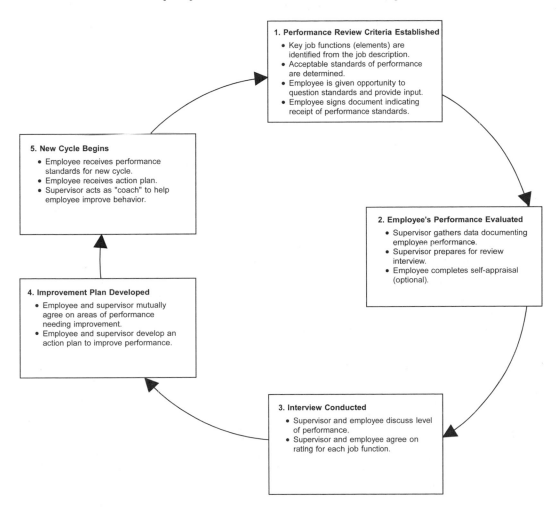

1. Performance Review Criteria Established
- Key job functions (elements) are identified from the job description.
- Acceptable standards of performance are determined.
- Employee is given opportunity to question standards and provide input.
- Employee signs document indicating receipt of performance standards.

2. Employee's Performance Evaluated
- Supervisor gathers data documenting employee performance.
- Supervisor prepares for review interview.
- Employee completes self-appraisal (optional).

3. Interview Conducted
- Supervisor and employee discuss level of performance.
- Supervisor and employee agree on rating for each job function.

4. Improvement Plan Developed
- Employee and supervisor mutually agree on areas of performance needing improvement.
- Employee and supervisor develop an action plan to improve performance.

5. New Cycle Begins
- Employee receives performance standards for new cycle.
- Employee receives action plan.
- Supervisor acts as "coach" to help employee improve behavior.

Developing a Performance Review System

Step One: Clarify Your Expectations

The first step in the performance review process is to select the significant job elements particular to the employee's position. Almost all organizations have job descriptions detailing the duties and responsibilities of a particular job. These descriptions can be an excellent source of information when selecting the basic job elements to use in the review process.

107

While job descriptions may have extensive details particular to the specific job, typically performance appraisal documents will only have five to seven categories, or elements. Within those categories, descriptions for acceptable performance are to be detailed. To be most effective, these job elements should be jointly reviewed and agreed upon by both the supervisor and the employee. In addition to understanding the specific elements of the job, the employee must also be familiar with the levels of expectation, or standards for performance, for each particular element. Standards of performance describe how the job will be done. It is important that the employee understand both the basic elements of the job and the expectations for acceptable performance. Knowledge of the standards for acceptable performance helps ensure employee success on the job. According to Ella Fitzgerald, "It ain't what you do, it's the way that you do it."

Step Two: Set Performance Standards

Job elements describe what must be done to accomplish the job. Performance standards describe how the job will be done. Together, they provide a guideline for the employee's performance and a basis for reviewing the employee's success on the job. When setting standards for performance, it is important that the employee be involved in the process. This helps ensure that the employee understands the standards and also helps motivate the employee to achieve or exceed the standard. When standards are being set, it is a good idea for both the supervisor and employee to initially set the standards independently. Then, after setting standards individually, the supervisor and employee should compare their standards and mutually agree on acceptable standards. If many people are doing the same job, representatives of the group should initially set standards of performance for the job. Next, representatives should present their agreed on standards to the supervisor. Together, they mutually agree on the standards for acceptable performance.

What follows is an example of performance standards and job description for the position of administrative assistant.

Job Description: Administrative Assistant

1. Answer telephone calls and route calls to party requested.
2. Take messages or route to voice mail when requested party is not present.
3. Screen visitors.
4. Schedule appointments.
5. Use word processor for routine reports and letters.
6. Receive and route incoming mail.
7. Maintain filing system.
8. Maintain department calendar.
9. Maintain follow-up system for appointments, calls, and correspondence.

Performance Standards: Administrative Assistant

Job Elements	Performance Standards
Answer telephone	Answers calls by the third ring Takes messages or routes calls to voice mail
Greet visitors	Welcomes visitors and requests that they sign in Gives visitor badge to each visitor Notifies employee that he/she has a visitor
Maintain department calendar	Keeps accurate, up-to-date master calendar for all department functions/deadlines Notifies department employees of significant changes to calendar
Process incoming mail	Opens correspondence unless marked "confidential" Routes all mail to correct department/employee the same day mail arrives
File correspondence	Files all department correspondence within three working days of receipt
Type correspondence and reports	Inputs all written correspondence by time requested and creates documents that are free of grammatical and spelling errors

Step Three: Determine the Rating Scale

Once the job elements have been set, and acceptable standards for performance have been mutually agreed on, the next step involves determining a scale to allow the supervisor to differentiate between levels of performance. Organizations use a variety of rating standards to determine an employee's level of success. The following sample is a simple system used to rate performance:

Job Elements	Performance Standards	Exceeds Standard	Meets Standard	Does Not Meet Standard	Comments
1.					
2.					

Another system commonly used by organizations uses five rating standards:

Job Elements	Performance Standards	Consist. Exceeds Standard	Often Exceeds Standard	Meets Standard	Sometimes Meets Standard	Does Not Meet Standard	Comments
1.							
2.							

When determining a rating system, it is important to describe what each of the gradations used in the system means. For example:

Consistently Exceeds Standard: Employee's work consistently exceeds the levels of performance set for this standard.

Often Exceeds Standard: Employee's work usually exceeds the levels of performance set for this standard.

Meets Standard: Employee's work consistently meets the levels of performance set for this standard.

Sometimes Meets Standard: Employee's work is consistently below the levels of performance set for this standard.

Does Not Meet Standard: Employee's level of performance is unsatisfactory.

Here is another example of a performance review rating system:

Job Elements	Performance Standards	Above the Standard	Meets the Standard	Less Than Standard	Needs to Improve
1.					
2.					

Above the Standard: Job performance that consistently and significantly surpasses the required job standards.

Meets the Standard: Regular and consistent work habits that fully meet the standard or requirements of the position.

Less than Standard: Occasional work that meets minimal requirements of standards; need for improved performance.

Needs to Improve: Work frequently completed at less than standard level; immediate improvement necessary.

Step Four: Begin the Appraisal Process

During the rating period, the supervisor should be continuously gathering information about the employee's performance. Every attempt should be made to obtain information regarding the employee's performance at regular intervals throughout the rating period, not just the week before the appraisal interview. Evaluating an employee's performance continuously throughout the rating period helps ensure that the information gathered is fair, accurate, and representative of the employee's performance throughout the year.

When gathering information about an employee's performance, be aware of two pitfalls: the tendency to overrate a favored employee and unfairly underrate a challenging employee. In some cases, supervisors overrate an employee whose actual performance does not truly measure up under close examination. For example, some people are awarded high ratings based on their past record or because they get along well with the supervisor and other team members. Some are overrated because they may present themselves well, dress impressively, or be a glib talker. Some employees may have accomplished little of consequence throughout the year, but accomplish something outstanding two weeks before the performance review interview and are awarded a higher rating than they deserve.

On the other hand, some people may be rated lower than their actual perform-ance on the job warrants for a variety of reasons. Sometimes people receive lower ratings simply because they are different. For example, people who raise questions and are not afraid to disagree with the boss are often rated lower than employees who conform and accept the system. People whose personality traits differ signifi-cantly from their supervisor's may be unjustly rated lower. Just as some mediocre employees who perform an outstanding job the week before the performance review interview are awarded a higher rating than they deserve, some employees are unjustly awarded a lower rating simply because of a mistake occurring shortly before the annual review process concludes. Although the employee may have per-formed admirably throughout the year, the one mistake wipes out the employee's track record for performance, and a lower rating is assigned.

Documentation. Unfortunately, conducting performance reviews is not the only task assigned to supervisors. Typically, because it is not a routine completed on a daily basis, we tend to put it toward the bottom of our daily "to do" list. To be objec-tive, however, we cannot leave the data-gathering process until the day before we are scheduled to conduct the employee's annual performance review. It is important to periodically review the employee's job elements and performance standards and make notes throughout the year regarding the employee's level of performance. This can be as simple as occasionally jotting down a few quick lines, noting evidence of either exceptional or unacceptable employee performance. Then date the note and drop it into the employee's file. When it comes time to rate the employee, com-pleting the performance appraisal form will require less time and effort because you have noted levels of performance periodically throughout the year. Further, ade-quate documentation collected at intervals throughout the year helps ensure that the supervisor remains objective and does not rate the employee based only on performance immediately prior to the end of the review cycle.

Of course, if you have concerns about an employee's performance, do not wait until the end of the performance review cycle to address the issue. Coaching and counseling throughout the cycle is far more effective than waiting until the end of the cycle and then presenting the employee with a list of concerns that you have had throughout the year. Remember, there should be no surprises during the perform-ance review interview. If you have concerns about an employee's performance, the employee should already be aware of these issues.

Self-Appraisal. Some organizations encourage employees to be active participants in the appraisal process by evaluating and rating their own performance prior to the assessment interview with their supervisor. In such organizations, employees are reminded throughout the year to review their standards of performance and document areas where they feel they have exceeded the standard. Approximately one month before the employee's annual review, the employee is reminded to begin preparing for the review interview by completing the performance review form and rating him- or herself as objectively as possible. Employees need to be cautioned about both rating themselves higher or lower than they deserve. They must be advised to compare their performance against the standards of acceptable performance and not to a coworker's on-the-job performance.

Organizations that promote self-appraisal as part of the annual review process cite increased productivity, higher morale, and greater rapport between supervisor and employee as benefits of the program. Employees who participate in the review process are more familiar with their standards of performance for their job and work harder to exceed the standards. Further, employees who complete the self-appraisal are better prepared to actively participate in the performance review interview. When a supervisor reviews the employee's self-appraisal, it communicates to the employee, "I value your input." The truth is, supervisors cannot be everywhere and see it all. Encouraging the employee to complete the self-appraisal process helps the supervisor by providing more documentation about the employee's performance. On the other hand, employees who have not participated in any part of the review process show up at the review interview ready to have their supervisor "pass judgment" on their performance. An employee who does not agree with the supervisor's appraisal of his or her performance may become defensive and argumentative.

Step Five: Get Ready for the Interview

Conducting performance reviews that make a difference and are of value to the employee requires thorough prior preparation. Consider the following factors:

- **Think about time and location.** Pick a time of day convenient to both parties and schedule the meeting in an area where the door can be closed and the conversation kept private. Make it known to others that unless there is a crisis, you do not want to be interrupted during the review interview with the employee. Conducting a productive annual review takes concentration and interruptions can distract both the supervisor and the employee. Consider also the arrangement of the furniture. If possible, try sitting at a round table or side-by-side with the employee. Sitting across from your supervisor, who is seated behind the security of a desk, can be intimidating for some employees. Sitting side-by-side helps equalize the situation and is more conductive to open communication between supervisor and employee.

- **Complete all required paperwork in advance of the review interview.** Make sure that you have reviewed all of your documentation and used it to complete the performance appraisal prior to beginning the review interview. Have all the necessary forms ready and available so that you can conduct the entire interview without having to interrupt the process to find an additional form. If you are going to consider the employee's self-appraisal, leave the actual recording of the rating until you have given the employee time to provide input into the process.

- **Determine your approach.** It is a good idea to determine, prior to the time the employee arrives, how you will conduct the review interview. If the employee has completed a self-appraisal, ask for it now. The most straightforward method for proceeding with the interview is to start at the beginning and go through the job elements one at a time. The supervisor compares his or her rating with that of the employee's for each element, and then mutual agreement is reached on the rating for that element. Another way of handling the review is to first look at areas where the employee has met or exceeded the performance standard and then progress to areas where the employee may need to improve. Whatever approach you decide on, make sure that you have thought through the process first and are thoroughly prepared when the employee arrives. Adequate planning will help you feel prepared and confident as you begin the interview with the employee.

- **Plan your closing.** It is important to give thought as to how you will conclude the review interview. Remember, what you say last sticks with the employee as he or she leaves the review and returns to the normal working environment. Plan to summarize the areas where the employee met or exceeded the standard. Offer praise and encouragement, if appropriate. Review areas of concern you may have with the employee's performance. End the interview by encouraging the employee to give some thought to areas where he or she did not meet, or minimally met, the standard. Suggest that the employee meet with you again in a week's time to complete a plan of action that will help the employee raise the level of performance in areas where acceptable standards were not met. Plan to end the interview on a positive note, perhaps by conveying to the employee your appreciation for his or her contributions to the company.

Tips for Conducting the Review Interview

Create a positive climate. To help the employee relax, it is a good idea to begin the interview with a few minutes of light, easy conversation. Perhaps start with a comment about a recent event at work, a sporting event, or something in the news. Beginning this way helps build rapport with the employee and may help the employee overcome his or her initial nervousness. As stated previously, sitting at a round table or side-by-side further equalizes the situation and enhances rapport with the employee.

Ask questions and listen. The employee must be encouraged to talk in order for the performance review to be effective and of value. Many employees are hesitant about participating in an annual review, feeling that it is their supervisor's job to determine their ratings and their job to accept the ratings without question. Using open-ended questions such as "Will you tell me about occasions when you have exceeded this element?" will provide you with further documentation and convey to the employee that the review is a two-way process involving both the supervisor and the employee.

To build rapport with the employee, supervisors must not only ask for employee input, but truly listen. By that, we mean listen without interrupting and listen with an open mind. While we may have already decided an employee's rating, the employee may well be able to present information that will change our perception about his or her performance in a particular area. Listening with an open mind tells the employee "I value your input" and helps build rapport with the employee.

Focus on performance. To remain objective, avoid such descriptions as "attitude," "not professional," and "unreliable" when describing an employee's performance. These terms are vague, mean something different to everyone, and are hard to measure. Further, employees understandably become defensive when a supervisor tells them they have a "bad attitude" or are "not professional." They immediately begin searching for exceptions to convince you otherwise.

Instead, focus specifically on the job elements and the performance standards. Measure the employee's level of performance against the performance standards indicated in the performance review document. People are more receptive to negative feedback when it deals specifically with the standards indicated in the review document. They do not accept negative feedback when it attacks them personally. Under no circumstances should an employee's performance be compared with the performance of another employee. Comparing employees' performance builds resentment between employees and never achieves the outcome you desire.

Avoid confrontation. When discussing an employee's level of performance in comparison with the performance standards indicated in the review, avoid confrontation and argument. It is true that there may be a disagreement between how you have rated the employee and how he or she has rated him- or herself. To get further information, ask questions and listen. Arguing will destroy the rapport you are trying to build with the employee and limit the two-way communication you are trying to establish. The truth is, you are the supervisor, and both you and the employee know this. You have the authority and the power of your position. You have the right to determine the employee's rating. However, arguing and using your power to override the employee will not create the effect you are striving for. The employee should leave the performance review with a clear picture of his or her level of performance and an understanding of how that performance could be improved in the future. Ensuring that communication remains two way helps guarantee that the performance review interview will meet the needs of both the supervisor and the employee and result in a "win-win" situation for both people.

Emphasize an employee's strengths. It is normal to be preoccupied with thoughts about performance areas where you would like to see the employee improve. Do not overlook the employee's strengths, though. Acknowledge what the employee does well and build on these strengths. For example, a supervisor might be concerned with the number of errors in e-mails typed by an administrative support employee. However, the same employee routinely handles a large volume of incoming calls efficiently, greets customers warmly, schedules appointments without conflicts, and generally demonstrates a high level of performance in all areas of responsibility other than written correspondence. The supervisor conducting the assistant's performance review should recognize areas of performance that meet or exceed the standard and offer praise, if appropriate. This helps strengthen the relationship between the employee and supervisor. It also increases the employee's degree of confidence in his or her own ability to perform the job responsibilities. Further, the employee does not leave the performance review interview thinking that you are dissatisfied with his or her performance in general.

Identify areas for improvement. Discuss areas of concern you have with the employee's performance relative to a particular job standard. It is important to acknowledge specifically the performance that does not meet the standard. For example, you may note that the employee averages two to three errors per e-mail correspondence. It is important to have samples of the correspondence to demonstrate why you are concerned about the performance. The acceptable level of performance indicated in the employee's job standards is that all written correspondence is grammatically correct and error free.

Other than acknowledging the samples of errors on the e-mail correspondence, do not dwell in the past. Instead, focus on future employee performance. For example, you might ask the employee, "What can you do differently in the future to avoid these errors that make us look less than the professionals we are?" Generally, the employee will be able to come up with suggestions for improvement. If not, be ready to make suggestions or provide tips as to how the performance can be improved. It is always more effective, however, for the employee to generate his or her own ideas about how to improve performance. Many employees resent being told how to change their behavior. If, however, they are permitted to come up with their own solutions, they are more committed to making changes in their behavior that will result in increased levels of performance.

End the performance review interview positively. It is important to review the employee's strengths before the conclusion of the review interview and end on a positive note. Of course, you are concerned about the need for the employee's performance to improve in some areas. But you do not want the employee to leave thinking that the purpose of the review interview was only to address areas of concern. Acknowledging acceptable areas of performance helps ensure that the employee will continue to make an effort to meet or exceed the standards. Focusing only on the negative aspects of the employee's performance or ending the interview on a negative note will increase the likelihood that the employee will leave thinking, "Why bother? You don't think I'm making a real effort anyway. In the future, you'll get just enough from me so that I can collect my paycheck!"

Step Six: Develop the Performance Improvement Plan

Often, the employee leaves the review interview with a good idea about areas of his or her performance that are going well and a vague-to-general idea of areas where improvement is needed in performance. Typically, the supervisor breathes a sigh of relief after the interview and thinks, "Whew, I don't have to worry about that for another year!" It has been our experience that this is where the performance review process ends in most organizations. In order to be truly effective, though, it is necessary to go one step further. Either at the conclusion of the review interview, or ideally, at a later date, the employee and supervisor need to mutually develop a performance improvement plan.

A performance improvement plan describes a course of action taken by both the supervisor and employee that will lead to improved employee performance on the job. During the review interview, job elements in which the employee was not meeting minimum acceptable levels of performance were discussed. The first step in developing an improvement plan is to pick one or possibly two job elements to be worked on. Typically, if there is more than one job element requiring improved performance, the most critical one should be chosen first for the plan.

When considering the element to pick, think about the payoffs in terms of increased productivity, greater teamwork, and more profitability for your organization. Also, consider the degree of difficulty the employee will experience as he or she strives to improve performance. You may wish to select a relatively easy job element first. Targeting an easy element for improvement first leads to employee success. The feeling of success experienced by the employee should generate a positive feeling of confidence and help the employee rise to the challenge of assuming more responsibility and working on even more difficult goals.

Remember, if you initially select too many job elements for inclusion in the performance improvement plan, the whole process may seem overwhelming to the employee. Employees can tackle one or possibly two areas that are targeted for improvement at the same time. More than that may lead to a feeling of despair and the thought that "It's just too much to change. I'm not doing anything right!"

Tips for Creating the Performance Improvement Plan

Make the plan simple, practical, and easy to understand. Target one or possibly two areas in which the employee needs to improve performance. Provide examples of how the work will improve. For example, "The employee will correctly file all correspondence, using standardized office procedures, within three working days of receipt of the correspondence." When the employee is unsure about where to file the correspondence, he or she will ask a supervisor for specific directions regarding filing the document.

Include specific timelines for targeted behaviors. To ensure that both you and the employee have a clear understanding of when and how the behavior will be improved, include specifics regarding time. For example, "The employee will answer all incoming calls before the third ring. The employee will correctly route all incoming calls within five seconds. If a caller is placed on hold, the employee will verify every 30 seconds that the caller wishes to remain on hold and not leave a message or be connected to voice mail."

Identify training. Be specific about training that will help the employee improve performance. For example, you may wish to write in the employee's performance improvement plan, "Attend a class on Effective Telephone Techniques during the month of April." "Spend four hours with a customer service supervisor reviewing effective techniques for receiving/routing telephone calls before the end of May." In addition, be specific about whose responsibility it is to arrange the training for the employee.

Demonstrate a positive attitude. If you initiate an employee performance improvement plan thinking that it probably will not make much of a difference in the employee's behavior, that outcome is exactly what you will get! If, however, you are committed to helping the employee identify areas of concern and creating a plan that will help the employee further develop, you will most likely see an improvement in both the employee's behavior and attitude. We are convinced that when supervisors demonstrate a genuine interest in employee development and keep a positive attitude about the employee's ability to improve performance, that employee will be motivated to make changes in behavior.

Remember, making changes is tough, and tougher for some employees than others. If an employee is going to improve, there must be a support system in place. The employee may need additional coaching from the supervisor. Additional training may be required. More than anything though, encouragement is needed during a time of change so that the employee will have the confidence to experiment with new ways of doing things. Acknowledge signs of increased levels of performance, particularly in the beginning when the employee is making the first few tentative steps toward improvement. As the employee continues to make progress meeting the goals listed in the performance improvement action plan, recognize the growth with praise, encouragement, increased responsibility (demonstrating the supervisor's confidence in the employee), and, if appropriate, monetary rewards.

In conclusion, the most important aspect of any performance review process is obviously not the format or technique utilized, but the underlying attitude by which both the employee and supervisor view the entire process. If supervisors lack confidence in their ability to review employee performance, dread conducting review interviews, and see reviews as a waste of time and generally go out of their way to avoid the process, whatever evaluation system is in place will be a failure. However, when supervisors view performance evaluation as part of an ongoing process that can positively lead to improved employee performance, there are far-reaching benefits not only for the individual, but also the organization as a whole. Supervisors with that perspective no longer view conducting performance review interviews as "the job that nobody wants!"

My Personal Improvement Plan

Review Date: _____

1. My areas of strength during the last review cycle:

   _____

   _____

   _____

2. The job elements where I need to improve my performance:

   _____

   _____

   _____

3. My goals for improving my performance:

   _____

   _____

   _____

4. Action steps needed for me to accomplish my goals:

Action	Who is Responsible?	When
_____	_____	_____
_____	_____	_____
_____	_____	_____

_____   _____
Employee Signature   Supervisor Signature

_____   _____
Date   Date

☞ Tips for Success

Performance Reviews

1. Gather examples of performance, both positive and negative, throughout the year, not just the week before the performance appraisal is due.

2. Be positive. Remember to include documentation showing where the employee is doing a great job, not just in areas where there is room for improvement.

3. Make sure you are familiar with all the performance standards and rating criteria for the job before conducting the review process with the employee.

4. Plan your schedule so that you will not be interrupted when giving feedback to the employee. Doing so demonstrates respect for the employee and the process.

5. Pick a quiet, private location and give consideration to the seating arrangements. When possible, come out from behind your desk.

6. Ask for employee input. Listen. Listening conveys you care and value the employee's insights.

7. Focus on behavior. Remember, people cannot change their personalities, but can change their behavior.

8. Be specific about what improved performance looks like. Use examples.

9. Remember to look for positive changes in employee behavior and recognize the employee's success.

10. Put a date on your calendar to remind you to check back with the employee who is working on an improvement plan.

Chapter 10

Building a High-Performing Team

> "A house divided against itself cannot stand. There are only two options regarding the commitment to teamwork. You're either In or you're Out. There is no such thing as life in-between."
>
> — *Pat Riley, Coach of Miami Heat*

One of the challenges that every supervisor and manager has is the task of bringing people together to function as a team. In today's competitive environment, supervisors need to decide what will enable their work group to provide the highest level of quality, customer service, or task accomplishment. Although there are rare exceptions, in most situations, the ability to respond to quality and customer service is much stronger when people operate as a team.

Teamwork Defined

Teamwork is the actions of individuals, brought together for a common purpose or goal. The needs of the individual are subordinated to the needs of the group. In essence, each person on the team puts aside his or her individual needs to work toward the larger group objective. The interactions among the members and the work they complete is called teamwork. It is important to recognize that just because you are a supervisor with a specific group of people assigned to complete a specific organizational task that does not necessarily mean you are leading a team. A team is not just any group working together. Groups do not become teams just because someone labels them a team. We agree with Michael Jordan, who says, "Talent wins games, but teamwork and intelligence win championships."

Building a Team Is a Challenge

Most supervisors and managers will agree that there have been times in their careers when they have not been able to build a team. For whatever reason, the team just did not come together. Supervisors and managers are quick to rationalize why the group did not perform as a team. Some of the responses we have heard include the following:

- Team members lacked commitment.

- The long-term employees are more comfortable working independently.

- Some people refuse to change and work with others.

- The employees and/or the organization have tried teaming up before and it did not work.

- Upper management sends a message that they encourage teams but their non-supportive actions speak louder than words.

- The team has one, two, or more people that others do not want to work with. It takes more time to accomplish something as a team than it does working independently.

- No one on the team was accountable.

- The team had politically based membership, rather than performance-based membership.

- The team had low goals or expectations.

What Makes a Great Team?

In both our consulting practice and research, we have uncovered five characteristics that are common among all great teams.

Great teams have a common, shared goal. Team members are equally committed to a common purpose, goals, and working approach for which they hold themselves mutually accountable. As a supervisor or manager, you have the opportunity to set the goals for your team. This technique is used by the majority of supervisors. The supervisor tells the team what needs to be accomplished and how to accomplish the task, whether on this shift or in a specific work period. People need to know what needs to be accomplished.

What we also know is that if the team does not buy in to the goal and make a commitment to accomplish the task, there is a large chance the task will not be completed or not be completed correctly. As a supervisor, there are many times when management or a customer dictates a goal to you, i.e., we need 200 units shipped by Friday. In this case, as the extended arm of management, you do not have a choice. The task has to be completed. But you are better off asking the team if this is something they think they can accomplish by Friday. If team members say "No," the appropriate question would be, "What would we have to do, or do differently, to accomplish this goal?" In this particular example, a team member responded that if they could get the products from another internal department one-half day earlier, it would be tough but they would be able to accomplish the task. The supervisor was able to get the other department to provide the products a half-day earlier, and the shared goal was accomplished on time.

As the supervisor, you are better off asking and finding out what objections or concerns team players have about the goal than to assume it is a shared goal just because you told the group what needed to be accomplished.

The team has a positive vision of what the team is trying to accomplish. The term "vision" can be clarified as a clear mental picture of a desired future outcome. Someone on the team—either the supervisor, leader, or other team member—is able to convey a positive vision of the team's results. On a consulting project with a manufacturing company, a cross-departmental group of people came together to improve the level of quality in one of the organization's new products. It was evident at the first meeting that three members of the team really believed that management had empowered them to solve the problems. Although there was some cynicism from two team members, the strong belief from the three members that this team really could have a positive impact was enough to overcome the cynics and get all team members to pull together to solve the problems.

As a supervisor, whether you have a positive or negative vision of the future, you will be influential. For example, if you as the team leader *do not* have a positive vision of your team's ability to accomplish the goal, and no one on your team does either, there is a strong chance you will all be right!

Great teams are driven by performance challenges. It is the challenge that energizes a team to greatness, regardless of its location in the organization. A common set of demanding performance goals, or a significant accomplishment that needs to be completed, or a large problem that is having a negative impact on both people and the organization most of the time will result in an outcome of both high performance and a strong team. Teams thrive on performance challenges; they produce mediocre results without them.

Lack of performance challenges that are meaningful to the team members involved is one of the largest reasons why teams have failed. Almost every large organization can share horror stories about how teams have orchestrated one type of team disaster or another. In many of these situations, team members did not understand "why" teams were being formed. When there is a question of "why," you can guarantee that a challenging goal or accomplishment is also nonexistent. As a supervisor or manager, you need to ensure that your team is working on a challenging goal that is meaningful to each member of the team.

Great teams value and respect the contributions of each member. Team members need to recognize that each individual brings a unique gift or contribution to the team. Also, it is important that each team member recognize that it would be harder to accomplish the task without each individual's unique contribution. When we talk about value and respect, we have observed instances where value and respect for others do not transcend outside the team setting. For example, a supervisor stated to us that his most valuable technician was not someone he respected off the job. He went on to add, "But when it comes to producing high-quality parts and solving big problems, this person is the best!"

Great teams win. It does not matter whether you are on a sports team or in a business environment, great teams accomplish their goals or tasks. It is your challenge as a supervisor or manager to build a winning team. Anyone could win by being given ten ideal or perfect employees to do the job. The problem is that in real life, this never happens. And an even bigger problem might be that if it did happen, there would be no need for the supervisor!

In reality, most times you are given a mixture of people. A few may fall into the ideal/perfect category. The majority will fall into the middle-of-the-road type employees. They are not ideal/perfect, but they are not challenging either. Last, you will most likely have one or two challenging employees. These are the people who are *so challenging* that you find yourself lying awake at 3:00 a.m. asking the question, "Why do they have to report to me?" When employees challenge you, you will find many times that your value and respect for these people decrease.

It is important to understand that challenging employees are not bad. They are the people who help you strengthen your leadership skills. As you navigate your way through the challenges, do not take your eye off the individual's value and the contribution they can make to the team. When challenging employees buy in to the vision and common goal, they have the ability to become a middle-of-the-road or even an ideal/perfect employee.

Supervisors and managers need to develop the ability to take this blending of people and talents; formulate a positive vision; set a challenging, shared goal; and build value and respect for each team member's contribution. When this happens, you will find that your team's chances of winning increase tremendously.

Stages of Team Development

Stage One: Formation

In this first stage, it is actually safe to say that you have a group of people who work together, rather than a true team. People in this stage will gather together to share information, or to decide what actions will help individuals better fulfill their specific job functions, but there is not a committed focus toward a common goal. Some of the key characteristics of groups in this stage include the following:

- lack of honest communication
- members who are watchful and guarded
- minimal group work accomplishment
- learning of new jobs and roles
- hesitant participation
- uncommitted people
- unspoken concerns
- unclear roles and responsibilities

If you were the team leader observing these characteristics on your team, the question becomes, "What can I do to help move the team forward?" The following five suggestions will help move a team through the team development process:

- **Meet often.** When new teams come together, team members feel a lack of "belonging" to the team. Because of this lack of "belonging" and the unknown relationships, along with unclear roles and responsibilities, it is sometimes easier for individuals not to meet at all. Everyone will go on doing their own jobs without feeling a need to come together as a team. By meeting more often in the beginning of team development, the members get to know and trust each other earlier in the process.

- **Conduct introductions.** If people do not know each other well, it will be helpful to have people introduce themselves. As the leader, it is your responsibility to give people an opportunity to know each other.

- **Give a proper orientation to the team.** Any time a new member joins a team, this addition has the potential to send the team back to the forming stage. It is helpful to give new members the proper history and background of your team.

- **Clarify goals of the team.** We know that one of the key characteristics of a great team is a challenging goal. It is important that all team members be involved in the goal setting and clarification process.

- **Ask for commitment.** When teams are new, we do not know who is really committed to the team's goals and who is not. You will find it helpful to directly ask people for the commitment to helping the team be successful. You may also find it helpful to ask team members what they would like to personally achieve by being a member of the team.

Stage Two: Conflict

As members get accustomed to working with each other, conflict or feelings of hopelessness or helplessness may arise. We have listed some of the outward characteristics of this stage of team development:

- blaming
- competition
- lack of trust
- infighting
- whining
- feeling stuck
- polarization (i.e., day shift vs. night shift)
- minimal work accomplishment

These characteristics are not bad, but rather a natural course of direction in the team-building process. As the supervisor or manager, it is part of your job to know what you can do to help move the team forward. The following six suggestions provide specific guidance:

- **Address team members in conflict.** The worst thing you can do when conflict arises on your team is to ignore it. You may ask two team members to sit down and resolve their conflict, or you may sit down and play the role of a mediator in resolving the conflict. Either way, you are addressing the conflict, rather than ignoring it.

- **Maintain conversations in the "aim frame."** We advise supervisors in our seminars to be "aim frame" thinkers vs. "blame frame" thinkers. Aim frame thinkers ask two questions: "Where do we want to be?" and "How do we get there?" These two questions keep all conversations healthy and productive. Blame frame thinkers also address two questions: "What's wrong?" and "Who can we blame?" With these last two questions, we only have two guarantees: nothing will be accomplished and it will divide the group.

- **Meet often.** Groups in conflict will actually stop meeting because they would rather avoid each other than discuss the conflict. Force the group to meet and discuss the sensitive issues. Hold the tough conversation. Get to the bottom of the conflict. If you stick to the aim frame, it will go well.

- **Focus on results.** This is the stage when many managers spin their wheels concentrating on making the relationships "right." You will find it more productive to focus your energy on the results the team produces. When the team members are totally focused on results and are held accountable for the results, many of the relationship problems will be resolved by the individuals involved.

- **Eat together.** The last thing that people in conflict want to do is eat lunch together. This suggestion works because when people eat, they tend to talk about personal things rather than work. People begin to learn about each other as individuals, rather than "the guy from XYZ department."

- **Ask participants to sit in different seats.** Groups in conflict have set seat assignments that many times they will refuse to change because that may mean they have to sit next to someone they do not like. Prior to each meeting, tell people they have to sit in a different seat next to someone new. In fact, you might even lead by example. It works!

Stage Three: Functional Work Group

This stage occurs when teams get their jobs done. There is not a lot of conflict, but then again, there is not a lot of excitement either. Teams come together each day, do their assigned duties, and then leave. Some of the key characteristics of this stage include the following:

- getting organized
- establishing procedures
- displaying team cohesiveness

- using interactive dialogue
- confiding in each other
- confronting issues as a team

You may ask the question, "If the team is not broken, why try to fix it?" The reason is because a team in this stage is capable of much more. With a few adjustments, you can help improve the level of commitment, the level of productivity, and the amount of fun and satisfaction individuals gain by being a part of the team. Some actions to help the team move forward include the following:

- **Set new goals.** If the team is comfortable where they are, see if the team can come up with any new challenges. It is during the times when we are challenged that we succeed and do our very best.

- **Provide training.** In the functional work group stage, people may begin to feel like they have stopped growing. Find out what people would like to learn and help them promote their personal and professional growth.

- **Encourage innovation.** This is the stage when you will hear the line, "But we have always done it that way, why change?" Change creates growth in individuals and teams, and growth helps increase satisfaction.

- **Recognize what is right.** In this stage, supervisors tend to become involved when something is not right. This means that people only hear from you when something is wrong. Recognize those things that are also right.

Stage Four: A High-Performing Team

This is the stage where the definition of teamwork, listed at the beginning of this chapter, fully develops. You will begin to see some of the key characteristics of a high-performing team:

- mutual caring among members
- high energy
- aim frame discussions
- closeness
- common vision and purpose
- fun as a team
- creative problem solving
- high trust among team members
- continuous improvement

This time, the discussion is not centered on what you can do to move the team forward, but rather what you can do to help keep the team performing at high levels. Some ideas include the following:

- **Celebrate successes.** In watching great teams perform, we have observed that they will find a reason to celebrate every success. Part of their motivation is knowing they will recognize the superior accomplishments of the team.

- **Do a team audit.** When things are going great, most people will feel comfortable addressing the question, "What could we have done even better?"

- **Change your role to facilitator.** High-performing teams will operate whether the leader is present or not. Knowing that, become a facilitator, rather than the "supervisor." High-performing teams know what needs to be done.

- **Set new goals and vision.** If the group is not continually setting new, challenging goals, the team will lose its drive and motivation. People want to be a part of a team that is accomplishing something great.

- **Have fun.** There is no greater reward than being a part of a fun team!

Assessing Your Skills as a Team Leader

The following checklist provides you with a quick assessment of your current ability as a team leader. The 16 items outline some key abilities required for leading a team.

Team Leader Assessment

Read each statement and then place a checkmark (✓) in the box under the appropriate number to indicate your current ability. Ratings run from 1 (low) to 10 (high). Respond as you think a consensus of your team members would score your abilities.

	LOW									HIGH
	1	2	3	4	5	6	7	8	9	10
1. I set measurable goals.	❏	❏	❏	❏	❏	❏	❏	❏	❏	❏
2. I really listen to others.	❏	❏	❏	❏	❏	❏	❏	❏	❏	❏
3. I give clear directions.	❏	❏	❏	❏	❏	❏	❏	❏	❏	❏
4. I develop trust with and among others.	❏	❏	❏	❏	❏	❏	❏	❏	❏	❏
5. I inspire positive team performance.	❏	❏	❏	❏	❏	❏	❏	❏	❏	❏
6. I confront conflict in a positive manner.	❏	❏	❏	❏	❏	❏	❏	❏	❏	❏
7. I remain objective when someone disagrees with me.	❏	❏	❏	❏	❏	❏	❏	❏	❏	❏
8. I keep meetings on topic.	❏	❏	❏	❏	❏	❏	❏	❏	❏	❏
9. I effectively manage time in a meeting.	❏	❏	❏	❏	❏	❏	❏	❏	❏	❏
10. I provide a clear vision to team members.	❏	❏	❏	❏	❏	❏	❏	❏	❏	❏
11. I effectively delegate work to others.	❏	❏	❏	❏	❏	❏	❏	❏	❏	❏
12. I establish positive relationships with key employees and customers.	❏	❏	❏	❏	❏	❏	❏	❏	❏	❏
13. I am able to influence upper management.	❏	❏	❏	❏	❏	❏	❏	❏	❏	❏

Continued...

	LOW									HIGH
	1	2	3	4	5	6	7	8	9	10
14. I am patient with people who are slow or who challenge me.	❏	❏	❏	❏	❏	❏	❏	❏	❏	❏
15. I recognize the stages of team development and am able to move the team through the stages.	❏	❏	❏	❏	❏	❏	❏	❏	❏	❏
16. I have an ability to _____	❏	❏	❏	❏	❏	❏	❏	❏	❏	❏

Effective team leaders must realize that they don't know all the answers and that they cannot succeed without other members of the team. Work on improving any "low" ratings and maintain or even reinforce the skills of "high" ratings.

Leading Your Team Out of a Crisis

From time to time, every supervisor or manager will find they are in charge of a team in crisis. Crises come in many shapes and sizes. A few we have seen supervisors struggle with include team members who do not get along; company financial problems; morale or motivation at an all-time low; quality problems; customer service problems; departments at war with each other; and top management not supportive of a team or department.

The deeper the crisis, the more challenging it is for supervisors and managers to figure out how to solve the problems and put the team back on track. Many times, supervisors and managers do not know what action they should take. Many possible actions seem to have the potential to send the team into an even deeper crisis. Because of this lack of definite action, the supervisor or manager "hopes" that the situation will get better on its own. We can say that very seldom does the team come out of crisis on its own when the supervisor or manager is using the action of "hope." The following action steps will help you lead your team out of a crisis:

- **Face reality.** When a crisis hits and supervisors/managers are not sure what to do, the first inclination is to deny that the problem is as big as it really is. The animal that comes to mind is the ostrich. If we bury our head in the sand, the problem will not seem as large as it really is. But just like the ostrich, when we stick our head in the sand, we leave other parts of our body exposed. Face reality. The problem most likely will not go away unless you do something to solve the crisis.

- **Take action.** If you wait until your boss helps to solve the problem or until team members decide to help solve the problem, you may wait forever. What is worse is that supervisors and managers who do not take action to solve team problems are not doing their job. Be empowered. You have the ability to take responsibility to make decisions and actions that will lead the team from crisis. If you are not empowered to do this, then there is a good chance your team is going to remain in crisis.

- **Prioritize.** When teams fall into a crisis, there are usually many problems that may be impacting the team. You cannot fix all the problems at once, so it is in your best interest to get the team involved and prioritize the actions that need to be taken. If the team is unwilling to prioritize actions, then you will have to decide which problems to solve and in what order.

- **Focus on results.** When teams are in crisis, there is a tendency to focus on trying to fix the relationships that have broken down. While the thought or attempt is good, we have found it much more productive for floundering teams to focus on results. When everyone is focused on the purpose of the team and the results it must produce, many of the relationship problems will resolve on their own. If the team is not productive, there will always be relationship struggles.

- **Recruit the cream of the crop.** When teams go into crisis, it is usually the very best team members who leave. They join other departments or will find a new job in another company. Unfortunately, the most challenging team members never seem to leave. They would much rather tell everyone how bad things are than to do anything to change the situation. In a crisis, analyze your people assets and spend time asking the top performers to band with you and help solve the problems. Most people will stay in a bad situation if they know they can help improve the crisis, feel valued, and have a positive vision that tomorrow will be better than today.

- **Praise and recognize your people often.** The reason we emphasize this as a specific point is because when a team goes into crisis mode, and you are the leader of this team, you tend to focus your energy on what is going wrong instead of recognizing all the things that are going right. When people do not feel valued, and the team or organization is in a crisis, you start to hear team members say, "I don't get paid enough to put up with this crap." One way we can minimize this feeling in our team members is to value their contributions and recognize them for doing things right.

- **Tighten discipline.** When teams go into crisis, there are usually many things happening that are not conducive to good teamwork. For example, we might find members coming to work late, people coming to meetings late or not coming at all, work being completed with inferior quality, internal customer service lacking between departments, and last, people not taking responsibility to solve problems. When a crisis occurs, it is in your best interest as a supervisor or manager to tighten, not loosen, discipline. This means you need to hold people accountable for coming to work on time or producing quality parts. Without tightening the boundaries or setting detail standards, you send out messages to all team members that negative behaviors are acceptable.

- **Identify who is responsible and what role that individual will play.** In a moment of crisis, it is critical that you clarify who is responsible and what role that individual will play in leading the team from crisis. This point helps keep focus on the results. When a team is in crisis, you will usually find that team members are clear on what is wrong and who is to blame, but they are not clear on what needs to be done and who is responsible. As the supervisor, you can assign roles and responsibilities.

- **Over-communicate.** When a supervisor or manager is "in" over his or her head with team problems, there is a tendency to focus energy on operational, rather than leadership, tasks. You begin to utter these words, "All I do around here is put out fires." As a supervisor, your primary role is to support others. Increase your communication to team members: both information provided by you and information given to you from the team. Most of the time, your team has the ability to solve the problems if you utilize them as a resource. Increase your communication in a crisis, and it will lessen the negative impact of the crisis.

- **Maintain a positive mental attitude.** If you throw in the towel because you feel the situation is hopeless, then most likely your team members will view the situation as hopeless also. Not having a positive mental attitude can have a negative impact on a supervisor's or manager's career. If you have no hope of the situation getting better, but someone else does, either on the team or in the organization, your team members will begin to follow someone else. A supervisor or manager with no followers is not a leader.

We are the first to agree: teams are not for everyone or every situation. Nonetheless, teams usually outperform other groups or individuals. And teams perfect individual members' strengths and overcome their weaknesses.

Team Performance

1. Great teams have a clear mission, a strong vision, and great goals. Make sure your team has a common, challenging goal that makes team members stretch to reach.

2. Create an environment where the contributions of all team members are recognized and valued, not just the "stars."

3. Don't oil the squeaky wheel. Value creativity. Recognize and reward those who challenge "the way we always do things around here."

4. Confront conflict. If you stick your head in the sand and deny it exists, remember what part of you is exposed!

5. At every opportunity, try switching from being a directive leader to a team facilitator.

6. Promote cross-training to multiply the number of "experts" on your team.

7. Set goals with specific deadlines. Goals without deadlines are only a "hope."

8. People need to feel they belong. Praise and recognize your people frequently.

9. Success is not permanent. Focus on recruiting "the cream of the crop" as you anticipate the need for new team members.

10. Celebrate success!

Chapter 11

Selecting and Hiring Winners

"The world is full of willing people; some willing to work, the rest willing to let them."

– Robert Frost

One manager recently confided to us, "I don't know much about wrongful terminations, but I sure have made some wrongful hires in my time!" In the previous chapters, we have discussed the skills needed to effectively manage employees once they are on the job. In this chapter, we will review the skills needed to hire the right people. When the right person is in the right job, it makes all the other skills we have discussed in this book much easier to practice.

In addition, hiring the wrong people is very costly to an organization. These costs include (1) high turnover rates, (2) decreased productivity, (3) poor morale, (4) potential damage to the company's reputation, and (5) costs associated with recruiting, hiring, and training a replacement for a terminated employee. Your hiring decisions will be among the most expensive and long-lasting decisions you will make for your organization.

Assessing Your Interviewing Skills

As preparation for this subject, why not try the assessment tool below? It consists of some questions that will help you assess the current strength of your interviewing skills.

Interviewing Skills Self-Assessment

❑ Yes ❑ No 1. Have you ever hired a person who did not have the skills you thought they had?

❑ Yes ❑ No 2. After the interview, have you ever thought of something you wish you had told the candidate?

❑ Yes ❑ No 3. When the interview is complete, are you still confused about the candidate's qualifications?

❑ Yes ❑ No 4. Of the five people you have most recently hired, have any left for employment elsewhere?

❑ Yes ❑ No 5. Have you ever asked a question of a candidate and then later found out that the question was not legal to ask?

❑ Yes ❑ No 6. Do you ever find that you do not have time to adequately prepare for the interview?

❑ Yes ❑ No 7. Do you tend to do more talking than the candidate?

❑ Yes ❑ No 8. Have you ever found you did not hear the candidate's response because you were thinking of what question to ask next?

❑ Yes ❑ No 9. After the interview, have you ever thought of something you wish you had asked the candidate?

❑ Yes ❑ No 10. Have you ever protected your nervousness by sitting behind your desk or some other comfort zone of authority to conduct the interview?

There is no grading scale for this assessment. If you select a high number of "yes" responses, the greater will be your need to learn and practice effective interviewing skills.

Common Challenges Evident in the Interview Process

Although we are incredibly optimistic consultants, we want to begin with a few words of caution. In preparing for the interview, it is helpful to be aware of some of the most common errors that interviewers frequently make.

Talking too much. Studies indicate that most interviewers talk 50 percent or more of the time during an interview. An interview that is dominated by the interviewer fails to accomplish the most crucial purpose of the interview, which is to get information from the applicant. An effective interviewer will conduct the interview so that he or she spends only about 20 percent of the time talking and the applicant spends 80 percent of the time talking.

Telegraphing the desired response. Interviewers often lead or help the candidate get the "right answer" by telegraphing the answer that they want to hear. For example, the interviewer says, "How do you feel about working on teams? We have a very strong work ethic around here that values teamwork." Now, what would you say to this? "No, I think teams are a lousy idea!" Make sure that your questions are straightforward and do not telegraph the desired response.

Failing to know job requirements. You cannot conduct an effective interview without first knowing the specific job requirements. This is where effective preparation pays off. Too many interviewers do not have a complete understanding of the job or what it entails. These interviewers are at a significant disadvantage in being able to select the person with the right qualifications. Take the time to conduct a thorough job analysis that will clarify specific job duties, responsibilities, skills, knowledge, and abilities.

Jumping to conclusions. Interviewers often make the mistake of making quick judgments and jumping to conclusions before they have enough information to make a sound decision. If the applicant says one thing that does not fit with what you are looking for, it does not mean that they are not the right person for the job. On the other hand, if an applicant says something that you are very impressed with, this should not be the single contributor to your decision to offer the job.

Reacting to the "halo" effect. This common mistake is made when the interviewer happens to really "like" the applicant. Sometimes you will just "hit it off" with someone. A quick rapport is established and you seem to get along very well. You can almost build a friendship within the interview because the chemistry just seems to fit. This is when an interviewer may make the hasty judgment that this applicant would be "perfect" for the job. Beware, you may be under the "halo" effect: you have put a "halo" over the head of the applicant. He or she can do no wrong—even though he or she may be *wrong* for the job.

Being disorganized. Interviewers who do not take a systematic approach to the interview will be disorganized and may lose valuable time to get the information they need. Effective interviewers take an organized approach and plan out the interview sequence. This pre-planned structure ensures that the interviewer will be able to cover what is needed to make the best possible selection determination.

Now that you are aware of some of the most common errors made by interviewers, you are ready to prepare for the interview. The key steps in preparation include (1) conduct a job analysis to determine job requirements, (2) review the résumés and applications, and (3) plan the interviews.

Preparing for the Interview

Step One: Conduct a Job Analysis to Determine Job Requirements

One of the most critical aspects of preparing for the interview is to define the requirements of the job. During the interview, you will be determining whether there is a good match between the candidate's experience and the job requirements. Many interviewers rely on job descriptions and general assumptions to get their information about the job. Most job descriptions provide a general summary of the job duties and responsibilities. They do not usually go far enough in describing specific skills and abilities needed to do the job. To get a more thorough grasp of the true job requirements, outline your responses as you read through the following questions:

- What skills, knowledge, and abilities are absolutely essential to do the job?
- What specific education or training is required to do the job?
- What are the specific duties and responsibilities of the position?
- Describe key involvement with others (management, employees, customers, vendors, or peers).
- What are the potential sources of satisfaction or the pluses of the job?
- What are the potential sources of dissatisfaction or the negatives in the job?
- Is there a career path available? If so, what is it?

- What other job or career opportunities might be available to a person in this position?

- What specific behaviors or personal characteristics are important for this position? (Be specific in describing these behaviors. For example, if the position requires creativity, what specifically would be expected? Initiate new ideas for product development? Present a variety of approaches or solutions to solve problems?)

- What specific situational or environmental factors are required for the position? (Include things like long hours, overtime, shift work, weekend travel, relocation, physical requirements, office space, or work environment.)

Step Two: Review the Résumés and Applications

Once you have done a thorough job analysis, you are now ready to review the individual applicant's résumé, application, and any other pertinent background information. Note any unusual aspects of the person's work history or education. As you review the information, write out questions you can ask during the interview to get more data or to clarify information. Also, note areas where you can ask for specific examples. For instance, if the résumé indicates that the person has headed up a number of problem-solving teams, you can ask for specific examples of how he or she led the team, what problems or roadblocks were encountered, and what was ultimately achieved by the team.

The purpose of taking the time to review the applicant's information is not only to give you more data about the applicant, but also to help you prepare for the interview. A careful review of the applicant's material will assist you in formulating pertinent questions to maximize your time in the interview.

Step Three: Plan the Interviews

At this point, you should have a thorough understanding of the job requirements, a good sense of the individual applicants, and specific questions ready to ask in the interview. The last part of preparation before conducting the interview is to plan the interview schedule and arrange the appropriate physical setting.

In planning the interview schedule, you need to determine how much time you will spend in the interview. The average recommended time for an initial interview, after screening the résumé and the application, is 30 to 45 minutes. For highly technical or very involved positions, the interview may go on for one hour or more.

Once you have decided how much time you want to devote to the interview, you need to design a structure that will allow you to get to all the questions you want to ask. If you are going to plan for a 45-minute interview, determine how much time you want to spend in each area. For example, you may want to spend the majority of time on specific types of work experience to ensure that the applicant has a certain level of proficiency in a particular technical skill.

Plan ahead regarding how much time you will spend in each area and stick to your plan. If you alter your plan, you may find that your interview time is up and you haven't even gotten to the most important questions! (In the next section on conducting the interview, you will see an interview structure that will help you plan your time accordingly.)

The second part of planning for the interview includes planning for the appropriate physical setting. The most important aspect of the physical setting is that it be comfortable and relaxing. Remember, both you and the applicant will be a little, if not a lot, nervous. Creating a comfortable environment will ease the situation.

Furniture should be placed for easy conversation. If you are using an office with a desk, pull your chair around so that you are not behind the desk. Ensure that there will be no interruptions during the interview. Have whatever materials you will need available, including the candidate's résumé and application and your notes. Make sure that you are ready to conduct the interview. This means that you should clear your mind—and desk—of all other distractions. Plan on devoting your full attention to the applicant. This short interview may be the only time you have to make one of the most important business decisions you will have to make. It deserves your full attention.

Conducting the Interview

When conducting the interview, an organized approach must be followed if you want to get all the information you need in the allotted time. One way to achieve this is to follow an organized structure or format. The following organizational format will ensure that you get to the most critical questions. You will need to determine how much time you plan to devote to each of the elements of the interview structure.

Welcome/greeting. The purpose is to welcome the applicant and put him or her at ease. Welcome the applicant with a smile and a handshake. Introduce yourself and your title or position. Offer coffee, water, or other refreshments and guide the applicant to the interview location. Once you are both seated and ready to begin the interview, start the conversation with "small talk" to get the applicant to talk, "break the ice," and "open up." This could include "How was the traffic coming in this morning?" or "Did you have any trouble finding our office?" or any other non-controversial area of general interest.

Interview structure preview. The purpose is to let the applicant know what to expect and reduce anxiety about the interview process. The preview allows you to transition from the welcome to the actual interview. It tells the applicant what you have planned for the time that you are together. It should include the general areas you plan to cover and how much time you have planned for the interview.

The preview could go something like this: "Well, since we don't have much time today, I'd like to get started on the interview. Let me tell you what I have planned. I'd like to start with your work experience and then talk about your education. After that, I'll ask you to give me a self-assessment of your strengths and development needs. Then, I'll take some time to answer your questions and to give you more information about the position and our company."

Work experience. The purpose is to get specific information, examples, and illustrations of the applicant's work experience, job skills, and knowledge. Most interviewers will begin with the most recent work experience and work backward. However, another approach argues for beginning with the earliest work experience and moving forward. This approach will allow you to see the career path that was taken and to follow the applicant's thinking and line of reasoning in making his or her career decisions.

Ask questions to get details about what type of work was done, how it was done, and what results were achieved. Ask follow-up and probing questions to get more details. For example, if the applicant says that one of his or her duties included training, a series of follow-up questions might include the following:

- "How did you go about determining the content for the training?"
- "Give me an example of one of the key training points and how you presented it."
- "What kind of results did you achieve with the training?"
- "How did you measure your success?"
- "What might you do differently if you had the chance to do it over again?"

Education. The purpose is to understand the applicant's specific education and training and to see how that education relates to the necessary job requirements. You can use the same basic process to cover education as you did for work experience. By working chronologically, you are asking the applicant to "tell the story" of his or her educational background.

Self-Assessment. The purpose is to get the applicant's perspective of his or her own strengths and development needs. Ask the applicant to give you his or her perspective of what he or she considers to be personal strengths and the areas needing improvement. Most applicants are generally prepared for this question. However, if you ask good follow-up questions, you will be able to get some very valuable data.

Presenting information and answering questions. The primary purpose of this segment is to "sell" the employee on the job. At this point, you will have a good idea if this seems to be the right person for the job. If this is a top candidate, discuss the benefits of the job and how it will meet his or her needs. If you will not be seriously considering the applicant, you will not need to spend much time in this area. However, you do need to complete this section to ensure a fair interview and to promote good public relations.

Answer the candidate's questions and elaborate on information that will satisfy any concerns. Tailor the information that you have to present to the candidate's needs. Include information that is particularly important to the candidate.

Closing the interview. The purpose is to determine the applicant's level of interest in the job, explain next steps, and end the interview on a positive note. Determine if the applicant is interested in the position by asking directly, "What is your level of interest in the position?" Explore any doubts or reservations the applicant may have about the position or the company.

Explain the next steps. This could include who else you would like the applicant to interview with, when they will be notified about the next interview, or when the hiring decision will be made.

End the interview on a positive note by thanking the applicant for taking the time to speak with you. Clarify what the applicant can expect next. Do not make an offer or a rejection statement at this time. You will need some time to analyze your interview notes and to think through the process.

Questioning the Applicant

As we stated earlier, the goal of the interview is to get the best information possible so that the interviewer can make a good selection. The primary tool for getting good information is to ask good questions. There are two different types of questions: closed-ended questions and open-ended questions.

Closed-ended questions. Closed-ended questions are questions that can be answered with a *yes* or *no*. For example, if you asked an applicant if he or she likes his or her present job, the answer could simply be "yes" or "no." The disadvantage of using closed-ended questions in an interview is that they do not produce the maximum amount of possible information. Closed-ended questions begin with words like "Is," "Can," "Do," "Did," "Will," and "Are."

Open-ended questions. Open-ended questions are questions that need expansion to be answered. They usually start with words like "What," "Where," "When," "Why," "How," "Tell me," "Explain," and "Describe." The advantage of using open-ended questions is that you will receive more information rather than less. For example, if I ask, "Tell me what you really like about your present job?" I am going to receive much more information than I did in the closed-ended example.

The following examples illustrate how you can change closed-ended questions (CL) to open-ended questions (OP).

CL	Do you have good communication skills?
OP	What do you feel your key strengths are in the area of communication?
CL	Were you attracted to work here because of our benefits?
OP	What attracted you to seek employment with our company?
CL	Did you make any major mistakes in your last job?
OP	Can you describe a major learning point from your previous jobs?
CL	Have you ever had a personality clash with a boss?
OP	Tell me what you have liked and disliked about previous bosses.
CL	We have a very fast-paced environment here. Are you motivated?
OP	What type of business environment do you enjoy best?

There are many other useful open-ended questions for interviewing purposes.

- How would you describe your past job in detail?
- Tell me how you spend a typical day on the job.
- Why do you want to leave your present job?
- What are your greatest strengths?
- What are your biggest weaknesses?
- What are you doing to overcome them?
- On your past jobs, what significant contributions did you make?
- What specific tasks do you enjoy most? Why?
- What specific tasks do you like least? Why?
- Tell me about the most challenging project you have ever had to tackle.

Open-ended questions are powerful questions because they do not lead the applicant down a specific direction. If you asked the question, "Do you enjoy working on computers?" what candidate would disqualify himself or herself by saying *no*? But, if you asked an open-ended question like, "Tell me what you disliked in your last job," and the applicant responds that he or she disliked working on the computer all day, you have a pretty sound indication this may not be the best applicant for a position that requires extensive computer work.

A final note on your choice of questions: make sure that they are all questions that can be legally asked in an interview. It's a good idea to run your questions by a Human Resources representative to check for legality before you conduct the interviews.

Making the Hiring Decision

Now that you have taken the time to plan and conduct a thorough interviewing process, you are ready to make the selection decision. Since you have carefully analyzed the job, you will be able to quickly screen out unqualified applicants and select from the most qualified candidates.

Even with the extensive data you have, you may find it difficult to decide between the top two or three candidates. You may want to go through a rating and ranking process, assigning numerical measurements so that you can "add up" the qualifications of each candidate and select the candidate with the highest rating.

Ask some additional questions to make the final decision.

- *Accomplishments:* What was really accomplished on previous jobs?
- *Responsibilities:* Is this level of responsibility just right, too high, or too low?
- *Skills and knowledge:* Does the candidate have what it takes to do the job?
- *Strengths:* Are the key strengths present? Will these strengths add to the position?
- *Weaknesses:* Does each specific limitation impact the job? Is it offset by a necessary strength? Can this weakness be remedied through a brief orientation, learning on the job, or other training?
- *Stability:* Is this an important factor or not?
- *Compatibility:* Will this candidate be compatible with others in your department? Others in the organization?
- *Past behavior:* Is there repeated evidence or a pattern of successful performance?

Plan new employee orientation. Now that you have hired a new employee, it is important that you get the employee off to a good start. Make sure that you will be available to give your undivided attention to the new employee for the first few hours of his or her first day. If the new employee is forced to sit around doing nothing until the supervisor can find the time to get him or her started, you will not be providing a very warm welcome. Do not have a new employee report until you know you will have the time to properly prepare and introduce the employee to his or her work assignment.

The following checklist will help ensure that employees are properly oriented to a new company and job.

Welcome the new employee.
- ❏ Introduce the new employee to coworkers.
- ❏ Explain the function of each person you introduce.
- ❏ Give the employee a tour of the company and department.
- ❏ Explain where restrooms, coffee areas, and parking facilities are located.

Introduce the new employee to the job.
- ❏ Ensure that the new employee's working area, equipment, tools, and supplies are prepared and available.
- ❏ Work with IT to ensure that the new employee has full access to the company network, Internet, and any other required program.
- ❏ Provide the new employee with necessary training.
- ❏ Explain the use of phone, copy machines, and company vehicles; mail procedures; and/or supply procedures.
- ❏ Explain hours of work.
- ❏ Give new employee department telephone numbers.
- ❏ Review location of first aid equipment.

Coordinate with Human Resources Department. (If they do not cover these responsibilities, they should be covered by the supervisor.)
- ❏ Time cards/sheet guidelines
- ❏ Payroll procedures
- ❏ Probationary period
- ❏ Performance evaluations

- ❏ Holidays and time off
- ❏ Employee handbook
- ❏ Company ID card
- ❏ Security guards or security measures

☛ Tips for Success

Selection Process

1. Take time to understand your organization's hiring process.

2. Remember, the three primary purposes of the hiring interview are (1) get information, (2) give information, and (3) promote good public relations.

3. Let the job applicant talk. Plan on spending 80 percent of the time listening and 20 percent talking.

4. Do not give away the answers you expect by telegraphing the desired response.

5. Conduct a job analysis—know the job requirements.

6. Get the whole picture. Avoid jumping to conclusions.

7. Take time to plan the interview.

8. Use open-ended questions to get complete and thorough answers.

9. Know the law and ensure that you conduct fair and legal interviews.

10. Start your new employee off on a positive note by providing a warm welcome and thorough orientation.

Chapter 12

Facilitating Productive Meetings

"Meetings do not need to be punishment. After all, gatherings to discuss a subject of common interest are what parties are all about."

– Philip B. Crosby

Ask any group of managers and supervisors to list their top three most time-consuming activities, and "unproductive meetings" always surfaces in their lists. These same managers and supervisors regretfully admit that about half their time in meetings is wasted. Unfortunately, we never know ahead of time which half of the meeting is going to be the productive half. If it were known, we could plan accordingly and better manage our time!

One manager recently complained, "The biggest waste of time in our company is our management meeting on Monday mornings. The meetings are aimless and accomplish little." In today's hectic work environment, this manager isn't alone in his dislike for meetings that don't value an employee's time. Meetings that start late, don't accomplish much, and run late aggravate those in attendance and contribute little to the organization. In this chapter, we will talk about critical components for planning and leading a successful meeting. After reading this chapter and practicing these skills, you will find your confidence as a group leader growing as you successfully plan and conduct productive meetings.

To Meet or Not To Meet?

The first step in planning a successful meeting is to make an important decision. The decision is whether or not to even hold a meeting. Many meetings should *not* occur at all. For example, an inappropriate reason is to call a meeting simply for the sake of meeting. In today's world of information overload, meeting without a specific purpose is inexcusable.

Informational Meetings

Legitimate reasons for calling a meeting fall into two broad categories. The first category is for the exchange of information. Informational meetings are held for the purposes of coordinating activities, exchanging information, building morale, and selling a concept or idea.

The number in attendance at an informational meeting is determined by how many employees need to know this information. Generally, in informational meetings, the communication flow is one way, from the leader to the participants. In meetings of this type, the emphasis is presenting information the group needs to know. Leaders conducting informational meetings need to be thoroughly prepared, but usually will not be interacting with the audience. Their goal is to share with their audience the knowledge they have about a particular topic. Their success is determined by how well they deliver the information to the participants.

Decision-Making Meetings

The second reason for calling a meeting is to involve those in attendance in problem-solving, decision-making, or goal-setting processes. As these meetings involve the participants, the number in attendance needs to be limited to those members of the organization who are knowledgeable and will contribute to the decision-making process. Ideally, attendance at these meetings is limited so that participants all have the opportunity to contribute to the group process. Leaders of groups tasked with making decisions must know how to encourage those in attendance to express themselves and be creative in proposing solutions. Leaders must know how to generate participation, but also how to steer the group back when they stray from the task. Further, leaders of decision-making meetings must know what to do when emotions sidetrack participants or when a decision seems blocked.

Planning a Productive Meeting

Step One: Creating the Agenda

After determining whether a meeting needs to be held, and if it does, what type, the next step is to begin the planning. Every meeting should have an agenda. An agenda sends participants the message that I value your time enough to do prior planning. It lets participants know ahead of time what they will be doing during the meeting. If the meeting involves participant input, we recommend e-mailing an agenda out to the participants ahead of time. Participants then have an opportunity to prepare themselves for the meeting. They can make sure that they have all the data needed to make an informed contribution to the meeting. An agenda should include the following:

- **Start time.** Establish a start time and then begin right on time. Starting on time rewards those who are prompt and ready to start at the announced time. When you have a reputation for starting on time, people attending your meetings will show up on time!

- **Topics.** The topics to be covered at the meeting should be listed next, in the sequence in which they will be discussed during the meeting. Be brief here, including only enough information for participants to be able to identify the subject.

- **Break time.** If a meeting is scheduled to run more than 90 minutes, schedule in a short break. When participants start their break, be very specific about the time you will resume. Start again promptly at the announced time. People will get the message that you value their time and intend to keep the meeting moving productively.

- **Summary.** End every meeting with a short summary of the topics covered and the outcome. Although this activity doesn't take long, it helps participants focus on the content of the meeting and reminds them that the meeting accomplished something.

- **Follow-up.** After the summary, review participants' future responsibilities. Whatever participants have agreed to contribute, whether it be assuming responsibility for a task or gathering more information for a future meeting, needs to be reviewed before the meeting adjourns.

- **Adjournment time.** Having been held captive in too many meetings that ran long past schedule, please honor the adjournment time. Stick to your agenda. Work hard to keep the meeting progressing toward the established goals. End on time. If consensus on an issue is close, or if you know that the remaining agenda items can be covered quickly, ask the group's permission to extend the adjournment time by a few minutes. Otherwise, end the meeting as scheduled and plan another meeting to come to closure on the items that still remain an issue. As with starting on time, ending meetings on time will quickly build your reputation for being an organized leader with respect for others' time.

Step Two: Selecting the Participants

Generally, when deciding who should participate, the smallest number of appropriate people is the best guideline to follow. Consider the type of meeting you will be conducting. If it is to be an informational meeting, the participants will include all those who need the information. On the other hand, if the meeting will have a problem-solving format, then you should consider the following criteria when you select participants. Participants attending problem-solving meetings should have the following:

- **Expertise in the problem.** Select participants who have knowledge or technical expertise in the area that will be considered during the meeting.

- **Commitment.** Participants should have a mutual interest in solving the problem; therefore they will be committed to the problem-solving process.

- **Diversity.** When selecting participants, consider team members who have different facts, opinions, and feelings. They will contribute more creative solutions to complex problems.

- **Open-mindedness.** Participants attending the meeting will have diverse opinions. However, they need to be able to listen to one another and openly consider solutions presented by others.

Step Three: Arranging the Facility

Adequate prior planning in selecting and setting up a meeting room will contribute significantly to conducting a productive meeting. Consider the size of the room in relation to the number of participants. Will there be enough room to comfortably accommodate participants and any required furnishings and audiovisual aids? Check also to see that the heating/cooling, lighting, and ventilation are adequate for the size of your group and the activities you have planned during the meeting.

Determining what type of meeting you will be conducting (informational or decision-making), will dictate the arrangement of the furniture. Generally speaking, participants attending informational meetings can be seated facing forward so that they can maintain eye contact with the group leader. They may not need tables. Participants attending decision-making meetings should be seated so that they face one another. If participants are not all familiar with one another, have name tents for team members.

The Role of the Leader

As a leader of a group, you are responsible for creating an environment in which people can and do contribute to discussions that lead to recommendations. You are in charge of creating and maintaining conditions in which people feel free to contribute, arguments are minimized, and focus remains on the objective. Throughout the meeting, you are tasked with monitoring progress and providing the direction needed to keep participants on track. You will be continually analyzing the group's progress and refocusing the direction, if necessary, to ensure the group moves forward to meet its objective.

With practice, you can conduct a productive meeting and do it well. First, be prepared to lead. Make sure that you have the agenda ready, that the room arrangements are made, and that you are knowledgeable about the items that will be discussed during the meeting. Determine whether your meeting will have an informational or decision-making format. Second, make sure that you are familiar with the meeting process and your role as a leader. Third, believe in yourself. Management would not have assigned you the role of group leader if they did not believe that you could handle the situation. They respect your ability.

Next, view the role as a group leader as an opportunity to take additional responsibility within your organization. Being a leader takes more preparation than being a participant. Welcome the required extra effort as being an opportunity to excel and do whatever it takes to prepare yourself to lead the group.

Finally, aim for excellence. Set high standards. Expect excellent contributions from the members of your team. Lead by example. Your team members will respect you, recognize your effort, and contribute more to your meetings.

Rational Decision-Making Process

Your role as a leader of a decision-making or problem-solving meeting will require that you have an understanding of the Rational Decision-Making Process. This process provides a structured order and keeps participants' attention focused on the problem.

Step One: Analyze the Problem

First, spend time leading the group while they analyze the problem. During this time, participants will contribute their perspective about the problem or situation that has brought the group together. This is not a time for participants to suggest solutions. Ensure that all participants have the opportunity to share their views about the problem. This is important because people from different sections of the organization may view the problem from entirely different perspectives.

Step Two: Define the Problem

After all participants have had the opportunity to share their perspectives relating to the problem, define the problem. Lead the group to consensus on a clear definition of the problem. Once the problem is clearly defined, you are ready to start the process that will move the group forward to a solution or recommendation.

Step Three: State the Desired Outcome

At this point in the meeting, participants have discussed and defined the problem. It is now time to state the objective or the end result the participants want to achieve. For example, a group of supervisors may be trying to determine an equitable system for scheduling. After discussing concerns raised by employees regarding the schedule, the group determines that their objective will be to develop a schedule that gives employees an equal number of weekends and holidays off.

Step Four: Generate Alternative Solutions

There are a number of ways that alternatives can be generated. Typically, the most common method to generate a list of viable alternatives is by open discussion or brainstorming.

Step Five: Use Consensus to Reach Agreement

There are several reasons why leading a group to consensus is more advantageous than voting on a decision. Although voting is appropriate for larger groups, it generally should not be used in smaller groups, particularly when participants work with one another on a day-to-day basis. Voting creates winners and losers. Although both groups will continue working together after the decision is made, the losers may have a tougher time accepting the solution reached by the group. This is understandable, because their solution wasn't the one picked. Reaching agreement by consensus, however, maximizes the support of the decision by group participants. Although participants may not be in total agreement, reaching agreement by consensus leads to a decision that participants can support with a high degree of commitment.

When leading a group to consensus, make sure that all participants have time to present their position and are not interrupted. Encourage members to listen carefully and consider all proposed solutions. If a group seems to be deadlocked and not able to reach consensus, encourage them to look for the next most acceptable alternative.

Remember that differences of opinion are normal and to be expected. When a group has trouble reaching a decision, it is because the participants have a commitment to the outcome. If they didn't care, they would reach consensus quickly and not waste their time arguing their position. Your task as a leader is to help them go through the process of generating possible solutions, sharing their opinions, and reaching a decision that is acceptable to the group.

While the final decision reached may not be the most optimal one in some participants' minds, it should be one that they can support. Do not end the meeting without checking with those participants who raised differing viewpoints during the discussion. For example, ask John, "John, is this a decision that you can support?" If the participant says, "No," then ask, "What would need to be different in order to gain your support?" Continue the process until you are confident that the decision reached is one that will be supported by the group. While reaching consensus is a more time-consuming process than voting, it is a process that builds group cohesiveness and commitment to reaching a workable solution.

Brainstorming Process

Step One: List All Ideas Generated by the Group

Encourage group members to contribute their ideas, even if they think that they may not be workable solutions to the problem. To ensure that everyone is heard, only one person speaks at a time.

Step Two: Welcome Creativity

"Off-the-wall" suggestions and comments may seem completely off target, but may provide other participants the stimulus for generating a workable solution. Off-the-wall suggestions are often the jumping off point for devising novel solutions to complex problems.

Step Three: Make No Evaluation

Participants must not dismiss, criticize, evaluate, or judge team members' contributions during this phase of the brainstorming process.

Step Four: Limit Discussion

The intent of the brainstorming process is to generate ideas. Do not discuss ideas at this point as it slows down and limits the brainstorming process. Discussion should only occur when another participant needs clarification on a particular idea.

Step Five: Encourage Contributions

The more ideas participants contribute, the more likely it is that a workable solution will be devised. Continue to list participants' ideas, even though they may be repetitious. Duplicates can be deleted later. If the group needs stimuli to continue generating ideas, think of the five Ws and H—Who, What, When, Where, Why, and How?

Step Six: Record Ideas

Designate a recorder to write down all ideas generated, preferably on a flip chart or chalkboard so that participants can easily see all suggested solutions.

Step Seven: Rest on Decision and Incubation

Once consensus is reached and a decision is made, take some time to "sleep on" the decision. What seems like a novel solution to a complex problem today may not meet the needs of all concerned tomorrow. It is best to take some time so that participants and others affected by the decision have the opportunity to think through the aspects of the proposed solution.

Tips for Generating or Stimulating Discussion

When a group is trying to reach consensus on a solution, it is important that all the participants engage in discussion. Participants must feel comfortable and confident that their contributions will be heard. Facilitating a meeting in which participants have the confidence to contribute is challenging. Understanding the following techniques will help you lead the group in an atmosphere of free exchange and will maximize participant discussion.

Pick the right type of question. There are three general types of questions: general, specific, and direct. Each will elicit a particular type of response.

- General questions are broad and nonspecific. They are addressed to the group in general. They will elicit a wide range of general responses. Because of their nonthreatening nature, general questions are best used to start off the discussion in a meeting.

- Specific questions require answers that are focused and limited. It is best not to ask specific questions until participants in the group are comfortable and the discussion is flowing freely.

- Direct questions are asked of a particular individual. Like specific questions, it is best not to ask direct questions until you are sure that the individuals within the group are feeling confident enough to respond. Many people still remember back to their school days when they feared not having the "right answer" when the teacher called on them. They may "freeze" when called on directly. Until participants reach a point when they feel that their contribution to the group will not be a threatening experience, do not use direct questions.

Ask participants what they think. One particularly effective technique used to generate discussions is to ask members of the group to share their feelings or opinions about a particular topic. Questions such as "What is your thinking on...?" or "What made you come to that conclusion...?" or "Would you tell me more about your thinking on...?" will get participants involved in the discussion.

Ask for more explanation. When you don't understand a participant's contribution or you realize that members of the group aren't clear on an issue, ask for clarification. For example, "John, I'm not sure I fully understood your last comment. Could you explain it again for us?" or "Joan, this looks like it's confusing you. Would it help if Mike explained it again?"

Paraphrase participants' contributions. When your goal is understanding, paraphrase participants' responses. Questions such as, "If I understand it correctly, are you saying that...?" or "Mary, could you restate what you just said so that we can make sure we understand?" or "John is suggesting..." will help the group focus on what is being said.

Ask for a review of progress made. When many ideas have been presented, it is a good idea for you to summarize the information that has been presented, or ask a member of the group to do so. For example, "We've heard a lot of good ideas in the past hour. Would someone volunteer to summarize what we have come to agreement on?" or "Jack, you don't seem to be in agreement on this point. Would you please summarize your major objections?"

Support and encourage participants. When it becomes apparent that someone is not contributing, you might say, "Let's give Mary a chance to tell us her thinking on..." or "We understand your suggestions, Dale. Now, let's ask for Tom's thoughts on..." or "Before we go to the next point, I'd like to get Betty's opinion on this."

Refocus the group's attention. Periodically, when the group seems to be straying off task, to help them refocus, ask, "Are we on the right track here?" or "Is this one of the goals we identified?" or "Are we limiting our thinking. Are their other ways to get this done?"

Encourage examples. When the group is having trouble understanding a concept, ask for an example. Examples will help clarify issues and help members gain mutual understanding. "Maria, could you give us an example to help us understand?" or "Michael, I'm not sure that I'm understanding what you're proposing. Could you give me an example?"

Address differences of opinions. When it becomes apparent that a group member is not in agreement, address the participant specifically. Failure to acknowledge disagreement now may cause problems in the future. "Paul, I'm sensing that you are not in agreement with this proposed solution. Could you tell us why you don't agree?" "Elaine, I think you have a differing opinion. Please tell us your thoughts on this topic."

Check for group consensus. Checking for group consensus can be done periodically throughout the meeting. This helps the group come to closure on items already discussed and focus on items still under discussion. "We've covered five items this morning. Let's check to see if we're in agreement on..." "Before we take our break, let's check to see if we agree on..." "Is this solution one that we can all accept?"

Handling Difficult Behaviors

Occasionally, no matter how carefully prepared you are for a meeting, you will run into a challenging situation. Whenever you call a group of people together to make a decision, there is always the possibility that you will witness some interaction problems among group members. Being aware of the following typical distracting behaviors and then knowing techniques for correcting them will help you keep your meeting on track and productive:

- **The Experts.** These participants are "know-it-alls" who are only too willing to vociferously share their expertise with other members of the group. They offer their opinion frequently, regardless of whether it has been solicited. Their expertise can threaten other group members who may tune out and quit contributing to the group process. One way to handle experts is to acknowledge their viewpoint or opinion and then solicit input from other group members. "Peggy, we appreciate your thoughts on the proposed schedule change. Joe, do you have any other thoughts about the proposed changes?" Never argue with an expert. Acknowledge that you see the situation differently and ask that they remain open-minded during the problem-solving process. Suggest that they may wish to talk with you privately during the break to give you more information.

- **The Attackers.** Participants of this type argue, ask questions continually, and may challenge the group leader's expertise. Their tone of voice may be threatening or belligerent. They may have a meeting agenda of their own, and it most likely will not complement your agenda. The best way to deal with attackers is to acknowledge their disagreements. Arguing with them will only make them dig their heels in further and offer more resistance. Try saying, "Mike, I hear what you are saying and I commend you for having the courage to oppose this process. Could you give us more information about why you feel so strongly about this particular issue?" If the attackers continue, like the experts, you may ask them to talk to you further about their position either at the break or after the meeting.

- **The Distracters.** Some distracters ask too many questions. Their questions may not be related to the topic being discussed and sidetrack the group's progress. One way to handle a distracter who repeatedly asks questions is to use discretion when calling on participants. Call on other participants. If distracters continue to interrupt the group process with unrelated questions, acknowledge them and indicate that most likely their questions will be answered as the group works through the problem-solving process. Sometimes leaders and group members are distracted by people whispering. To alert whisperers that their activity is distracting, stop talking yourself. Usually, when there is no talking, whisperers get the message that they need to join the group. Another tactic is to physically stand near the whisperers. Again, this signals them that their personal conversation is distracting the group. You can also call on the whisperers directly and ask them to share their thoughts with the group.

- **The Complainers.** Sometimes group members come to the meeting with a negative mental outlook, more commonly known as a bad attitude! Rather than looking for solutions, they seem to find fault with everything. This can be intimidating for group leaders and creates a negative meeting environment. Instead of arguing with them and trying to persuade them to change their outlook, acknowledge their concern. "Jason, I am hearing that the possible solutions we've discussed are not acceptable to you. I am asking that you remain open as the group continues their discussion. If you still have concerns, let's get together at the end of the meeting." Acknowledge their concerns, but don't let their negative attitude become infectious and impede the group's progress.

- **The Non-Participants.** Group participants sometimes "tune out" the group. These participants may miss steps in directions, ask questions that have already been answered, or physically withdraw from the group. The best way to get non-participants back in the loop is to call on them directly. Ask them specific questions or solicit their opinion about the topic under consideration. Maintaining eye contact with them is another technique that will help ensure that they stay focused.

- **The Loudmouths.** Participants who are bad listeners, monopolize the conversation by talking too long, and interrupt frequently are loudmouths. Like attackers and distracters, they can be challenging for other group members. One way to handle loudmouths is to try thwarting them by calling on others. If they persist, try summarizing their responses and moving on. For example, "Connie, you feel that the best approach for us would be..." or "Mark, what are your thoughts on this subject?"

In closing, remember that individuals who can lead others to agreement on a common goal are effective managers and an asset to their organization. Upper management will recognize your ability to lead people and reward you with more responsibility. Increased responsibilities will enhance your opportunities for advancement within your organization. Like the acquisition of any skill, leading effective meetings takes practice. Using the techniques covered in this chapter, you will, with practice, be able to motivate participants to contribute, facilitate the group's progress as they reach agreement, and effectively lead a meeting in which participants leave saying, "That was a great meeting! We really accomplished our goal!"

Meeting Planning Checklist

When preparing for a meeting, review the specific tasks and then check each one off as it is completed.

Specific Task	Completed
Determine whether or not a meeting needs to be held.	
Decide what type of meeting is appropriate (information/decision).	
Decide who should attend the meeting.	
Select a meeting time.	
Select a meeting place.	
Develop an agenda.	
Notify participants of the meeting.	
If participants require preparation time, send agenda beforehand.	
Arrive early to check room arrangement.	
Check to see that all technology/equipment is operational.	
Start meeting on time.	
Review agenda with participants.	
State objective/outcome for meeting.	
Encourage participation.	
Keep group discussion focused on topic.	
Lead group to consensus.	
Summarize group progress.	
Decide what follow-up action is required.	
After meeting, write up minutes and distribute to participants.	

Meeting Facilitation

1. Before you plan to call a meeting, ask yourself this important question, "Do we need to meet, or is there a more efficient way to accomplish our goal?"

2. If a meeting is worth calling, an agenda is a must. The agenda signifies the importance of the meeting and lends structure and organization throughout the meeting.

3. Get the agenda out to participants prior to the meeting, allowing them enough time to focus their thoughts and do any advance preparation prior to the meeting.

4. Arrange the facility according to the type of meeting. If discussion is required, plan to have participants facing one another.

5. Begin and end meetings on time. Doing so conveys that you value the participants' time and intend to use it efficiently. Nothing is more frustrating for a timely person than showing up for a meeting at the announced start time and then wasting 20 minutes waiting up for other participants before the meeting begins.

6. In your opening statements, clearly state the desired outcome for the meeting.

7. Encourage participation. If you sense that there may be disagreement, even if nothing is said, have the confidence to call directly on individuals. For example, "Susan, I am feeling that you have some thoughts about this issue. Would you share them with us?"

8. Keep the discussion focused. If needed, remind participants about the goal for the meeting and redirect comments that do not relate to the current discussion.

9. Make every effort to come to agreement by consensus, not voting. Periodically check in with participants to see if they can support decisions under consideration.

10. Summarize progress and review responsibilities at the end of the meeting. Don't end until participants are sure about the next steps and their individual responsibilities.

Chapter

13

Developing Consensus

"A genuine leader is not a searcher for consensus but a molder of consensus."

– Martin Luther King, Jr.

We recently developed a training program for a manufacturing client that supplies products for the defense industry. They were interested in training because their biggest customer had just told them, "You've got some problems with quality that you need to fix. Don't just make this a management fix. Get your people involved. They know firsthand where to make the changes. Listen to them. If you can't make these changes, you may be dropped from our list of vendors." This was the first time we had specifically heard a customer dictate how a problem would be solved within a company! All of a sudden, our client had a real interest in learning how to use consensus to creatively solve problems.

Global competition, mergers, acquisitions, changes in governmental regulations, and increased customer demands all spell constant change for organizations. "Selling" change to employees at all levels within the organization is easier when employees are involved and feel ownership related to the change. Getting input and recommendations from employees requires that a supervisor be able to achieve group consensus.

Historically, up until about 20 years ago, employees did not expect to be involved in management decisions. In fact, many employees did not want to be asked to provide their opinion on decisions that affected the company. That was management's job. As one old-timer stated to us in an interview, "You'll have to pay me more money if you want me to do management's job. That's why they make the big bucks." In today's workforce, an employee who does not want to be involved in the decision-making process is in the minority. Based on the authors' experience in conducting employee opinion surveys, it is almost guaranteed that when employees are not involved in the decision-making process, the organization's level of morale and motivation will decline.

It is critical that today's managers and supervisors be responsive to the rapidly changing events going on around them within their organization, the economy, and the environment. Leaders must be effective at creating a dynamic system comprising networked teams of knowledgeable workers. To be effective in today's workplace, the role is shifting from making decisions to empowering others to make decisions.

Consensus Defined

Consensus is a state of mutual agreement among members of a group where all legitimate concerns of individuals have been addressed to the satisfaction of the group. Consensus requires that everyone be heard and understood. There is a common misconception that consensus management means that all decisions, no matter how significant, must be made by the group coming to consensus. This is not the case. There will always be times when it is appropriate to make decisions without getting others on the team involved. One example of decisions that would be more appropriately made by the manager working independently is deciding whether a team member should be coached or terminated. A second example where independent decision would be more effective is where there is a short window of time available to execute the decision. Consensus building takes time.

Often, when we discuss consensus with managers, they tell us they reach consensus with their team by taking a vote. Consensus is not about taking a vote. Consensus means that all members on the team have discussed their concerns, feel heard, and feel strongly that they can live with the outcome of the decision, as well as publicly supporting the decision. If consensus is taken to its extreme, it means one member of the team can veto the decision. Consensus works best when all members of the team are clear on the team's mission and vision, and are able to put personal interests aside to enable the team to accomplish team goals.

Benefits of Consensus Building and Shared Decision Making

There are many benefits to consensus building and shared decision making. Some of the benefits and advantages of consensus building and shared decision making include the following:

- **Greater diversity of opinion.** When team members are involved in the decision-making process, there is opportunity to hear different viewpoints. Different viewpoints are critical to a manager's success. If everyone thinks just like the manager, it makes the decision process easier, but it also increases the chances of being blind-sided by something that was never considered because there was no avenue to generate differing viewpoints. With differing viewpoints and critical examination of the decision, the manager increases his or her chances of making a good decision.

- **Shared responsibility.** When the time is taken to involve team members in the decision-making process, team members feel a greater level of responsibility in creating a successful outcome. One of the classic employee lines when a decision fails is, "Well, it sure wasn't my idea. If they'd asked me, I could have told them it would never work." By working through team members' concerns and objections, there is a higher level of team member commitment to make the decision a success.

- **Better teamwork.** Although consensus building, at times, can be messy, if leaders will follow through with the process, consensus building can ultimately lead to a stronger team. People who have listened to differing viewpoints, feel their viewpoint has been legitimately heard, and have been involved in determining the course of action usually feel a stronger bond to the team.

- **Greater understanding.** One of the great questions employees love to ask is, "Why are we doing this?" or "Who was the genius who made this decision?" What they are really saying is, "I don't understand why this decision was made and why I need to change in order to turn this decision into a reality." When employees are involved in the decision-making process, there is a greater understanding of the "why" behind every decision.

- **Faster implementation.** Although consensus building takes longer to make the decision, it is always faster to implement once the decision has finally been made. To leave the group out of the decision-making process, we can make decisions as rapidly as we can think. The problem with making individual decisions is that if team members are needed to execute the decision, it always takes longer to successfully turn the decision into action because the people who are needed to implement the decision do not feel ownership for the decision's success.

- **Greater long-term success.** When employees feel they have been involved in determining the course of action, the chances for success are bound to increase. One specific area where we see a higher chance of success is when employees run into a roadblock or a problem. When team members have been involved in determining the course of action, they will usually find an appropriate solution when they encounter a problem. If team members have not been involved in the decision, they may have decided that the decision will not work, sometimes even before the implementation process begins.

Advantages of Individual Decisions

As we mentioned earlier, not all decisions should be reached by consensus. Individual decisions also have advantages. Some of the advantages include the following:

- **Decisions can be made quickly.** The best part about making an individual decision without input from others is that we can make decisions quickly. When time is of the essence, we can make three decisions in under a minute and do it all while we are driving to work. The only thing left to do is tell people what needs to be done. Although individual decisions are quick to make, they almost always take longer to implement if the actions of others are needed to successfully implement the decision.

- **Decisions are confidential.** There are times when decisions have to be made confidentially. If a team member needs to be terminated, it is not in the team's best interest to bring a group of people together to make the decision. Discussing one employee's inadequacies is inappropriate in a group setting.

- **Decisions are critical to the organization's success.** If decisions are critical to the organization's success and the leader feels that the right decision has to be made immediately, then it may be more appropriate to make an individual decision. Some decisions that may be more appropriately made by an individual or select group include setting standards, making choices when others are unwilling to take a risk, and determining a course of action when values conflict.

- **Decisions have individual responsibility.** If no one else needs to be involved in turning the decision into a success, then it is far more beneficial to leave the group out of the decision-making process. We recently interviewed a salesperson who stated that he had made the decision to get each client proposal out to the client within two days of the request. In this case, the salesperson put together his own sales proposals. No one else needed to be involved in creating a successful outcome.

Leading a Diverse Group to Consensus

As consultants, we are frequently retained to help build teamwork among groups of people who do not work well as a team or who have a difficult time making group decisions. The skill we most frequently use to enhance teamwork is building consensus. Often, when there is disagreement among team members, it is centered on small pieces of large issues. Recently, we worked with a bank that had a major disagreement at the senior management level over who was their "real" customer. In their mission, the bank stated that they were a commercial bank; their primary customers were businesses. Several members of the senior management team were not happy with the mission statement because various branches of the bank had a large number of individual customers rather than business clients as described in the mission. When the mission was re-worked, the group was able to come to consensus by changing the mission statement to:

> "We are a locally based commercial bank providing creative financial solutions and exceptional service to the businesses and individuals in the communities we serve. For every challenge, a solution."

The four critical factors in leading a diverse group to consensus are listed below:

- **Create a compelling positive vision of the outcome.** When we use the word "vision," it is just a fancy word for a clear mental picture of the outcome. A great analogy of a clear picture of the outcome is the box top of a jigsaw puzzle. When you build a jigsaw puzzle, you always know exactly what you are trying to build because you have a clear mental picture of the outcome. Without the box top, it would make jigsaw puzzle building very frustrating. As the manager, if you cannot see how to bring the group to consensus, how can you expect a fellow team member to create a positive outcome. By interviewing members of the team and collecting different viewpoints, a manager will begin to see the common denominators among team members that will enable the group to reach a consensus decision. The critical factor is that the manager or supervisor must see the positive outcome, many times long before the rest of the team sees the team's ability to come to a consensus decision.

- **Have a high level of confidence that you can make a positive difference.** To be successful in building consensus, you have to have a deep-seated belief that you can lead the group to consensus. As Mark Twain stated, "Whether you think you can or think you can't, you are right." If you do not have a positive vision, and you do not believe you are the person who can lead the group to consensus, others on the team will read your lack of confidence and it will undermine your ability to create a successful group process. One manager recently asked us, "What happens when you feel you don't have the confidence to lead the group to consensus?" In a situation where the manager lacks confidence, we recommend meeting with individual team members one-on-one until you truly understand each team member's "real" concerns. Once you have interviewed each team member, create a graph of where agreements and disagreements exist. Where you find disagreements, generate solutions that can help facilitate the consensus-building session.

- **Develop the ability to communicate with empathy.** The ability to communicate to all team members with empathy is one of the most critical success factors in leading a group to consensus. By definition, empathy implies that the listener has the ability to understand what message the communicator is sending. Empathy is different from sympathy. Sympathy implies that you acknowledge a person's emotion. For example, "I am sorry to hear that your car was stolen." Empathy implies I care and I want to understand. For example, "I am sorry to hear that your car was stolen. It's a real hassle to be without wheels. I know how you must feel." To be effective in leading a group to consensus, you do not need to be able to feel what each team member is feeling. But you do need empathy and the ability to understand what each team member is communicating.

- **Focus on the "aim frame."** When groups disagree, many times they slip into a discussion of what is wrong with the current situation or the proposed topic of conversation. Sometimes it can even get nasty with some team members blaming others for the situation. When groups have a difficult problem to resolve and are trying to come to a consensus, it is helpful for the manager to focus the group in the aim frame. Focusing on the aim frame asks the group two questions. The first question is "Where does the group want to be with the decision or what is the ideal outcome?" The second aim frame question is "How do we get there?" If groups are steered by the manager or facilitator into the aim frame, even some of the most difficult topics to discuss will remain in a positive focus.

Preparing for the Consensus-Building Session

Conduct a comprehensive assessment of the situation. Before leading a team meeting where consensus on an issue is to be attained, it is important for the manager or facilitator to have a full understanding of where all team members are coming from regarding the topic. One of the challenges for managers is that after they work with team members for a period of time, they believe they know what each team member thinks on the issue to be discussed. This attitude of "knowing" where team members stand will lead to getting blindsided in meetings and the inability to bring the group to consensus. Part of the inability to lead the team to consensus stems from the team members' belief that the manager or facilitator does not understand his or her perspective. The underlying purpose of conducting a formal or informal interview with each team member, prior to the consensus-building session, is to gain an accurate understanding of the team's reality.

Interview each member of the team when possible. When the number of people is too large to interview everyone, we recommend interviewing the widest range of diverse opinions possible. To ensure that you have a full understanding of the issues, ask the people you interview if there are other team members you should also talk to in order to ensure mutual understanding. If others are selecting who you should talk to, be aware that you may be receiving only one side or understanding of the issues. Understanding the diversity of the issues enables the manager to facilitate many different points of view.

Ensure both informal and formal leaders are included in the assessment process. Remember, informal leaders without titles often are influential and persuasive with their peers. When it comes to building consensus, everyone on the team has a stake in reaching a mutually agreeable decision and should be held responsible for the successful implementation of the decision. Do not leave team members out of the process.

Get the toughest people involved up-front; ask for their commitment/help in the interview. Everyone has worked with a really difficult employee at least once. With really difficult people, there is a tendency to leave them out of the decision-making process until the last possible moment because they are so hard to involve in the process. Leaving difficult people out of the decision-making process is a big mistake when it comes to building consensus. In fact, to be successful, it is helpful to get them involved first, rather than last, in the process. Go to the difficult people, interview them, and in the interview tell them that you need their help in bringing the group to a mutually agreeable decision.

Determine what questions to ask in the interview process. The following are several questions we have found useful to ask when conducting an assessment and gaining the background information needed to build consensus:

- How would you describe the current situation the team is facing?

- What are your concerns as we move through the decision-making process?

- What do you see as the opportunities or possible solutions in bringing the group to consensus?

- From your perspective, what would be the ideal outcome? If not ideal, what could you live with and also publicly and actively support in regard to this decision?

- What are the group's "undiscussables"? *(These are the types of concerns that group members will talk about one-on-one but will not publicly bring up to discuss as a team.)*

- If you were in my shoes, what would you do to bring this group to a consensus decision?

- If we were to resolve this one issue, would you then be able to support the rest of the group's decision? (Ask this question if there are specific points of disagreement.)

- If this solution is not acceptable or agreeable, then what do you suggest?

- If we do not come to agreement, what happens?

- Is there anyone else you would suggest I speak with to ensure I have a full understanding of the issues?

Develop the Agenda

To lead a consensus-building meeting, it is helpful for the leader to formulate an agenda. An agenda produced in advance will help keep the team focused and on track. Invariably there are always some team members who toss out tangents that are designed to take the group off track. A well-formulated agenda allows the leader to maintain control, focus, and purpose of the discussion.

Meeting Procedures for Reaching Consensus

You have conducted an assessment of the situation. You think you understand the issues and concerns. You have a positive vision that you can lead the group to consensus. Now all you have to do is hold the meeting. These suggestions will assist you in assigning roles and setting up the meeting room for optimum success.

Arrange seating to facilitate face-to-face interaction. Each member of the group needs to be in a position where he or she can see all other members of the team, and vice versa. As the facilitator, set up the room so that the chairs are in place prior to the group's arrival. Ensure that no one is seated with his or her back to the facilitator. When the facilitator cannot see the eyes of all participants, it is much more difficult to lead the group to consensus. Usually the most difficult people will try to sit with his or her back to the facilitator. Do not let this happen! If people sit down in places where face-to-face interaction is not possible, it is appropriate to ask them to move.

Review the team's purpose for the meeting. It only takes a few minutes, but these minutes may save the group hours. Clarify agenda topics, priorities, and time limits. Review the purpose of the meeting so that all members are focused on the goal.

Ensure that all people know each other. It is easy to take for granted that all members of the group know each other. Make sure that everyone in the group is properly introduced.

Select members for the facilitator, minutes-taker, timekeeper, and monitor. You may think that it would be easiest to assign the roles to team members prior to the start of the meeting. To assign the roles prior to the meeting is a mistake because some members of the group will think that the outcome of the meeting has been orchestrated from behind the scenes. Usually, the facilitator has been assigned. Allow team members to select who will fulfill the other three roles.

Set standards for interpersonal behavior. The group should agree on certain standards of behavior. Listening with the intent of understanding another person's perspective is the key to collective decision making. Group leaders foster the consensus process by valuing and encouraging individual differences, which can reduce and perhaps avoid arguments, competition, and judgments.

Once the "nuts and bolts" have been taken care of and participants are familiar with the consensus decision-making process, it is time for you to take the lead. The following tips will help ensure your success.

Facilitation Tips to Ensure Success

Start off on a positive note. We start each consensus-building session by asking team members, "What is going well or right since the last time the team met?" The reason for starting off with the question is it helps pave the way for a positive consensus-building discussion. Even in teams where there is a lot of disagreement and controversy, there are always things that are going well and it helps the consensus-building process to recognize what is going right.

Let the group generate issues/concerns they feel need to be discussed. As the manager or facilitator, you have brought the topic to the table for discussion. It is important that the manager and facilitator ask team members what the issues are surrounding the topic they would like to see discussed. If the manager tries to control the discussion, it will be impossible to reach consensus. Generate a list of the issues and then help the team isolate the common themes.

Isolate the specific areas of disagreement. Before the consensus discussion commences, the issues of disagreement are always large because people speak in generalities. Once people start really listening to each other and exploring the common ground, the issues of disagreement usually turn out to be small, not large.

Deal with only one issue at a time. Because of the diversity of opinions, consensus building can easily throw an on-target discussion off track. As the manager or facilitator, it is critical that you deal with only one issue at a time or you will hopelessly wander from topic to topic and never reach consensus.

Create an action plan. Once consensus is reached, it is critical that an action plan be created. The actions need to be clarified so that team members understand (1) what the action is, (2) when it needs to be accomplished, and (3) who is responsible for the accomplishment of the action item.

Set future time and date to meet. A follow-up meeting needs to be set to track progress of the decision or there will be a tendency for the group to slip back to old habits that were in place prior to the consensus-building session.

Although the ability to successfully bring a group to consensus is one of the most difficult skills we have presented in this book, we are confident that like all skills, with practice, it can be mastered. As organizations continue to ask employees to do a lot more with a lot less, the need for a leader who can build consensus will continue to grow. Practice the skill. It will be well worth your time.

☛ Tips for Success

Consensus and Decision Making

1. Begin with a clear vision of the outcome you desire.

2. When the group isn't able to come to agreement, focus on the "aim frame." Refer back to the vision and ask, "Where do we ultimately want to be?" or "How are we going to get there?"

3. Before leading the group, do your homework. Interview a cross-representative sample of participants before bringing the group together. This will prevent you from being "blindsided."

4. Remember to include negative thinkers. Get them involved from the outset. There is a much greater chance of them buying in to the solution if they are involved.

5. Prepare an agenda.

6. Consider the room arrangement. When possible, seat participants so that they can see other group members.

7. Keep the discussion focused. Deal with only one issue at a time.

8. When stuck, try to isolate specific areas of disagreement.

9. If the group generates ideas that do not pertain to the current discussion, "park" them on a flip chart to be dealt with later, or at another time.

10. Remain positive. It is critical that you have a deep-seated belief that you will be successful at leading the group to success.

Chapter 14

Managing Conflict

"The pure and simple truth is rarely pure and never simple."

— Oscar Wilde

Understand that as a supervisor or manager, no matter how carefully you plan, periodically you will have to deal with conflict. Whether it be conflict between employees, with a vendor, or with a customer, conflict has a way of uniquely appearing, demanding that we acknowledge and deal with the challenge. Just as you would not ignore poorly produced products or inferior job performance, you can't afford to ignore conflict. While it is unrealistic to think that you can create a conflict-free environment, you can learn more about how to resolve issues so that conflict doesn't overwhelm you and impact your company's productivity. The intent of this chapter is to give you the tools that you need to understand what causes conflict, how to deal with conflict, and how to keep conflict under control in your organization. With practice, you will become confident in your ability to resolve conflicts that typically arise in the day-to-day operations of an organization.

Defining Conflict

First of all, understand that conflict is a fact of life and is here to stay! Wherever you have groups of people working together, you are going to experience conflict. Know that this is a normal occurrence and that the better you understand conflict, the better you will be able to effectively deal with the challenges inherent in supervising people.

Many relatively successful supervisors and managers have a fear of conflict. Much of their fear stems from misconceptions about the subject of conflict. One way of diffusing that fear is to explore and shatter some misconceptions that are commonly associated with the subject of conflict. Learning more about dealing with conflict will help reduce your fear of conflict and enhance your business, family, and social contacts.

Common Misconceptions about Conflict

If you ignore conflict, it will take care of itself. In most cases, nothing could be further from the truth. While it may be true that in some cases you can choose to ignore conflict, recognize that this is a coping strategy, not a solution to conflict. For example, if you continue to accept substandard products from a vendor without trying to resolve the quality problem, you avoid conflict. If, however, the substandard products delay your production or result in an inferior final product, you may have avoided conflict but cost your organization in the long run. Most often, when conflicts are ignored, things usually get worse. Generally speaking, it is best to develop a plan to deal with challenging situations and not assume that conflict will resolve itself.

Conflict results from poor management. Relationships in the workplace are diverse and subject to periods of disharmony. Confident supervisors know that some tension in the workplace is normal and have a positive attitude about their ability to resolve conflict. For example, relationships are sometimes stretched when employees perceive that others are not working as hard as they are. If one employee consistently takes longer breaks than is permitted, as a supervisor, you must deal with this. If you choose to ignore it, the conflict will escalate and other employees will become resentful. If, however, you address and correct the problem with the employee abusing the break time, you will gain the respect of your other employees. Taking the opportunity to coach and counsel employees regarding inappropriate behavior increases your effectiveness as a manager and helps reduce potential conflict.

Anger is a destructive emotion. Anger, like other human emotions, exists and is neither positive nor negative. Anger in the workplace does not have to be thought of as being bad. Anger only exists where there are strong emotions. If people didn't have a commitment and care about an issue, they would not exhibit anger. If, however, anger is vented appropriately, it can help people move forward and resolve their conflict. It is important to note here, however, that we are not condoning angry outbursts in the workplace. Our goal is to help you understand that anger emerges from passion, and passion in the workplace is not a bad thing. When conflict is addressed, anger subsides and often the team emerges even stronger than before the anger surfaced.

All conflict must be resolved immediately. In some cases, a rush toward resolution of conflict may actually limit your success. Some conflict is best managed by a series of interventions, not a quick fix. It is important to maintain a vision of the big picture and not try to find a solution for every conflict. For example, when your staff complains about their workload, it is best to thoroughly explore their concerns. You will find it helpful to involve the group in a problem-solving session where you can discuss their feelings and explore alternatives. Denying the problem by refusing to discuss it will only make the conflict worse.

Conflict indicates low regard for the organization. Actually, just the opposite is true. If people didn't care about their organization, they would not expend the energy. Generally, conflict occurs in areas where people have a deep concern. Conflict can help clarify emotions and serve as a tool for helping determine an organization's core values. It is not uncommon for conflict to occur between departments within an organization. Employees dealing directly with customers may have difficulty relating to employees in other departments, such as accounting. Both departments accuse the other of missing the "big picture" or not really caring about the company. In reality, employees in both departments care deeply about the organization. Bringing both sides together to discuss their concerns will help the two departments resolve their differences and will actually make the organization stronger.

Stages of Conflict

We find it helpful to view conflict in three different stages. By viewing conflict in stages, you will find it easier to determine the severity of the conflict and its impact on the organization. Once the level of conflict is determined, it becomes easier to determine a plan of action and work toward a realistic solution.

Stage One Conflict

Conflict at Stage One is real, but often not intense. Typically, people working together will have different goals, values, and unique individual needs. In Stage One conflicts, people feel discomfort and possibly anger, but do not get very emotional about the conflict. Once the problem has surfaced, facts and opinions are shared openly and the parties involved generally feel a sense of optimism about their ability to resolve the problem. In Stage One conflict, communication is typically specific and clear because the people and the problem are not intertwined. Brainstorming activities will work well at this level, because people are willing to discuss the problem specifically and leave out the personalities.

Tips to help managers and supervisors resolve Stage One conflicts:

- **Get employees involved to carefully examine the conflict.** Get both sides talking and ensure that they both listen to one another.

- **Make sure that employees stick to the issues.** Don't let either party bring up emotional issues from previous conflicts. Deal only with the facts relating to this particular conflict. Ask whether their reaction is in proportion to the problem.

- **Help employees identify points of agreement first.** Working from the points of agreement, try to identify and resolve the points of disagreement. Help employees see the big picture and get beyond their issues of conflict.

Stage Two Conflict

Conflict at the Stage Two level becomes characterized by a win/lose attitude. The wins and losses characteristic of Stage Two conflict seem greater because the people involved are emotionally tied to the problem. How one looks in the eyes of others is suddenly very important. At this level of conflict, people keep track of their verbal victories, witnesses take sides, and sides begin to keep track of their wins and losses. Whereas conflict can be handled at Stage One with various avoidance or coping strategies, these strategies will not work when dealing with Stage Two conflict.

Tips to help diffuse conflict at the Stage Two level:

- **Interview for accuracy.** Interview all parties individually or independently so that you know the issues prior to bringing together the people who are in conflict. When you accurately know all the issues and perceptions, you will be in a better position to resolve or mediate the conflict.

- **Create a neutral atmosphere.** Create a safe, neutral atmosphere in which to discuss the conflict. Seat participants in a circle, not across from one another. Seating participants close to one another, without the security of a table or desk between them, helps set the right tone for conflict resolution.

- **Keep the group focused in the "aim frame."** Groups focused in the aim frame ask two questions: "Where do want to be?" and "How do we get there?" Focusing the group on these questions will reduce finger pointing and blaming.

- **Focus on the facts.** Use whatever time it takes to make sure that you have all the details. Make sure that you clarify any generalizations. Ask participants to clarify who "they" are and how many times "always" means.

- **Encourage teamwork.** Each participant is equally responsible for finding an acceptable alternative to resolve the conflict.

- **Focus on points of agreement and look for middle ground.** At this point, do not suggest compromise. Typically, people involved in Stage Two conflict are emotional. To them, a compromise may mean giving up and may feel like a loss. Keep exploring alternatives until both parties can agree on a solution.

- **Recognize that helping people resolve conflict takes time.** Allow enough time for each party to express all their concerns regarding the conflict. Take what time is needed to find a solution to the conflict that is agreeable to all parties. Rushing or forcing a resolution may create a quick fix, but not a lasting solution to the conflict.

Stage Three Conflict

When conflict escalates to Stage Three, both being right and wanting to punish wrong become increasingly important. Sides are drawn and people rally around their cause. The conflict becomes all-consuming and parties involved make it the center focus, expending a large amount of their effort and energy in their commitment to their cause. In true Stage Three conflict, issues are intense and there is little middle ground. Sides polarize and insiders try to persuade outsiders to join their cause. Both sides enlist support by promoting their cause as being what is best for the organization. In truth, as the conflict escalates, both sides become increasingly more committed to winning and frequently lose sight of what damage their conflict is inflicting on the organization.

When Stage Three conflict reaches the point that it severely impacts organizational morale and productivity, outside intervention is needed. If the conflict is limited to one area of the organization, a neutral party from another area within the organization could be called in to mediate the dispute. If, however, the conflict permeates the entire organization, it is best to call in mediators from outside the organization. Regardless of where the mediating team comes from, they must be seen as neutral by all parties involved in the conflict.

Mediators will be required to sift through many layers of emotion to get down to the underlying facts. Facts surrounding the incidents that initially started the conflict may have become clouded and obscure as the conflict escalated. Mediators should first interview representatives of each side privately. Once the mediator has the facts, both sides will be brought together and the mediator will attempt to get agreement on the facts. Working with both sides, the mediator will then seek consensus on an acceptable alternative to end the conflict.

Tips for dealing with conflict at the Stage Three level:

- **Make a commitment to get all the details.** This will require time, but the outside intervention team must make sure that they commit to interviewing as many people as necessary to ensure that they get the facts right. This will require sifting through a great deal of information clouded by emotion, but is a critical step.

- **Recognize and understand the intensity of individuals' commitment to their cause.** From an outsider's point of view, you can logically think through the conflict. Know that to those personally in the conflict at this level, logic and reason will not necessarily persuade them to think differently. Concentrate on getting agreement on the facts and mediating a solution that is acceptable to both sides.

- **Once the conflict is resolved, concentrate on corporate goals.** Conflict at this level is intense, and a period of healing will be required after it has been resolved. Make sure that both sides understand the need to commit to their organization's goals. As a manager or supervisor, recognize the skills of your employees and the contributions they make for the benefit of the organization. Redirect energies away from the conflict that polarized sides and impacted negatively on the organization. Focus on the future and what all employees can contribute toward common organizational goals.

Conflict Stages

Stage	Characteristics of Conflict Stages
One	1. Individuals agree to meet and discuss the facts. 2. Both sides believe they can resolve the conflict. 3. Individuals can discuss the problem without involving personalities. 4. Parties involved stick to the facts and work toward a solution. 5. Individuals agree on a solution and implement it positively.
Two	1. A sense of competition exists between both sides. 2. Parties focus on "winners" and "losers." 3. The facts become obscured by personalities. 4. The language used is emotional and general. (Phrases such as "They always," "She never," and "They are such" obscure facts and intensify emotional responses to the conflict.)

		5. Parties are more willing to continue the conflict for the sake of making themselves look good than they are to entertain attempts to resolve the conflict.
Three		1. Parties are obsessed with "winning." 2. Attempts are being made to "get rid" of others. 3. Sides become polarized; each side attempts to attract followers. 4. Leaders or spokespersons for each side emerge. 5. Corporate good becomes secondary to the goal of each side winning. 6. There appears to be no common ground, issues have escalated to only black and white options, solutions seem unattainable.

Conflict Management Styles

Different types of controversies call for different types of conflict management styles. We will briefly discuss five main management styles for dealing with conflict. Once you have a basic understanding of these different styles, you can select the one most appropriate for the specific conflict.

Management Style One: Withdrawing

In choosing the withdrawing or avoiding style of conflict resolution, little value is placed on either self or others. A manager using this style will withdraw and may pretend that conflict isn't happening. Sometimes, though, this can be an appropriate style to use. If more time is needed to study a conflict, or if the issue is relatively unimportant, this style works well. If, however, a manager uses this style as a response to all types of conflict, tense situations may escalate and the manager will quickly gain a reputation for doing nothing when conflict divides parties. Two departments, for example, may be in conflict with one another for what they perceive to be budgetary inequalities. The vice president responsible for both departments chooses to ignore the comments heard from each department about the other. Rather than diminish, the feelings of mistrust and resentment continue to grow between the departments until lack of internal support between the departments begins to negatively impact the entire organization.

Management Style Two: Smoothing

Parties may decide to use a smoothing style of conflict management when it is important to maintain a positive relationship. Smoothing places a high value on the wants and needs of others and a lesser value on self-gratification. This strategy places less emphasis on differences between parties involved in the conflict and greater value on reaching common ground. One party may decide to oblige the other in order not to "rock the boat." The obliging party may decide that attempting to confront the issue may cause damage to the relationship and that the outcome would not be worth jeopardizing the relationship. The obliging style results in a win/loss outcome. In this case, one party has decided that obliging the other party is worth the loss in order to maintain the relationship. Taking this calculated loss is fine as long as one party does not build resentment against the other. For example, a small start-up company may put up with a rude customer because they need the business. Eventually, though, as the business grows, employees at the firm will resent having to continue the relationship with the rude customer.

Management Style Three: Forcing

The forcing or dominating style of conflict management is just the opposite of the smoothing or obliging and results in a win/lose outcome. Parties using this style place a high value on self and a low value on others. This style is appropriate to use when the issues are minor or a quick decision is needed. This strategy may also be employed by someone having greater expertise or authority in an area than the other side. In this case, one side dictates the outcome for the other side. Although this method quickly resolves conflict, care must be taken to ensure that the losers do not feel bullied. In other words, just because one party can mandate a solution, it may not be the best approach because the losers will build resentment and harbor hostility. The dominating style of conflict resolution, used repeatedly over time, does nothing to foster cooperation and may actually escalate conflict in an organization. A manager, for example, repeatedly handles all scheduling conflicts relating to job assignments by dictating who will do what. Over a period of time, this leads to resentment and a feeling that, if given the chance, employees could themselves do a better job of examining job assignments and resolving the conflict equitably.

Management Style Four: Compromising

This style of managing conflict is a middle-of-the-road solution. Parties involved in compromising tactics place neither high nor low value on either self or concern for others. Often, this approach is used when other methods have failed, yet both parties are still desirous of a positive outcome. At this point in the conflict, both sides have reached the point where they are willing to give up something in order to resolve the problem. Compromise results in a lose/lose outcome. Compromising tactics work best when issues are complex or when there is an equal balance of power between the parties involved. Using the avoidance example from the paragraph above, the vice president responsible for the two departments arguing over the budget would call representatives from both departments together. Each side would then present their facts, feelings, and suggestions for change. Working with the representatives, a compromise is devised that more equitably distributes resources. Although neither department got all that they wanted, both departments would support the compromise solution.

Management Style Five: Collaborating

This style is best used to solve problems when issues are complex. Parties using this style of conflict resolution have a high regard for both themselves and others. In other words, both parties are committed to a win/win outcome and willing to work together to derive that outcome. When using the collaborating style to resolve conflict, both sides must be willing to examine their differences factually and reach a solution that is acceptable to all. Parties using this style work hard to think creatively and come up with an acceptable solution. Their goal is to gather as much factual information as needed to generate a solution acceptable to all parties. This style takes time and will only work if both parties are committed to the outcome. For example, over a period of time, workers in a small office have become divided. Each side feels that the other is not working as hard and not contributing their fair share to the organization. Under the leadership of the manager, both sides sit down to talk about their feelings and examine solutions. Objectively, they look at various job responsibilities, realign some responsibilities, and commit their support to a united team effort.

Methods for Resolving Conflict

Methods	Results	Appropriate if...	Inappropriate if...
Withdrawing	Person tries to solve problem by denying its existence. Results in win/lose.	Issue is relatively unimportant. Timing is wrong. Cooling off period is needed. Short-term use.	Issue is important and will not disappear.
Smoothing	Emphasizes area of agreement. Differences are played down. Surface harmony exists. Results in win/lose and in variations of resentment and defensiveness.	Same as above. Also when preservation of relationship is important.	Reluctance to deal with conflict leads to evasion of an important issue when others are ready and willing to deal with the issue.
Forcing	One's authority, position, majority rule, or a persuasive minority settles the conflict. Results in win/lose if the dominated party sees no hope for self.	When power comes with position of authority. When this method has been agreed on.	Losers have no way to express needs. Could result in future disruptions.
Compromising	Each party gives up something in order to meet midway. Results in lose/lose if "middle-of-the-road" position ignores the real diversity of the issue.	Both parties have enough leeway to give. Resources are limited when win/lose stance is undesirable.	Original position is unrealistic. Solution is too watered down to be effective. Commitment is doubted by parties involved.
Collaborating	Win/win. Abilities, values, and expertise are recognized. Each person's position is clear, and emphasis is on joint solution.	Time is available to complete the process. Parties are committed and trained in use of process.	Not enough time or abilities. Commitment is not present.

Handling Conflict Positively

One of the challenges of dealing with conflict is to help people maintain healthy relationships *during* and *after* periods of conflict. Simply resolving the problem is not enough. The people involved must be satisfied with the outcome, and attention must be given to their emotional well-being. If these two areas are not addressed, chances are other problems will surface within time. The following tips will help you maintain healthy relationships during periods of conflict:

- **Acknowledge conflict.** Workplace conflict happens. Effective supervisors acknowledge conflict and take steps to helping employees resolve conflict.

- **Encourage participation.** As conflict escalates, the people involved become consumed with their cause and the good of the organization becomes secondary. Managers and supervisors can help people overcome problems that split groups by encouraging participation. Getting parties involved to admit ownership of the problem and work toward resolution helps build commitment to the good of the organization.

- **Create a safe environment.** Creating a neutral environment in which both parties can present their facts, discuss the problem, and suggest ideas for resolving the conflict is one way to support and encourage participation leading to conflict resolution.

- **Encourage commitment.** Reminding people that collectively "we" own the problems and collectively "we" have the power to resolve them is a good technique for encouraging commitment to ending the conflict.

- **Question to determine the facts.** Conflict, by nature, gets emotional. Although people may not intentionally lie, their perspective colors their perception of the facts. As a leader during conflict resolution, keep listening and questioning to make sure that you have the facts straight. As people passionately present their case, this will be a challenge.

- **Listen, listen, listen.** During periods of conflict, listening skills are critical. It costs you nothing to listen and gives you a much better perspective on the problems surrounding the conflict. As managers and supervisors, we are used to doing the talking. We feel confident when we are in charge of the conversation. As a leader dealing with conflict, however, we need to stop talking and start listening.

- **Listen objectively.** In order to support people during conflict, don't argue with their facts. Instead, keep questioning, making sure that all parties have an opportunity to be heard before any decisions are made. Typically, when the facts are separated from the opinions, it becomes easier to think crea-tively and propose alternative solutions leading to an acceptable solution to the conflict being discussed.

- **Focus on the problem, not the people.** This is a challenge, because in Stages Two and Three conflict, the people and the problem are intertwined. Personalities align with one another, and the details surrounding the facts or situation that originally started the conflict become obscured. As a leader, you must work hard to keep the people issues separate from the facts. Insist that parties focus on the facts. If emotions flare and parties begin attacking one another personally, steer the discussion back to the facts. Insist that par-ties listen to one another as they present their facts. Get agreement from both parties on the facts. Sticking to the facts plays down emotional responses and enhances the problem-solving process.

- **Take more time to reach a decision, if necessary.** Although we are not rec-ommending avoidance as a problem-solving technique, declaring a "timeout" at some point in the conflict resolution process may be helpful. Occasionally people become so passionate about their cause that they lose their perspec-tive. Sometimes the facts needed to resolve a problem are not available. Leaders must communicate why they are delaying the decision so that the parties involved maintain their confidence in their leadership.

- **Follow up.** Initially, after conflict has been addressed and resolved, it is usual for things to appear to be going more smoothly. Don't assume this will last. Periodically check back with both parties to ask how things are going. If issues emerge, get both parties together again and address the concerns before the situation escalates.

Finally, recognize that despite all that you do to keep your leadership positive and focused on organizational goals, conflict in the workplace will be inevitable. If we worked only with machines, conflict would not be a challenge. As we work with people, though, it can be expected that relationships will be stretched from time-to-time and we will be faced with the task of helping people resolve stressful situa-tions. Use what you have learned in this chapter to confidently counsel, mediate, and lead during a time of organizational conflict. Your ability to help others deal ration-ally with conflict will identify you as a valuable team player within your organiza-tion. Remember that conflict does not have to be feared, nor spell disaster for a team. Knowing what you now do about conflict resolution, recognize it as an oppor-tunity to practice and further enhance another one of your supervisory skills.

☛ Tips for Success

Conflict Resolution

1. Don't ignore conflict. Chances are, if left alone, the conflict will escalate, not go away.

2. If you work with people, there is potential for conflict. This is no reflection on your ability as a supervisor or manager. What will distinguish you is your ability to confidently deal with workplace conflict.

3. Before attempting to resolve issues, make sure you know the facts. The best way is to talk with employees one-on-one to learn firsthand about their perceptions regarding the conflict.

4. Remember to listen more than you speak when resolving conflict. As a manager or supervisor, we are accomplished problem solvers. When the conflict revolves around people and feelings, it is critical that you listen, listen, and then listen some more.

5. Make every attempt to remain objective and neutral. Your team is looking to you as a role model. They will be influenced by how you resolve conflict. If you are calm, objective, and solution oriented, you are demonstrating positive techniques for resolving conflict.

6. To help ensure that you remain objective, focus on the problem, not the people involved with the problem. Doing this helps you stay detached from the emotion surrounding the conflict and helps you better focus on positive outcomes.

7. During periods of conflict, help employees refocus their attention on your team's goals. When you emphasize goals and outcomes, it demonstrates your commitment to resolving the conflict and focuses energy back on the reason we are in business.

8. If you reach a "stalemate" when attempting to resolve conflict, declare a "time out." Giving those involved a time to cool off may help all parties better focus on solutions.

9. When resolving conflict, attempt to utilize the collaboration method, which strives to achieve a solution that is mutually acceptable to all parties. Using the collaboration style helps ensure that neither party in the conflict feels like the "loser."

10. Once the conflict is resolved, periodically check back with the participants to make sure that there are no further issues.

Chapter 15

Negotiating for Win/Win Results

> "Let us never negotiate out of fear. But, let us never fear to negotiate."
>
> – *John F. Kennedy*

Managers and supervisors frequently face situations requiring negotiation skills: agreeing on appropriate schedules and deadlines for projects, solving problems with clients, setting the salaries of employees, acquiring more personnel for the department, and maintaining high customer service standards with staff. Utilizing effective negotiation skills is the only realistic and successful approach to meet the challenges of today's rapidly changing environment. In this chapter you will learn what negotiation is, as well as the supervisory skills you need to be a great negotiator.

What Is Negotiation?

What do you think of when you hear the word "negotiation"? Unions and management locked in a heated debate regarding wages and benefits? Sports figures threatening to switch allegiances unless they get their specified millions? Labor and management locked in a 12th-hour contract struggle for a 4 percent raise? Experience demonstrates that most of us think of negotiation in this win/lose type of scenario.

At a San Diego State University–sponsored seminar on negotiation, the following question was posed to participants: "How often do you negotiate?" The choice of answers included "Often," "Seldom," or "Never." Surprisingly, over 36 percent of the respondents answered "Seldom" or "Never." Unfortunately, this was a trick question! The correct answer is "Always." Everything in life is negotiated, under all conditions, at all times—from asking your significant other to take out the morning garbage to merging into a freeway lane in rush hour traffic; from deciding with an employee what time frame to schedule the completion of a project to deciding which television program to watch with your family. Every aspect of your life is spent in some form of negotiation.

Gerard I. Nierenberg, the author of the first book on the formalized process of negotiation, defines negotiation as, "Whenever people exchange ideas with the intention of changing relationships, whenever they confer for agreement, then they are negotiating.[4]" Using this definition, most of us are constantly involved in negotiations to one degree or another for a good part of any given day. Negotiation should be considered as a positive way of structuring the communication process.

Negotiation's Possible Outcomes

A negotiation will end in one of five possible outcomes. The outcome will be one of lose/lose, win/lose, lose/win, win/win, or no outcome. In most occasions, our goal should be a win/win outcome.

Outcome One: Lose/Lose

Lose/lose is the outcome when neither party achieves its needs or wants and is reluctant to negotiate with the same counterpart again. For example, you make an offer to a candidate you feel is a match for your company. Your ideal candidate accepts your offer, but a few days before the new employee is due to start work, he calls to inform you that he has accepted a better offer from another company. At the moment you received his call, you felt you lost. The candidate did take the other job, but it did not turn out like he expected. He wishes he had accepted the first job offer and feels he lost out in the negotiation.

Outcome Two: Win/Lose

The second and third possible outcomes of negotiation are the win/lose and the lose/win. The difference between the two is which side of the fence you land on. In some negotiations, you will be the winner and your counterpart will lose. In other negotiations, the roles will be reversed. If you have ever lost a negotiation or been taken advantage of by another, you know that the feeling is not pleasant. The significant problem in a win/lose or lose/win outcome is one counterpart walks away without accomplishing his or her needs or goals. And more importantly, the loser will likely refuse to renegotiate with the winner. Ultimately, this sets up the potential for a future lose/lose outcome.

---

[4] Nierenberg, G. (July 1991). *The Art of Negotiating: How to Become a Skilled Negotiator.* Pocket Books.

An example of a win/lose relationship would be a supervisor who continually asks an employee to work overtime or on weekends but is never willing to give that same employee a day or time off when requested. This one-sided relationship destroys respect, morale, and trust.

Outcome Three: Lose/Win

Remember, when you create a lose/win or win/lose, the loser, if given the choice, will most likely refuse to negotiate with the same counterpart again. During a six-week course in Negotiation at San Diego State University, one of our students continually created win/lose outcomes, with himself always in the winner's circle. By the sixth week, there was not one person in the class who would negotiate with him. Creating win/lose or lose/win is not good business!

Outcome Four: Win/Win

In almost all negotiations, the goal we should strive for is to create a win/win outcome. This is an outcome where the needs and goals of both counterparts have been met. Also, both counterparts walk away with a positive feeling and are willing to negotiate with each other again. A supervisor who asks an employee to work the weekend, but then grants the employee's request to take time off to attend his daughter's graduation later in the week is a great example of a win/win outcome. In the negotiation workshops we present, it is rewarding to see the excitement in participants' faces when they both realize they have created a win/win outcome.

Outcome Five: No Outcome

The fifth possible outcome is no outcome: neither party wins or loses. For example, a person who owned a large commercial piece of real estate decided to sell his property. The reason for selling was that the city government was considering rezoning the area where the property was located. The property owner felt the rezoning was going to lower the property value. A real estate agent was called to list the property. In the meeting, the real estate agent, who was a member of the zoning commission, told the property owner that they had received erroneous information and no rezoning would take place. The agent recommended that the owner hold on to the property, rather than sell. The property owner accepted the agent's advice. In this particular negotiation, nothing happened.

Creating a Win/Win Outcome

Creating a win/win outcome is possible. Follow these keys for success for win/win solutions.

1. **Do not narrow your negotiation down to one issue.** If you do narrow the negotiation to one issue, then you have created a situation where you have a winner and a loser. The most common example of narrowing a negotiation down to one issue is arguing over the price of something. With supervisors, the most typical issue is money. Most supervisors believe the most important thing to employees is money. There are so many other factors that can be brought into the negotiation. Some examples are job assignments, recognition, status, perks, awards, vacation, timing, quality, other goods and services, etc.

2. **Realize your counterpart does not have the same needs and wants as you do.** If you do not take this factor into consideration, then you negotiate from the framework that my loss is my counterpart's gain. With that attitude, it is virtually impossible to create a win/win outcome.

3. **Need to really believe #2 in your heart.** Experience shows most novice negotiators acknowledge their counterpart most likely does not have the same needs and wants as they do, but when they get into an actual negotiation, the acknowledgment vanishes from their mind. For example, most supervisors forget about the power of daily recognition or valued contributions and just focus on what raise they can or cannot give an employee. Supervisors focus on money because that is what they think employees desire the most. In creating a negotiated outcome, in most instances, it will be in your best interest to have a cooperative attitude to help develop a win/win atmosphere.

Negotiation Resources

Resource One: Time

Time is a valuable resource for supervisors and managers. Most people think of negotiation as an event that has a definite beginning and ending. Furthermore, we find that most people consider the negotiation to start and end with the actual interactive process between the two counterparts. Nothing could be further from the truth.

Recently, one of our seminar participants asked for advice on what strategy she should use when agreeing on appropriate schedules and deadlines for projects. All the options she had considered dealt with the actual face-to-face meeting. What she had not considered was all the pre-planning and information gathering that creates a powerful negotiation. These included documenting her workload, prioritizing projects, delegating the work properly, and having a clear vision of the goals she wanted to achieve prior to the meeting. Most negotiations, like life, are a continuous process that begin long before the actual negotiation takes place.

Time plays a critical role in negotiations for all supervisors and managers. Most often, negotiations will conclude in the remaining 20 percent of the time allowed. This element of negotiation is an interesting rule that seems to apply to life in general. It is called the 80/20 rule, or Pareto's Law (named after Vilfredo Pareto, the Italian economist and sociologist who created it). Pareto's Law says, "Twenty percent of what you do produces 80 percent of the results, and conversely, 80 percent of what you do produces only 20 percent of the results."

In negotiation, this means that 80 percent of your results are generally agreed upon in the last 20 percent of your remaining time. We consistently see this in the seminars we present. As the participants negotiate with each other, the seminar leader periodically tells the participants how much time they have to conclude their negotiation. Normally, the majority of the negotiations are concluded in the last remaining two minutes. Here are two suggestions that will help you bring time to your side of the negotiations:

- **Have patience.** Since most concessions and settlements will occur in the last 20 percent of the available time, be patient. Remain level-headed and wait for the right moment to act. As a general rule, patience pays. It may be that the thing to do when you are not certain is to walk away or do nothing.

- **Realize deadlines can be moved, changed, or eliminated.** As a deadline comes near, do not panic. Change your deadline. Have you ever wondered how many of the people who are running to the Post Office at the last minute on April 15 have refunds coming back to them? Even with the lack of a refund, people still have the opportunity to file an extension, giving them another four months.

Resource Two: Information

Most often, the side with the most information will receive the better outcome in a negotiation. Why then, do we fail to get adequate information prior to the start of a negotiation? Because, as we mentioned earlier, people tend to perceive the negotiation as the actual interaction between two counterparts. We seldom think about the information that we need until it hits us like a ton of bricks in the actual negotiation.

A negotiation is not an event, it is a process. It starts long before the actual face-to-face encounter. One reason you have to start much earlier is because during the actual negotiation, it is likely that one side or the other will conceal their true interests, needs, and motivations. Your chances of getting this information during the actual negotiation is relatively remote.

How do you get this information? You start early. The earlier you start, the easier it is to obtain information. People will offer much more information prior to the start of any formal interaction.

Where do you get this information? From anyone who has any knowledge that will help you in your negotiation. This may be using the Internet to research facts and statistics, talking to someone who has negotiated with your counterpart in the past, talking to your counterpart, or gaining inside information from friends, relatives, coworkers, etc.

The benefit of gaining your information prior to the negotiation is two-fold. First, with your information in hand, it gives you the opportunity to listen for your counterpart's needs, wants, and motivations. This also includes listening for what is being omitted. Second, it has been proven that the side with the most information will probably receive the better outcome in the negotiation.

Resource Three: Power

When we discuss power in seminars, we sometimes see disgust written across the faces of some participants. The word "power" has received a negative connotation for many years. It has received this reputation because most people, when they hear the word "power," contemplate one side overbearing and dominating the other. We define power as the ability to influence people or situations. With this definition in mind, power is neither good nor bad. It is the abuse of power that is bad.

Most people have more power than they think. We believe there is a link between one's self-esteem and the amount of power one feels they have. It has been demonstrated that people with high self-esteem feel they have more viable options in negotiations. People with low self-esteem do not perceive themselves as having viable alternatives. This is the same for people who feel they lack the power to act. Powerless people become apathetic, which means they do not stand a fair chance when they take their baggage into a negotiation. When entering into a negotiation, there are some rules to remember about power:

- **Seldom does one side have all the power.** Even in a situation where you are going to banks asking for a business loan, you, the entrepreneur, still have power—the power to decide which bank you will apply to, the power to decide what interest rate you will pay, and the power to decide if you will put up your home as collateral.

- **Power may be real or apparent.** I *(Peter)* am reminded of the days when I was a proctor in the Sociology Department at San Diego State University. Cheating was a problem, but I had never made a focused effort to stop the offenders. I figured I would use multiple tests on the final and it would all come out in the wash. Unfortunately, I did not have time to scramble the test on the final and I had to resort to Plan B. As I was passing out the tests, I made an announcement that on this final, I would uphold the university's "policy" on cheating. As I completed handing out the test, one bold student asked what the university's policy was on cheating. My response was simple, "If you need to ask, then you do not want to know." This was the first time I ever saw all 60 students with their heads staring at their own paper! Does the university have a policy on cheating? I do not know. But in this situation, whether the power was real or apparent did not matter: the students perceived I had the power.

- **Power only exists to the point that it is accepted.** On a flight home from Europe, all the ticketing agents in the economy class had at least a 20-minute line to check baggage. The business class and first class had not one person. The Business and first class ticketing agents were looking off into space like they were mentally rehearsing their policy and procedures manual. Not wanting to wait in line, I *(Jane)* took my baggage and ticket up to the business Class window and got my seat assignment. (I would have gone up to the first class counter, but I did not want to push my luck!)

- **Test your power.** You will never know how much power you have until you test reality. The chances are you have more power than you think.

Advance Preparation

In negotiations, advance preparation is critical. The more prepared you are, the better off you will be. Also, it will be in your best interest to have a clear set of goals going into the negotiation. You can then set your goals based on the information you collect. The following sheet provides a guideline in collecting the information you will need.

Negotiation Worksheet

Your Side	Counterpart's Side
Topic:	Topic:
Available Facts:	Available Facts:
Negotiable Issues:	Negotiable Issues:
Position on Issues:	Position on Issues:
Needs of Negotiators:	Needs of Negotiators:
Strategies and Tactics:	Strategies and Tactics:

Listening Skills: A Powerful Key

Unfortunately, not enough negotiators know how to be good listeners. And negotiators who are poor listeners miss numerous opportunities. Statistics state that the normal, untrained listener is likely to understand and retain only about 50 percent of a conversation. This relatively poor percentage drops to an even less impressive 25 percent retention rate 48 hours later. This means the recall of particular conversations will usually be inaccurate and incomplete.

Since listening skills are taken for granted by many negotiators, many communication problems develop. To be a good listener, you must attempt to be objective. This means you are going to try to understand the intentions behind your counterpart's communication, and not what you want to understand. With everything your counterpart tells you, you must ask, "Why did he tell me that?" "What does he think my reaction should be?" and "Was he being honest?"

The best negotiators almost always turn out to be the best listeners as well. Why does the correlation exist? Invariably, the best negotiators have been observers of the communication skills, both verbal and nonverbal, of their counterparts. They have heard and noted how other negotiators effectively use word choice and sentence structure. They have also practiced listening for the vocal skills such as the rate of speech, pitch, and tonal quality.

Attentive Listening Skills

Great listening does not come easily. It is hard work. The following suggestions will help you receive the true meanings your counterparts are trying to convey. Including them as part of your management skills will lead to more effective, efficient, and productive negotiations.

- **Be motivated to listen.** When you realize that the person with the most information will usually receive the better outcome in a negotiation, you have an incentive to motivate yourself to be a better listener. It is wise to set goals for all the different kinds of information you would like to receive from your counterpart. The more you can learn, the better off you will be.

- **If you must speak, ask questions.** The goal is to get more specific and better refined information. To do this, you will have to continue questioning your counterpart. Your questioning sequence will be moving from the broad to the narrow, and eventually you will have the information to make the best decision. The second reason to continue asking questions is it will help you uncover the needs and wants of your counterpart.

- **Be alert to nonverbal cues.** Try to not only listen to what is said but also to understand the attitudes and motives behind the words. Remember, the negotiator does not usually put his or her entire message into words. For example, there is considerable difference between the auditory and behavioral cues emitted by the negotiator. While his verbal message may convey his or her honesty and conviction, his or her gestures, facial expressions, and tone of voice may convey doubt.

- **Let your counterpart tell his or her story first.** The old adage "People like you so much more when they are doing the talking" is applicable here. Ask questions to learn more about your counterpart and build rapport early on in the negotiation.

- **Do not interrupt while your counterpart is speaking.** Interrupting a speaker is not good business for two reasons. First, it is rude. Second, you are very likely to cut off valuable information that will help you at a later point in the negotiation.

- **Fight off distractions.** When you are negotiating, try to create a situation where you can think clearly and avoid interruptions. Interruptions and distractions tend to send negotiations back to square one or at least create the possibility of a severe setback. Employees, peers, children, animals, etc., all have the possibility of distracting you and forcing your eye off the goal. If you can, create a good listening environment.

- **Do not trust your memory.** Write everything down. Any time someone tells you something in a negotiation, write it down. It is amazing how much conflicting information will come up at a later time. If you are able to correct your counterpart or refresh his memory with facts and figures shared with you in an earlier session, it will give you a tremendous amount of credibility and power. Writing things down may take a few minutes longer, but the end results are well worth the time.

- **Listen selectively.** With a questioning goal in mind, you can listen for words and nonverbal cues that add to the information you are seeking. When you hear specific bits of information, such as your counterpart's willingness to concede his or her price, you can expand with more specific questions.

- **Give your counterpart your undivided attention.** When negotiating, it is important to look your counterpart in the eye when he or she is speaking. The goal is to create a win/win outcome and have the counterpart willing to negotiate with you again. To do this, your counterpart needs to believe you are a fair, honest, and decent person. One way to help achieve this goal is to pay close attention to your counterpart. When he or she is speaking, look eyeball-to-eyeball. Watch what message the eyes are sending. What is the nonverbal behavior? Many experienced negotiators agree that with careful attention, you can tell what your counterpart is really thinking and feeling. Is he or she lying or telling the truth? Is he or she nervous or desperate to do the deal? Careful attention and observation of your counterpart will help you determine his or her true meaning.

- **React to the message, not the person.** It was mentioned in an earlier point that we want our counterpart to be willing to negotiate with us again. This is not going to happen if we react to him or her and offend his or her dignity. It is helpful to try to understand why your counterpart says the things he or she does. If you are going to react, pick on the message and not your counterpart personally.

- **Try not to get angry.** When you become angry, your counterpart has gained control in triggering your response. In the angry mode, you are probably not in the best frame of mind to make the best decisions. Emotions of any kind hinder the listening process. Anger especially interferes with the problem-solving process involved in negotiations. When you are angry, you tend to shut out your counterpart.

- **It is impossible to listen and to speak at the same time.** If you are speaking, then you are tipping your hat and not getting the information you need from your counterpart. Obviously, you will have to speak at some point so that your counterpart can help meet your needs and goals. However, it is more important for you to have your counterpart's frame of reference. With you having your counterpart's information, you will be in control of the negotiation. When you are in control, you will be acting and your counterpart will be reacting to your proposals. It is usually better to be the one in the driver's seat.

In conclusion, when you want to improve your listening skills, a good rule to remember is that you have two ears and one mouth. You should use them in their respective proportions. To succeed in negotiations, one must understand the needs, wants, and motivations of one's counterpart. To understand those needs, one must hear. To hear, one must listen.

Strategies and Tactics

Here are five of the 101 strategies and tactics that appeared in Peter B. Stark's and Jane Flaherty's book, *The Only Negotiating Guide You'll Ever Need.*[5] Strategies and tactics are the tools of negotiation that help you maintain or gain leverage.

Strategy One: Principle of Walk Away

We are fond of the saying, "In any relationship, the side with the least commitment to continuing the relationship will have the most power." If you have the ability to walk away from the bargaining table when the tide turns, you will have more leverage.

---

[5] Stark, D. B., & Flaherty, J. (2003). *The Only Negotiating Guide You'll Ever Need.* New York: Broadway Books.

Example:

Recently Peter's wife, Kathleen, bought a daybed for their daughter. The price of the bed was advertised on sale for $177. When she went to pay for the bed, the salesman told her there was an additional $25 delivery fee. Kathleen was upset about the fee because she had scheduled me to pick up the bed in my company truck. She left the store with the $25 delivery fee still intact, because the clerk said that the fee was non-negotiable, whether they delivered it or not. In fact, the clerk said if they did not charge the fee, they would lose money on the bed.

Kathleen went home and called two other outlets of the same store. To each one, she stated she wanted to buy the daybed advertised on sale, and if she picked it up herself, would there be any delivery charge. In each case, the other outlets said no. Armed with this information, she called the first store and requested to have the delivery charge removed, or she would cancel the transaction and take her business to another outlet. They agreed.

One week later, when we went to pick up the bed, the clerk behind the counter stated that the person Kathleen had talked to did not have the authority to remove the delivery charge. After going back and forth, Kathleen finally said, "Just give me my $177 back and we will buy the bed somewhere else." At that point, the clerk gave in and waived the fee.

If you are always able to walk away, you will retain the ability to create a win/win outcome.

Strategy Two: Principle of the Higher Authority

Being the person who does not have the final say in a situation can create a very powerful position. In this principle, someone has to go to someone else to gain final approval. More times than not, I have seen an experienced negotiator work the best deal he could, then run off to a higher authority. Usually, the negotiator will come back from the higher authority with instructions for an even better deal.

Example:

A president of a corporation works the very best deal he can on a piece of machinery. The initial price of the equipment was $450,000. He gets the salesperson to concede to a price of $428,000 with three months of use before the first payment. The president agrees to the deal but needs to take it to his board of directors for final approval.

The president comes back from the board of directors with the approval to sign the contract at not more than $425,000. He even went back to the salesperson and apologized for the board being so tough. In this case, the board could have been real or apparent.

Strategy Three: Principle of Splitting the Difference

When two parties are still apart on an issue and the negotiation seems to be at a stalemate, one can offer to split the difference with the other counterpart.

Example:

Seller: You are selling your car and you do not want to come down any further than $5,000.

Buyer: You want to buy the seller's car, but you do not want to pay any more than $4,800.

Solution: Since you are $200 apart, either the buyer or the seller could offer to split the difference ($200 divided by 2) and do the deal for $4,900.

Strategy Four: Principle of Is That Your Best Offer?

A great way to practice your negotiation skills is to simply get in the habit of asking salespeople, "Is that your best offer?" You will be amazed how many times the price will be lowered or an added benefit provided in response to this question.

Example:

An IT buyer is purchasing six new laptops and asks the salesperson, "Is $1,199 your best price per unit on this model?" The salesperson responds, "They are going on sale for $999 next month. Let me check with my manager to see if I can get you that price today if you buy all six." Simply by asking, the buyer saves $200 per unit.

Strategy Five: Principle of Never Saying Yes to the First Offer

Have you ever felt that you paid too much for something? The chances are you felt that way because you did not have to fight hard enough for your outcome. When someone says yes to your first offer, you walk away with one of two feelings. First, you think you paid too much. If that feeling is not enough to make you have buyer's remorse, you probably will think something is wrong with what you just bought.

Example:

Supervisor: "Would you be willing to start for $12.50 per hour?"

Employee: "Sure, $12.50 an hour is great. When do I start?"

In this case, the employee would be better off responding, "Since I currently make $12.50 an hour, I would need to make at least $13.50 before I considered switching positions."

☛ Tips for Success

Negotiations

1. Recognize that everything in life is negotiable! From deciding who takes out the garbage in your house to determining what price you will pay for a product or service to merging your car in rush-hour traffic, everything is negotiable.

2. Go for win/win outcomes. Find out the needs and goals of your counterpart. Yes, you do have a vested interest in helping your counterpart meet his or her needs and goals, especially if you ever have to negotiate with that person again.

3. Aim high. The outcomes will always be better with high aspirations.

4. Have sound strategies and tactics. If you know the strategies and tactics plus the counter strategies and tactics, you will always be able to maintain a balance in the negotiation.

5. Plan ahead and research well. If you wait until you enter the negotiation to do your planning and research, you will be like a ship out at sea without a sail and rudder. You will move with your counterpart, but without strategic direction.

6. Listen more than you speak. To create a win/win negotiation, you will need to understand needs and goals of your counterpart. It is impossible to do so without being a great listener.

7. When you do speak, ask great questions. The more you learn and understand about your counterpart's needs, the easier you will find it to create a win/win negotiation.

8. Learn to effectively read nonverbal communication. Remember, only 7 percent of the total message comes from the spoken word.

9. Utilize strategies and tactics. Strategies and tactics are the negotiator's tools that help maintain or gain leverage.

10. In most negotiations, you will have the ability to walk away. Remember, the side with the least commitment to the relationship usually holds the most power.

Chapter 16

Delivering Extraordinary Customer Service

> "There is only one boss. The customer. And he can fire everybody in the company from the chairman on down, simply by spending his or her money somewhere else."
>
> – *Sam Walton*

We recently conducted an extensive training program for the local division of a large international company on the art of providing extraordinary customer service. As we began the training program, we asked each class of participants this question: "In the customer's mind, what constitutes great service?" Throughout the program, there was a consistency in each group's responses to the question, with the following topics being mentioned most often.

What Constitutes Great Customer Service?

Treat Customers as Real People. Without exception, treating customers as real *people* emerged as the number one example of how companies committed to providing their customers with outstanding customer service. In today's age of electronic wizardry, it is not uncommon to be able to complete an entire business transaction with a company without ever having spoken with a live human being. This is great, if your needs are routine and you are proficient in navigating through a maze of digital challenges before finally making the right connection to solve your problem.

In other words, if at 11:30 p.m. you are wondering what the balance on your charge card is, accessing an automated system to find out your current balance is a real plus. If, however, you have just opened your most recent statement, only to find that you have been billed twice for the same transaction, you definitely want to connect with a live person who will assure you that they will fix the problem, right now! Even though customers can proficiently utilize an automated system, what they really value is finally making a connection with a person within a company who values them, treats them with respect, and fixes their problem.

Watch Your Attitude. So often we hear a customer comment, "The person I talked with had a lousy attitude!" Research consistently shows that customers stop doing business with a company for the following reasons.

- They moved away.

- They developed friendships with other companies.

- They left for competitive reasons—better pricing, more services, etc., from a different company.

- They were dissatisfied with the products or the service.

- They left because of an attitude of indifference on the part of an owner, manager, or customer service representative.

What is especially interesting is that the list above is presented in descending order, from the least mentioned reason for leaving to the most frequently mentioned reason for stopping doing business with a company. While less than 3 percent of the respondents in the survey sited moving as a reason for stopping doing business with a company, as many as 65 percent sited an attitude of indifference as their reason for leaving.

Attitude is all in the customers' perception. And just what is their perception? It is important to understand that for our customers, their perception is reality for them. Whether it be good, bad, or neutral, their perception is very real for them. And just how do they form their perception? To keep it simple, a customer forms his or her perception when the expected service fails to meet, meets, or exceeds the expectation of what they expected to get. We can go to extraordinary lengths to help ensure that we provide a great product or service, but if our customer meets with a representative of our company who demonstrates a lousy attitude, the customer will leave with the perception that the company does not really care about its customers.

Fix the Problem the First Time. Customers are quick to acknowledge that from time to time, problems arise. It is not so much the problem that customers have trouble dealing with, but how the problem is solved. No one has time in his or her hectic schedule, nor patience, for problems that just will not go away. Nothing is more frustrating than having to deal on an ongoing basis with a company that just cannot seem to resolve a customer complaint.

It is estimated that approximately 70 percent of customers experiencing dissatisfaction with either a product or service will do business with your company again if the problem is resolved in their favor. The reason for their continuing loyalty to your company, even after a problem existed, is that customers build trust with a company that has taken care of their problems in the past. They feel confident that should problems arise in the future, your company will again resolve them to their satisfaction.

Be Honest with Customers. So much of a customer's perception about customer service deals not with the product or service, but with the relationship between the customer and the company. Customers enter into a relationship with a company with the basic assumption that the company will deal with them honestly. Companies do not build customer loyalty solely by being honest with customers. Customers expect honesty. Customer loyalty is built when it costs a company something to be honest. Do the right thing, always, and the right thing is to be honest with customers—all customers, always.

Practice the Art of Follow-Up. Customers today expect to be treated with dignity and honesty and to have their problems resolved in a timely manner. What they do not expect, and what companies committed to providing customer service are routinely providing, is the practice of the "follow-up" call. Companies that are dedicated to providing memorable customer service see the follow-up call as one more opportunity to interact with the customer and leave the customer with a positive feeling about the company.

Following a challenging transaction in which the customer experienced difficulty getting his or her needs met, a representative from the company calls to check in with the customer. The company representative asks if the problem has been resolved to the customer's satisfaction. Companies committed to following up after difficult transactions know that this gives them the opportunity to check in with the customer to see if the problem has been resolved to the customer's satisfaction. If the problem has been adequately handled, the customer will most likely be impressed that the company cared enough to check back with him or her. If the problem has not been resolved to the customer's satisfaction, the company is provided with yet another opportunity to correct the problem and satisfy the customer.

Developing a Customer Service Strategy

When we conduct customer service seminars, we ask the participants, "What is the purpose of business?" The response most frequently made is, "The purpose of business is to make money!" While all of us in service-related fields are attentive to the bottom line and looking to make a profit, there is much more to the picture than just profits. Certainly, profits are a must in order that we stay in business. There is little arguing the fact that without profits, we will eventually go out of business. However, successful companies in today's super-competitive market know that focus on profits alone will not ensure prosperity. Successful companies, rather than dwelling strictly on profits, focus on how to win over and keep a customer loyal for life. In addition to strategies designed to attract and keep customers, these companies focus on creating an experience in which customers are so satisfied that they tell other customers. No amount of advertising can do for you what happy customers can do by telling others about their positive experience with your company! The following pages will describe strategies designed to attract, win over, and keep a customer loyal to your company for life.

Understanding the Customer Service Triangle

The ultimate goal in creating a service culture should be to focus the energies and talents of every member of the organization on the quality and service they provide to the customer. It is important to note that the quality and service standards evident in a company will be defined and determined not by the organization, but by the perceptions of the customer. Profitable companies know that creating a service culture is much more than just having a "customer service" department that functions well in most circumstances. Companies that have highly effective customer service strategies know that in order to be successful, every employee, regardless of whether he or she has direct contact with customers, must be fully committed to making sure that things turn out right for every customer. If we expect every employee, wherever they are in the organization, to be totally committed to putting the customer first, there must be a clearly defined and easily understood customer service strategy. Such strategies typically consist of three things: (1) a vision of the service we will provide our customers, (2) people who are committed to providing top-notch customer service, and (3) systems that are customer friendly.

Customer Service Triangle

Visually, using a pyramid as a model, the customer is at the center, or more specifically, the very reason for our existence. Without the customer, ultimately, we have no business. At the three points of the pyramid, supporting the customer, are (1) vision, (2) people, and (3) systems.

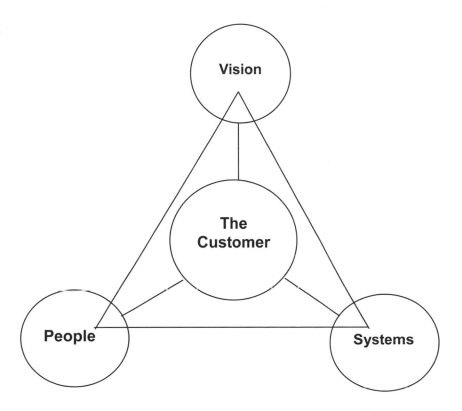

Pyramid Point One: Vision

When it comes to providing quality customer service, you must first have a vision, or a clear mental picture of what that service looks like. It is impossible to deliver extraordinary customer service unless all employees have a clear understanding of the company's standards for and commitment to providing service to its customers. One way to understand vision is to use the analogy of a jigsaw puzzle. Just as you cannot recreate the puzzle without looking at the box top, you cannot expect outstanding customer service unless all employees have a clear mental picture as to what that service looks like.

Defining what you are trying to ultimately accomplish with and for your customers helps your people understand the rhyme and reason of the work they do for your organization. Companies with well-defined customer service vision statements clearly convey to employees the idea of "what's important around here." Even employees who do not interact with customers on a day-to-day basis see the "big picture" and make decisions accordingly.

Perhaps the biggest advantage of having a vision, though, is that it provides a detailed definition of what good service means, both as it relates to the company and the customer. When a vision is clearly communicated to employees and is consistently used as a measure, is the company's chances of getting great reviews from its customers accelerate dramatically.

Clearly, having a well-thought-out customer service vision is critical. A clear vision identifies the following:

- Who are our customers and what do they want?

- How will our employees interact with our customers?

- What are our organizational values? What's important here?

Pyramid Point Two: People

You can have a great vision, but without the right people to bring it to life, the whole strategy can backfire. Unfortunately, in reality, it only takes one poor employee to destroy what would have otherwise been great service. To help ensure that each customer leaves with a favorable impression, the following factors must be considered:

- **Hire the right people.** Take great care to hire the kind of employee who can provide the service spelled out in your vision. A person can have degrees, credentials, and expertise, but if he or she is not nice to people, customers will not form a positive perception about your company's service. In the selection process, kindness, caring, compassion, and unselfishness should carry more weight than years on the job, salary history, and educational background. In addition, hire people who demonstrate a high level of personal self-esteem. People who have high self-esteem will treat your customers more positively. It is extremely difficult to treat someone with courtesy, dignity, and respect when you do not feel that about yourself.

- **Place the emphasis on the outcome, not the function.** Everyone in an organization has a function that he or she performs. They may answer phones, take orders, fill orders, schedule work, invoice the customer, etc. Companies that exceed customers' expectations are masters at placing more emphasis on the outcome than the job function. Looking for ways to satisfy customers' needs becomes more critical than following company procedures to fulfill one's job functions. Regardless of the job description, serving the customer is everyone's responsibility.

- **Value those who service the customer.** There is a saying that goes, "If you are not directly serving the customer, you had better be serving someone who is." Unfortunately, often customer service positions hold little value in an organization. Frequently, they are entry-level positions held by people who are anxious to get the experience behind them and move up in the organization. Companies like Starbucks Coffee and In-N-Out Burger know that customers' contacts with representatives make a lasting impact and hire employees accordingly. Once hired, those companies continue to place a strong emphasis on the value of the contribution to the company made by the customer service representative. These companies have figured out that to the customer, the front-line employee is the company. A company can have a great customer service strategy, but if the front-line employee does not live up to it, the customer leaves disappointed, perhaps never returning again.

- **Provide training for those who serve the customer, either directly or indirectly.** There is a high turnover rate in customer service positions. People leave these positions because they feel undervalued, overworked, and frequently, not trained adequately to handle customers' demands. Leaders in service-oriented organizations know that it is critical to provide new employees both formal and informal training opportunities. Certainly, a new employee must become familiar with the company's product, policies, and procedures. Just as important, though, is that the new employee become familiar with the company's philosophy regarding customer service. Nordstrom, a company noted for its outstanding, personalized customer service, practices both formal and informal training. To help new employees learn the Nordstrom philosophy, the company relies heavily on socialization with the new employee's peers and supervisors to teach that unique brand of customer service delivered by Nordstrom.

Service leaders also understand that producing exemplary service means ensuring that everyone—not just the customer contact person, but anyone who has an impact on customer satisfaction—has a thorough knowledge of what it takes to get the job done right. To help build this level of understanding, many organizations cross-train their employees and require all employees, regardless of their level in the organization, to spend time on the "front line" interacting directly with customers. Creating "switch-hitters" gives companies a greater service capacity. Requiring employees other than customer service representatives to interact with the customer helps all employees understand the challenges faced by customer service representatives. Further, it says to the customer service representative, "We know firsthand that you have a challenging job and we value your contributions."

Pyramid Point Three: Systems

In addition to having a vision and great people, systems are needed to deliver the service and product to the customers. The service systems are the logistics, policies, procedures, and tools the employees have at their disposal to deliver the service to the customer. Whether a system has been formally designed, or just happened, one thing is sure. Eventually, a system will evolve. When systems evolve on their own, they will usually evolve in a pattern of corporate self-convenience, becoming corporate, rather than customer friendly. What is the difference? A customer-friendly service system is one that makes things easy for the customer. A corporate-friendly system is one in which systems are designed for the ease of the organization and its employees, not the customer. The organization may run smoothly, but customers may not feel that the system is working to benefit them.

The following tips can help you develop customer-friendly systems:

- **Develop a service blueprint or plan.** Examine your cycle of service. Start by identifying the processes involved in the delivery of the service and estimate the time needed to deliver the service. Add to the blueprint steps that customers must take to complete their transactions. After developing a service blueprint, many organizations have been able to visualize how unfriendly their systems are. Blueprinting systems has shown organizations just how many forms, policies, and procedures stand between the customer and the employees' ability to deliver outstanding service. Strive to fine-tune systems so that the delivery system appears, from the customers' vantage point, almost effortless.

- **Listen to your customers.** Once you have developed and implemented service systems, listen continuously to feedback from your customers. Customers' needs and expectations change over a period of time. Value their input and respond accordingly. One industry that has become an expert at meeting customers' ever-changing expectations is the fast-food industry. Not only have they responded to the frantic pace at which we live our lives by delivering fresh, hot, tasty food within 90 seconds of our placing an order, but they all have "value" meals competitively priced. In addition, many now are including the nutritional value of the food, either on the menu or on the paper wrapping the food product. This industry knows that continuously seeking customer input and responding to their expressed needs guarantee a place in the highly competitive fast-food market.

- **Remember the customer is ultimately the boss.** Getting people to focus on the customer when designing systems is no easy challenge. It seems to be human nature to design systems that are originally customer friendly, only to see the systems, over a period of time, be modified to become more convenient for departmental or organizational considerations. Blockbuster and Hollywood Video had a lock on the DVD rental market, until Netflix changed the game by offering to deliver movies to our mailbox and letting us keep them as long as we want them. Ultimately, if customers do not like the service and delivery model you provide, they can and will fire you!

Managing Customers' Perceptions

Customers make decisions about who they do or who they do not do business with based on their perceptions. What is customer perception? The customer's perception is the difference between what the customer expected and what he or she received. When customers interact with a company, they leave with either a positive, neutral, or negative image of their transaction, based on their expectations. The challenge is how to manage the transaction with each and every customer so that they all leave with a positive impression about the interaction.

Just how do customers form their perceptions? The following list identifies common methods customers use when forming their perceptions:

- **Comparison.** Today's consumers are highly informed, competitive shoppers and know price, value, and quality. Using the Internet, with a few key strokes, they can compare what you have to offer with your competitors. If your product or service is competitively priced and good value for the money, what may be the deciding factor for the customer is the quality of the service received from customer service representatives in your company. All things being equal, customers want to do business with people who treat them with respect and convey to the customers that their business is valued.

- **First experience.** When it comes to providing great customer service, first impressions are critical. Often when a customer's first interaction with a company is positive, the customer gains confidence in the organization and does not look for reasons to find dissatisfaction with the company. Initially connecting with an employee who is positive, cheerful, and intent on meeting the customer's needs does a lot to build customer confidence and loyalty. Or initially, was the online ordering experience easy to complete and the delivery as expected?

215

- **Past experiences.** Customers doing business with a company expect a certain type of service based on their past experiences. If the last time they did business with you they experienced a battle trying to achieve their needs, they will approach the next encounter with you armed for battle.

- **Reputation.** Companies that have great reputations for providing quality services experience fewer customer challenges and more positive interactions with their customers. Why? Because when you have a great reputation, people trust that you will fix problems to their satisfaction.

- **Media.** To a large extent, the media helps shape our perceptions as a consumer. We have learned that faster, bigger, quieter, smoother, etc., is better. The media, through advertising, allows us all to be informed, educated consumers. We form perceptions based on a company's ability to deliver what the media says we have a right to expect. Social media can make or break a company. One consumer review can spread to thousands of consumers and create an even longer lasting image of a company than any news piece or paid advertisement can.

Regardless of what we think about the service we provide, what ultimately counts is the customers' perception about that service. Customers' perceptions are reality for them. Managing our delivery system so that customers' unique needs are met, or delivering service that exceeds their expectations, is our challenge. It is important to note that in today's competitive marketplace where customers are continually expecting more for their dollar and more in the way of service, if you deliver all that you say you are going to deliver, and in the time you said you would deliver the product or service, the customer will not be raving about your company. After all, you just gave him or her exactly what was expected. Competition today is brutal, and you do not get customer points leading to long-term customer loyalty unless you deliver more than the customer expected.

Dealing with Angry or Difficult Customers

Even if you followed all the recommendations previously given for providing great customer service, the truth is that you would still occasionally encounter an angry or difficult customer. In reality, they are out there and some of their anger has nothing to do with you; you just happened to be in a position where they could vent and take it out on you. From experience, we have found the following ten tips to be helpful in dealing with that occasional challenging customer who seems determined to ruin your day:

- **Develop a positive mental attitude.** When a difficult customer wants to go one-on-one with you, make a decision to stay positive. Say to yourself, "I can handle this. That's why I'm here. Not just anyone can do this job. I'm the right person for the job." Giving yourself positive messages like these does two things. First, it helps increase your confidence while dealing with challenging circumstances. Second, it helps you convey a more confident presence in front of the difficult customer. When customers sense you are confident with the situation, they often calm down and become more open to your suggestions for resolution of their problem.

- **Let the customer unwind.** We sometimes jokingly say, "You can tell an angry customer, but you can't tell them much. Don't try!" Trying to interrupt an angry customer will only escalate the situation. Most likely, the customer has been rehearsing what he or she is telling you long before actually making contact with you. From the customer's perception, he or she has been abused, inconvenienced, or in some other way, wronged. This customer needs you to know all the details and does not want you to try to stop the conversation, even if you think you have a good solution. From experience, we advise that in these difficult situations you let the customer unwind.

- **Respond first with a personal level of interaction.** When customers are "venting," they want two things to happen. First, they obviously want their problem solved. In addition, most angry customers have a need for you to understand how their problem with your organization personally impacted them. Responding with "I understand how upsetting that must have been" or "I'm concerned about what happened, let's look into it" conveys to an angry customer, I care about not only the problem, but how the problem has affected you. In today's competitive market, successful service organizations are finding that connecting with customers on a personal level is one way to attract and keep loyal customers.

- **Reward the customer.** When customers complain, thank them! Research indicates that approximately 96 percent of all customers who have complaints about either your service or products do not complain directly to you, but rather, take their business to a competitor. Research further indicates that unhappy customers will tell eight to ten people about their dissatisfaction about your organization. With today's social media, the potential to tell hundreds or thousands of people about their unhappiness in an instant is reality. This type of advertising is not what your company wants! So next time you encounter a challenging customer, thank the person for giving you the opportunity to fix the problem. Remember that once you have fixed the problem to the customer's satisfaction, most challenging customers will remain loyal to your organization. The reason? They trust you to take care of future problems.

- **Keep your cool.** Your response in dealing with an angry customer helps set the tone for the interaction with you. If you lose patience and become angry with him or her, the situation is sure to escalate. If the customer raises his or her voice, lower yours. Lowering your voice forces the customer to lower his or her voice in order to hear you and has a general calming effect on a difficult situation. Some customers may be particularly difficult for you, but not so challenging for other coworkers. When you need their support, ask for help.

- **Stay objective; do not get hooked.** Some difficult customers, for whatever the reason, delight in the fight. In order to engage you, they dangle a hook, such as, "You folks never do anything right" or "You're always screwing up my account. Can't you get anything straight?" They want the challenge and have put you in a position where you feel you need to defend yourself or your company. Once you do, the hook is set and the fight is on. Make a conscious decision not to bite the hook. To help you refrain from the fight, visualize a rusty fishhook baited with something foul and say, "The hook is nasty. I'm not biting!" Instead of defending yourself or your company, ask questions like, "What is it that appears incorrect?" or "Could you give me the information I will need to verify that?" Asking questions refocuses the customer on the problem and gives you the opportunity to address the customer's specific concerns.

- **Offer alternative solutions.** Before the angry customer begins to interact with you, most have already decided how you are going to resolve the problem for them. The problem is, that in many cases, their solution and your solution may vary. When attempting to rectify problems, the greater the number of viable alternatives, the greater the likelihood that one of them will satisfy the customer. In some cases, you will need to tell the customer "No." It is more palatable, for example, to say, "We are not able to do that, but we can credit your account if you return the item, or we could repair the defective product for you. What would you prefer we do?" Customers feel more in control if they are allowed to select from more than one potential solution.

- **Take immediate action.** Difficult or angry customers want something to happen—right now! Chances are they have been doing a slow burn for some time about their perceived mistreatment. Saying "Sounds like there might be a problem. We'll look into it and get back to you" will only further incense them. Be specific about what you will do. Even if you cannot resolve their problem immediately, tell the person what action you personally will be taking. Give a specific time frame so that he or she knows what to expect, and when it will happen. For example, "I am not able to access that information, but the people in our customer service department will be able to help you. I think that I have all the details they will need to research this problem. I will give the information to customer service and you can expect a call from a representative within the next four hours. If you still have questions after talking to them, please give me a call. Will this work for you?" Assuring the customer that you are taking some action, even though the entire problem may not be quickly resolved, helps diffuse challenging situations.

- **Bring the incident to a polite close.** When you have determined an acceptable course of action, review the steps that will be taken to resolve the customer's problem. Check with the customer to see if you can help in any other way. Finally, close the conversation by once again thanking the customer for bringing the matter to your attention and giving you the opportunity to resolve the problem.

- **Follow up to ensure satisfaction.** Organizations that are intent on raising their levels of customer service often make it a practice to follow up with difficult or challenging customers. After the matter of concern has been resolved, they often check back with the customer a week or so later to determine if the actions taken have been satisfactory to the customer. In most cases, the customer is satisfied and pleased that their business matters enough that you would call back to check the outcome. In those cases where the customer still is not content, remember that this follow-up call gives you yet another opportunity to make it right!

Providing great customer service is not easy. Today's customers are better educated about their rights, more demanding, and increasingly raising their standards for what is acceptable service. It is getting tougher to impress them with anything less than outstanding, memorable service. Although challenging, today's successful organizations know that they must rise to the challenge in order that not only their product but their commitment to service set them apart from their competitor. Attracting customers is easy. Keeping customers loyal to your organization is the challenge. With so many choices, customers will continue to do business with companies that not only provide a great product, but great service. Upholding high levels of service will help ensure that when a customer declares loyalty, it is with your company!

☞ Tips for Success

Customer Service

1. Start first with a clearly defined vision of what customer service in your area of influence looks like. Make sure that each member of your team has the same vision.

2. Help each team member understand both the "big picture" related to customer service and how what they do contributes to creating happy, satisfied, loyal customers.

3. Interview and select new employees cautiously. Make sure those you hire can meet high customer service standards and deliver the service you have spelled out in your vision.

4. Listen to input from your front line people or those closest to the customers. They know best what the customer expects and often can make specific recommendations to improve service.

5. Be a role model for providing excellent customer service, both externally and internally. The way members of your team treat customers reflects the way you treat customers.

6. Make sure you value and recognize the efforts of those on your team who consistently deliver high-quality service. Consistently delivering top-notch service in a demanding marketplace is not easy.

7. Look for alternatives when dealing with challenging customers. The more options you can offer the customer, the more opportunity you have to demonstrate that you understand and intend to fix their problem.

8. Stay objective when dealing with angry customers. Don't bite the hook! Listen for facts and look for solutions.

9. Remember, no matter how great your service is, it only takes one person to destroy great customer service. Watch your attitude and the attitudes of those on your team.

10. Confirm customer satisfaction. Practice the art of following up to ensure satisfaction.

Chapter 17

Solving Problems Creatively

> "The significant problems we face cannot be solved at the level of thinking we were at when we created them."
>
> *– Albert Einstein*

Supervisors are typically forced to address problems early in their supervisory career. In fact, you were probably hired or promoted because you demonstrated a good grasp of how to solve problems. Effective supervisors are good problem solvers. This chapter offers some models and tips to help improve your problem-solving abilities.

It Starts with a Positive Attitude

You all know people who take a problem and then blow it all out of proportion. Instead of taking a proactive approach to solving the problem, they take a reactive approach and make the lives of those who are in contact with them absolutely miserable. Problems are not only a part of the job; they are a part of life. The only person who truly does not have any problems is a dead person. We suppose that could mean the more problems we have, the more alive we really are!

A good goal for supervisors is to be a person who views problems with a positive attitude. One thing we can promise, problems do not get any easier with a negative attitude. There are at least five characteristics that people possess who approach problems with a positive attitude.

- **Searchers.** These people search for ways something can be done. They are "possibility thinkers." They look for possibilities and solutions rather than focusing on why something cannot be done. You do not hear phrases like, "It can't be done here," "That won't work in our company," or "They'll never buy in to it upstairs." Instead, you hear possibility thinkers saying things like

"Why not try it," "Just give it a go," or "Let's try something new." Now ask yourself, who would you rather work for?

- **Visionaries.** These people do not let problems defeat them. Negative people are usually paralyzed by problems. When problems come up, they see no other solution. Positive people see problems as minor roadblocks. Positive thinkers know that a better road map is needed to get around the roadblock. If the first course ends with a roadblock, they will look for another path.

- **Courageous.** These people are not afraid to take a risk. Positive people do not have a "prove it to me attitude" before they try something new. They have the courage to try new things and the willingness to learn from mistakes.

- **Focused.** These people point out the positive possibilities change can bring. Negative people usually focus on all the possible disadvantages of the change. Most of us have experienced this scenario: you recommend a solution in a meeting and the negative person is always the first to throw cold water on your suggestion.

- **Optimistic.** These people are optimistic that they can find a solution. If you do not think you can find a solution, you are defeated before you even start. Positive thinkers believe that they are bigger than the problem, not vice versa.

Job Function versus Job Responsibilities

One of the greatest understandings an employee can have is that there is a significant difference between his or her job functions and his or her job responsibilities. Each employee has a specific job function that he or she was hired to do. Job functions are usually well-outlined on job descriptions. For example, an employee who is a welder may have a job description that states he or she will successfully weld each part onto a main assembly. The employee is evaluated by how successfully the welds hold the parts to the main assembly. There is most likely a quality inspection to help maintain high-quality standards.

The difference between function and responsibility is that job responsibilities are much more expansive than job functions. For example, what happens if the welder sees a quality problem on another area of the main assembly? Or, what happens if the main assembly manufacturers do not provide a clean enough surface for the welder to weld to? If the welder solely focuses on the job function, he or she would technically not have to say anything that does not relate to the specific job function—welding. But, if the welder assumes responsibility for building a quality assembly and satisfying the customer, then the job responsibilities say that he or she must help correct or at least point out any problems that are seen.

This is a powerful concept, particularly for problem solving in organizations. The minute employees start saying "That's not my problem because it is not in my job description" is the same minute the organization starts decaying. A company cannot thrive and grow when employees do not take the responsibility to do whatever it takes to satisfy the customer or to uphold a core organizational value. If everyone does not understand what his or her ultimate responsibility entails, the organization will not retain profitability.

Today, there are too many organizations in business that are willing to do whatever it takes to satisfy problems. If you allow people to only satisfy their job function, you are cutting your own throat and then, eventually, the throat of your organization.

Effective supervisors understand the difference between their job function and their job responsibilities. The acceptance of broad job responsibility allows for better and more creative problem solving. These supervisors also encourage the acceptance of job responsibility by their employees. It is this combination of responsible supervisors and employees that make up creative and innovative organizations.

A Problem-Solving Model

Most people do not like problems and try to get rid of them as fast as they can. Their natural tendency, when faced with a problem, is to pick the first reasonable solution that happens to come to mind. Unfortunately, the first solution may not be the most appropriate one and may even lead to larger problems. The following problem-solving model allows for a larger number of alternatives and increases the probability that the final solution will be the best one.

Step One: Define the Problem

The first step in any problem resolution process is to define what appears to be the problem. Write out a problem statement that describes what is going on.

Step Two: Gather Facts, Feelings, and Opinions

The second step is to gain as much information as possible from as many different sources as possible. This step gives you the opportunity to "get smart" and understand the dynamics of the problem. What is happening? Who is involved? What is the impact of the problem? Who does it affect? What are the causes of the problem?

Step Three: Identify the Real Problem

After you gather the facts, feelings, and opinions, it is important to determine whether you are working on the real problem or only a symptom of the problem. This may require restating the problem in a totally different format. Be willing to start over with the real issues if that is what it takes. Why spend valuable time trying to solve something that is not the problem in the first place?

Step Four: Generate Possible Solutions

The next step requires generating as many solutions as possible. In this stage, the goal is to generate alternatives. Avoid any judgment or evaluation of solutions at this point. *(Later in this chapter we will discuss brainstorming and fishbone diagrams as ways to generate a variety of alternatives.)*

Step Five: Evaluate Alternatives

After you have generated as many alternatives as possible, you want to start deciding which alternative will be the best solution. Now is the time to be critical about the different alternatives. Be cautious or hesitant when everyone agrees on which alternative to take. When no one is willing to challenge the prevailing viewpoint, you are likely to find yourself in the midst of something known as "group think," where some team members have concerns, or disagree, but no one wants to speak up and go against the prevailing viewpoint. So the decision is implemented even though people really believe that it is not the right decision. Critical evaluation and honesty allows for better decisions and will ultimately result in a better solution to the problem.

Step Six: Select the Best Alternative

Once you have evaluated all the alternatives, you are then ready to pick the one you think will solve the problem in the best way. Most people start at Step One by defining the problem and then move right to Step Six by making a choice. If we do Steps Two through Five correctly and thoroughly, Step Six should be relatively easy.

Step Seven: Gain Approval and Support

Any time you are going to change something, you will always need to rally approval and support. Do not think that the only thing that needs to be done is to select the alternative and then implement it. The negative thinkers will come up with obstacles and a "show me" attitude that must be overcome. It helps if you involve such thinkers in the beginning of the problem-solving process so that they become part of the solution and not part of the problem.

224

Step Eight: Implement Decision

After support has been developed, you are finally ready to implement the decision.

Step Nine: Evaluate Results

If you do not have a follow-up or monitoring system in place that allows you to check results, the chances for success diminish. If people do not know how the results are being measured or that they are going to be held responsible, problem solving becomes a difficult task. When things go right, recognize success. When things go wrong, go back to Step One and start the process again.

These steps in problem solving are known by most experienced problem solvers. Unfortunately, they are frequently not practiced by supervisors. The pressures of the job often result in managers circumventing some of these steps, and successful problem resolution suffers as a result. Go through the full problem-solving process and save yourself time in the long run. Also, you will be assured of getting the best possible decisions.

Cause of Problem or Just Symptom

One of the key questions to address when you are trying to come up with solutions to a problem is whether the cause is really the real cause or just a symptom of the problem. For example, a common problem supervisors face is a lack of quality in production. When asked what the cause of this quality problem is, many supervisors respond that the cause is a lack of motivation among workers.

Once you identify a cause, the next question is "Is that really the cause or just a symptom of the problem?" In this particular example, quality is probably not the true cause of the problem, but just a symptom. Some of the true causes that can be manifested through the disguise of motivation are listed below:

- The employee has not had the proper training.
- The importance of quality has not been communicated.
- There is a lack of coaching and counseling when poor quality occurs.
- There are no consequences for poor quality.

One of our clients was dealing with the problem of poor attendance at their educational seminars. They felt the possible causes of the poor attendance might be due to the following:

- The fees were too high.
- The time of the seminar was wrong.
- They were not spending enough effort on marketing.

After they looked at their organization's two-year track record, it seemed clear that they were not having any problem recruiting and enrolling new members. The problem they were having was retaining people once they were enrolled in the organization. After a careful look at their programs and the feedback given to them by participants, it became clear that poor attendance was a symptom of the real problem, which was poor quality of the educational programs and materials. This realization allowed the client to rethink their programming and to redesign their materials to be better suited to their customers' needs. This change resulted in overall increase in attendance and more repeat customers.

Cause-and-Effect or Fishbone Diagram

One simple and effective technique used to identify causes of problems is the cause-and-effect diagram. It is also referred to as the fishbone diagram. Begin by writing the problem on the right-hand side of the paper and draw a box around it. Then draw a straight line and an arrow that points to the box with the problem inside. Start adding what you feel are the main causes of the problem along either side of the straight line.

What follows is an example of a fishbone diagram. "Low Sales" is stated as the problem. Potential causes are listed on either side of the straight line—Economy/Environment, Quality of Product, Aesthetics of Product, Salespeople, Delivery Schedules, and Price. The economy could be one cause. Poor quality or missed delivery schedules might be another. Salespeople not doing certain things might be still another cause.

Once the major possible causes are identified, you can begin to note possible reasons or implications of the various causes. For example, one of the causes of low sales could be the salespeople. What could contribute to salespeople being the cause? Maybe they are not properly trained *or* they are not following up with customers *or* they are not calling on enough new accounts.

Use the cause-and-effect or fishbone diagram to analyze problems and their causes. This is also a useful technique to use with your department or team. When a small group contributes to creating the diagram, you will come away with a number of perspectives and some good ideas. Once the primary causes are clearly identified, research is conducted to confirm the cause. When the cause or causes of the problem are clear, brainstorming for solutions comes next.

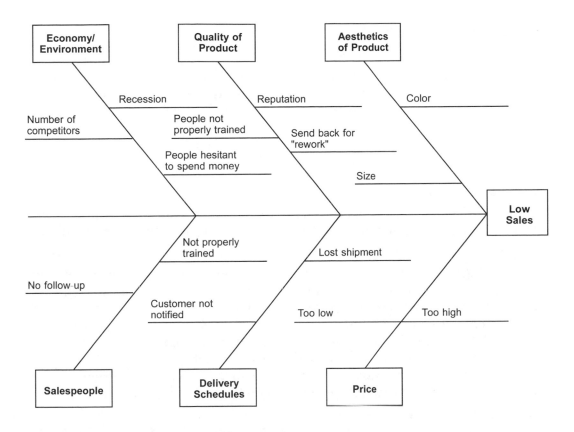

Brainstorming for Solutions

Brainstorming is a process where people use their collective and creative-thinking power to generate ideas. The objective is to generate a list of ideas, topics, or solutions related to a specific subject or problem. There are several advantages to the brainstorming process.

- It involves everyone who may know something about the problem, because the more people you have participating, the better your chances of coming up with the widest possible list of alternatives.

- Brainstorming promotes creativity. Every idea is accepted; wild ideas are encouraged.

- It generates a large quantity of solutions.

It would be helpful to check the seven steps for successful brainstorming as listed in Chapter 12.

Roadblocks to Problem Solving

Even when an organized problem-solving model, like our nine-step model, is used, people often encounter certain conceptual blocks that inhibit the problem-solving process. These conceptual blocks relate largely to individual thinking processes and to the ways problem solvers use their minds when facing problems. Improving your problem-solving skills is often thought of as gaining more information. However, being exposed to more information alone will not improve problem-solving skills. Many of us are challenged with conceptual blocks, or mental obstacles that constrain the way the problem is defined and the number of alternative solutions we find to be relevant. These blocks are largely unrecognized or unconscious, so the only way individuals can be made aware of them is to be confronted with problems that are unsolvable because of them. The following conceptual blocks can hinder our problem-solving ability:

- **Unilateral thinking.** Beginning with a single problem definition, unilateral thinking then pursues that train of thought until a conclusion is reached. No alternative definitions are considered. All the alternatives generated are consistent with the original thought pattern. It is very similar to digging one hole and drilling for oil. If you do not hit pay dirt, keep drilling deeper. In contrast, multilateral thinking is thinking that generates alternative ways of viewing a problem and thus produces multiple definitions. Instead of drilling the oil well deeper, multilateral thinkers drill wider; they pick different places to drill for oil.

- **Past experiences.** A major obstacle to innovative problem solving is that individuals tend to define present problems in terms of problems they have faced in the past. Current problems are usually seen as variations of some past condition. Alternatives proposed to solve the current problem are alternatives that have proven successful in coping with past problems. This becomes limiting when you are facing a completely new set of problems.

- **Forest or trees.** Can you differentiate the forest from the trees? Another conceptual block is the inability to differentiate or separate the major problem from irrelevant problems or background information. Inaccurate, misleading, or irrelevant information must be filtered out to correctly define the problem and to generate appropriate alternative solutions.

- **Artificial constraints.** Just as difficult as it is to filter out noises and to add missing details, it is also difficult for many people to avoid ignoring information. That is, they often constrain or place boundaries around problems so that they are unable to use information before them. The following questions illustrate this point:

- How many animals of each species did Adam take with him aboard the Ark?

- If you had only one match and you entered a room to start a kerosene lamp, an oil heater, and a wood burning stove, which would you light first?

- Do they have a Fourth of July in England?

- Two men played chess. They played five games and each man won three times. How do you explain this?

- A mama bull, papa bull, and a baby bull were in the barnyard. Which one did not belong there?

How long did it take you to answer these five questions? Now check the following "correct" answers to see how you used the "hidden" information.

- None. Adam did not take animals on the Ark. Noah did.

- You would light the match first.

- Yes. Everyone has a fourth of July. Not every country celebrates it as a holiday.

- They did not play each other.

- There is no such thing as a mama bull.

- **Fear of asking questions.** Some people are afraid to ask questions for fear of being perceived as ignorant or naive. Yes, asking questions is a risk. But, in the long run, the person who does not ask questions is the one who appears ignorant.

- **Biases against thinking.** There is a particular conceptual block in our culture against the kind of thinking that uses the right hemisphere of the brain. Left hemisphere thinking is concerned with logical, analytical, linear, or sequential tasks. Thinking using the left hemisphere is apt to be organized, planned, and precise. The emphasis in most formal education is toward left hemisphere thought development.

A number of researchers have found that the most creative problem solvers are able to solve problems in both the right and left hemispheres, switching from one to the other as needed. Creative ideas arise most frequently in the right hemisphere, but must be processed by the left.

Conceptual blocks cannot be overcome all at once because most blocks are a product of years of habit-forming thought processes. Overcoming them requires practice and thinking in different ways over a long period of time.

Problem Solving

1. Be optimistic in approaching the problem. Remember, that for most things, somehow, somewhere, there is a better way.

2. Focus your energies on what can be done, not on what cannot be done.

3. Recognize that your job responsibilities are always much larger than your job function when it comes to solving problems.

4. Generate as many possible solutions to the problem as you think of through brainstorming.

5. Evaluate and select the best alternative.

6. Determine whether you are solving the real problem or only a symptom of the problem.

7. Gain approval and support of team members who are involved before implementing the decision.

8. Transform yourself from a unilateral thinker to a multilateral thinker. Multilateral thinking generates alternative ways of viewing a problem.

9. Challenge "sacred cows" where knowledge justifies it.

10. Ask questions. The more information you have, the better you will be at solving problems.

Chapter 18

Creating a Motivating Environment

"What I do best is share my enthusiasm."

— *Bill Gates*

A frequent complaint from many supervisors is that their employees lack motivation. Supervisors feel this lack of motivation is responsible for most of the problems they encounter, from tardiness to a lack of productivity. The big question is, "How do I motivate my employees?" This chapter will define motivation and explore how to use it in the workplace.

One of the first questions we need to address is, "Is it really possible to motivate anyone?" Most people will agree we can motivate ourselves, but many of us have tried a myriad of different ideas and we still have not created motivation in another person. This is because you cannot motivate anyone! What you can do is create an environment that is conducive to motivating someone. You can also create an environment that will demotivate someone. Motivation is an internally generated phenomenon. It is a feeling that each of us develops internally and it causes us to act. As supervisors, our focus should be on how we can develop an environment and a relationship with our employees that foster the action of motivation.

What Is Motivation?

Motivation can best be described as the internal drive to fulfill a need. Each of us has specific needs. These needs translate into drives that we act on through specific behaviors. Drives are action-oriented and provide an energizing thrust toward goal accomplishment. As we act on the behaviors (through drives), we satisfy our needs. As our needs are satisfied, the intensity of the drive subsides. A more succinct explanation is that people do what they think they have to do in order to get what they think they want. As supervisors, if we truly want to motivate individuals, we have to fully understand their needs and goals. If we can understand the needs and goals of our employees, we have a good possibility of showing them the appropriate behaviors that will help them satisfy their needs. And those appropriate behaviors will be the behaviors that satisfy our needs and goals.

There is a big difference between internally generated motivation and just getting someone to move. Technically, the term "motivation" can be traced to the Latin word "movere," which means to move. Motivation is an *inner state* that energizes and activates, or moves, a person toward a goal. Historically, supervisors have been quite effective in providing the external motivation to get employees to move: "If you don't work faster, you will be fired." Most likely, the employee will begin working faster because he or she does not want to lose the job. But is the increase in productivity due to an inner push or an outside threat from the supervisor? The supervisor was able to move, not motivate, the employee. Most likely, the employee will produce just enough not to be fired, but the employee will not produce what he or she would be truly capable of if internally motivated.

Creating a Motivational Environment

The best supervisors have the most productive people who are also happy. The real challenge for supervisors is to design incentive systems that encourage high performance *and* also engender high employee morale. To accomplish this objective, supervisors should employ two general approaches to employee motivation.

- **First, they should examine the overall system of rewards in their organization from the employees' point of view to ascertain its potential for motivation.** This is best done by asking the question, "What do my employees expect when they complete a task?" This expectancy theory basically proposes that people regulate how much effort they put into their work based on what they expect to get out of it. More specifically, this theory states that employees will be motivated to perform well if they believe that meaningful rewards or recognition will result from their hard work and that there is a reasonably high probability that hard workers can become high performers.

- **The second approach focuses on shaping employee behaviors so that they are consistent with the expectations of management.** This is referred to as operant conditioning or reinforcement theory. Behaviorists argue that if we want to understand why employees do the things they do, we should examine the events that occur after a behavior that encourages or discourages similar future behaviors.

Positive Reinforcement

Positive reinforcement consists of linking desired behaviors with positive outcomes. When an employee does something you like, you should respond in a manner that is rewarding to that person. How can you motivate a marginal employee to improve? The following six-step model shapes behavior with positive reinforcement.

Step One: Describe the Goal or Target Behavior

The target should always be related to performance. What specifically must the individual do to become a high performer? Answers such as work faster, be dependable, or take initiative are too general. "Answer the phone in a more professional manner" should be replaced with, "When you answer the phone, say, 'This is XYZ Enterprises, Donna speaking. How may I direct your call?'" State the goal or target behavior clearly.

If the target behavior is actually a complex chain of behaviors, divide it into a chain of smaller successive behaviors. It is best to find a smaller series of steps that you can reward rather than to wait to reward the individual when the entire task is completed. In other words, acknowledge small successes.

Step Two: Check the Technical Skill Level

Make sure the individual possesses the technical skill required for the job. If low performance is due to lack of natural ability or training, provide the training and information to set the employee up for success.

Step Three: Select a Meaningful Reward

Make sure that you know your employees well enough to provide an appropriate reward that will be meaningful to that person. For some employees, additional responsibility can be motivating; for others, it might be verbal recognition. Still others may be energized by being given the responsibility to train a new team member or comp time off after the completion of a challenging project.

Step Four: Provide Positive Reinforcement

Make all positive reinforcement based on the employee moving closer to the target behavior you desire. If the employee receives the same reward at performance level two as at performance level five, the supervisor's reinforcement actually discourages improvement. This is what happens when everyone in the organization is given the same raise as a reward.

Step Five: Administer Immediate Rewards

Administer rewards immediately following each improvement in behavior. In animal studies, one can imagine how little learning would take place if a reward would be delivered two hours after a desired behavior had occurred. While this principle appears obvious in animal research, it is frequently violated in everyday management practice. Most managers and supervisors give positive feedback when it is convenient for them, not when the employee would be most reinforced by it. Feedback on the negative consequences of an employee's performance is often delayed for months by the supervisor. No wonder we have problems with motivation!

Step Six: Use Intermittent Reinforcement

As the desired behavior becomes a reality, change from a continuous reward structure to an intermittent reinforcement schedule. Administering a reward every time a given behavior occurs is continuous reinforcement. Administering rewards on an intermittent basis means administering the same reward each time, but not every time it is warranted. Neither approach is clearly superior, but they both have trade-offs. Continuous reinforcement represents the fastest way to establish new behavior. In contrast, partial reinforcement is a very slow process and it is resistant to extinction. For example, an employee who is praised every time an accurate report is written will quickly learn that you value accuracy. But what happens when you are on vacation and there is no one to offer that praise? That behavior becomes prone to extinction.

In contrast, partial reinforcement, although slow, is resistant to extinction. Gamblers in Las Vegas are excellent examples of partial reinforcement outcomes. Some people stay motivated to win long after they should have stopped an unsuccessful behavior!

Meaningful Recognition

Feeling appreciated and recognized are two of the most powerful motivators available to the supervisor. The question then becomes, "What is meaningful recognition?" Recognition is meaningful when tailored to the individual being praised. Instead of the usual "grip and grin" so many managers employ to thank someone for the job they have done, the manager should tap into the uniqueness the individual brings to the job.

One way to explain this uniqueness is to look at a painting an artist creates. This painting is a unique contribution, in many ways a gift that the artist is giving to society. If the artist is good enough, the painting might even have a commodity value.

Lewis Hyde, a poet and essayist, describes this concept when he states, "It is the cardinal difference between the gift and commodity exchange that a gift establishes a feeling-bond between two people, while the sale of a commodity leaves no connection.[6]"

If we only value and recognize the commodity side of our relationship with employees with the dollars we pay them, then we are undervaluing the uniqueness and gifted nature they bring to their jobs. Human work is not just a commodity. If we feel we are just a commodity and that anyone qualified could do our job, we begin to lose our motivation.

Our motivation intensifies when we, and others, recognize the gifted nature of our work. Try to value the uniqueness of each employee, recognizing that his or her work is a gift. Every employee has different strengths that we need to recognize. We cannot forget that motivation is a feeling. Recognizing people's unique strengths helps tap into that feeling.

Recognition Suggestions

The recognition suggestions on the following page were generated by seminar participants. It is well-documented that two of the strongest motivators available to supervisors are recognition and praise. If you are able to customize these ideas or suggestions, they will help you build a more motivated and engaged workforce, and it will cost nothing more than your thoughtfulness and time.

---

[6] Hyde, L. (February 12, 1983). *The Gift: Imagination and the Erotic Life of Property.* Vintage.

Recognition Suggestions

Brainstorming Results: Ways to Recognize Employees

- Ask employees for their opinions.
- Write a thank-you note to employee.
- Put a letter of recognition in employee's personnel file.
- Have your boss say thank you or send a letter of appreciation to employee.
- Do something unexpected (buy a coffee mug, bring flowers, etc.).
- Give a special parking place.
- Award "Employee-of-the-Month."
- Award "Employee-of-the-Year."
- Increase employee's responsibilities.
- Recognize employee's birthday or work anniversary.
- Give employee a special project.
- Take employee to lunch.
- Take employee to lunch with your boss.
- Post a memo of recognition in public area (company bulletin board).
- Attach a Post-it Note that says "Great!"
- Bring doughnuts or food.
- Recognize or praise employee or team in a group meeting.
- Give employee a plaque or something for public display.
- Write article about accomplishments in company newsletter.
- Give employee time off with pay.
- Provide employee with business card.
- Recognize someone via electronic mail.
- Listen—really listen—to employee.
- Share a reward you receive with your employees.
- Teach employee something new.
- Send employee to training.
- Have employee train or teach others.
- Have employee fill in for you during your absence.
- Call to say, "Job well done."

Ensuring High Motivation

There are several helpful suggestions to ensure that high motivation is obvious in your department. You can develop an environment that makes internal motivation a reality in your employees' lives.

Set high expectations with clearly defined objectives. When you ask people the question, "What accomplishment are you most proud of?" most will describe an accomplishment requiring significant effort to complete. Many managers think that pushing mediocre employees to higher accomplishments requires too much effort. There is no doubt, it does require tremendous effort. But the problem with allowing mediocre or poor employees to continue at their present levels is that the cycle of low motivation also continues. There is nothing motivating about mediocre performance. It takes guts to set higher standards and then hold your employees to them. As employees rise to meet the new standards, increased feelings of motivation are fostered in the workforce.

Reward people for meeting high expectations. If you set high standards for your employees, then you need to celebrate and recognize success when achievement occurs. One of the biggest complaints from employees is that they work incredibly hard to meet deadlines, and then no one recognizes them for their extraordinary effort. As you recognize and reward people for accomplishment, you must be sure the rewards you are bestowing are important to the recipients. As we learned earlier in the chapter, different things motivate different people.

Praise and recognize your employees often. This statement sounds so easy, and yet, it is incredibly difficult to practice on a steady basis. It is easy to find things that seem more important to do, like manage the cash flow, solve a customer's problem, pick up a new job, answer an employee's question, or complete a report. However, if time is not taken to praise and recognize your employees, motivation and morale will wane. Then you will have a lot more things to do!

Explain the "big picture." People are motivated when they feel they are making a significant contribution to the organization. Many times, employees do not understand how significant their contribution really is. One way to demonstrate an employee's contribution is to ask the question, "What happens when the employee does not do his or her job?" Often, when the employee does not do his or her job properly, it adversely affects someone else. That someone is usually another employee, department, or customer. You need to demonstrate how each employee's contribution is connected to the overall purpose of the organization.

Find out the needs and goals of your employees. Different things motivate different people. If you are going to successfully motivate your employees, you need to find out what is motivating to each employee. Employees may be motivated by challenge, recognition, promotions, responsibility, or learning something new. Once you identify what motivates your employees, you need to merge that individual's needs and goals into your needs and goals and then into the needs and goals of the organization.

Develop your self-esteem and the esteem of others. People with high self-esteem are more motivated and productive. We feel best about ourselves when we have challenged ourselves and have accomplished something. This means that you constantly have to set goals for yourself. Keep your employees involved in the goal-setting process. It is important for supervisors to remember that, by position alone, your behavior and actions have a tremendous impact on the way employees feel. Take the responsibility to help others feel heightened self-esteem.

Get others involved in the goal-setting process. If people are not involved in setting goals that affect their job performance, there is a strong chance that they may not be committed to the goals. Employees resent it when management sets goals that affect them without soliciting their input and then holds them responsible for achieving those goals. The problem with a goal not being "our goal" is that if we do not see the importance of achieving the goal, it is hard to find the motivation to act on the task. We tend to spend our energies on other tasks we perceive as more important; we tend to spend our energies on our own goals.

Develop a positive mental attitude. Being around a negative person is not motivating. Negative people tend to take energy away, not instill motivation. If your attitude is negative, it is probably a reflection of your vision. If things are getting worse, what is exciting and motivating about a negative future? Be positive—people will gravitate toward you, rather than push away from you.

Develop a "that's no problem" attitude. Have you ever worked with someone who could take a small problem and then blow it all out of proportion so that everyone could share their misery? There are some people who spend a lifetime looking for problems and then complain about them, rather than solve them. It does not take much of a person to handle life—or a job—when everything is going right. It does take a special kind of person to successfully handle an environment when things go wrong. The most valuable employees are the ones who can look at problems and come up with solutions. They say, "We have a problem, but that's no problem." Leo Buscalia, noted author, speaker, and professor, stated it the best when he said, "The most successful people in life are the ones with the greatest number of viable alternatives."

Be a positive role model. If you want to be a motivator, you need to be motivated. You cannot demand top performance from your employees if you are unwilling to give your very best effort. When employees witness your willingness to contribute extraordinary effort, they are much more willing to go the extra mile.

☞ Tips for Success

Motivation

1. Remember, motivation is something internally generated. It is impossible to motivate someone else. But you can create an environment where people find it easy to become motivated.

2. Take money off your list of motivators. If money does work, it is a short-lived motivator, usually only lasting until the first increased paycheck is cashed and spent. In most cases, you don't have much control over how much people are paid, but you do have tremendous control over your ability to recognize an employee for his or her contributions.

3. Make the reward meaningful to the employee. People are motivated by different rewards. Tailor your praise, recognition, or other motivator to the specific recipient.

4. Link your rewards to good performance.

5. Ensure that the employee has the capabilities to do the task you are asking him or her to do.

6. Administer rewards and feedback immediately following the positive behavior you desire.

7. Choose one idea each day from the list of Recognition Suggestions and pass it along to the people in your work group.

8. Maintain high expectations. Low or mediocre expectations that are accomplished are not motivating.

9. Get your employees involved in the goal-setting process. When it is also their goal, the opportunity for successful accomplishment increases.

10. Be motivated! You will never motivate anyone unless you are highly motivated yourself.

Chapter 19

Earning Followers in Your Leadership Role

"Management techniques are obviously essential, but what matters is leadership. Leading the whole organization needs wisdom and flair and vision and they are another matter; they cannot be reduced to a system and incorporated into a training manual."

– Anthony Jay

The title of this chapter makes an interesting point: it is difficult to be considered a leader if you have no followers. What makes this point so significant is that you *can be* a supervisor or manager and have no followers—all you need is employees. To take this point one step further, you can still be considered a supervisor, even if you are ineffective in your ability to direct the actions of your employees. But this is simply not the case for a leader. A leader must have followers.

Leader or Supervisor?

Historically, there have been countless attempts to define and differentiate leadership and management. Some have made statements such as "managers manage things, whereas leaders lead people" or "management is about efficiency, but leadership is about effectiveness." Other differentiations have stated that leaders possess "charismatic" or "heroic" qualities that allow them to influence people to positive change. In contrast, managers maintain the status quo.

When we ask supervisors and managers to distinguish between managers and leaders, the responses invariably paint a more positive picture for the functions a leader fulfills than for the functions a manager or supervisor fulfills.

A typical list of the differences between a leader and a manager/supervisor was generated by a group of participants at several of our seminars. The compiled information is outlined in the following chart:

Differences between Leader and Manager/Supervisor

Leader	Manager or Supervisor
Builds trust	Manages things
Motivates	Controls
Empowers people	Maintains power
Develops vision	Assigns goals
Has integrity	Plans
Develops commitment	Demands compliance
Coaches and counsels	Disciplines
Asks	Tells

When people look at this list, there is no question in their minds which role they would like to play in the organization. They want to be the leader! But our problems begin in this discussion when we ask the question, "Wouldn't a good manager motivate his or her employees?" The answer is most definitely "Yes." "Wouldn't a good manager also build trust with his or her employees?" Once again, most likely "Yes." On the other side of the coin, "Wouldn't a good leader also plan and even force compliance or discipline in some instances?" The reality of this discussion is that good managers and good leaders will probably rely on both sets of skills or behaviors at different times.

Let's look at an example to illustrate the value of being able to employ both leading and managing skills. A young man worked as an ambulance driver for two years and was then promoted to the position of field training officer. This meant that most of his time was spent working with people new to emergency medicine. As a field training officer, part of the job was motivating new employees to continually learn new aspects of emergency medicine. Another part was to coach and counsel people when things did not go right. He was also responsible for having a vision and developing a plan on every call they responded to. People said he was a great leader in very traumatic situations. A nervous rookie once said to him, "I feel calm when I work with you." The young man not only felt comfortable leading his partners, but also leading bystanders, police and fire personnel, and the patient's relatives. He encountered very few situations where he lacked the confidence that he could not handle the situation. But, on any given moment, he might change roles and become incredibly directive, many times even forcing compliance in the process. If the situation warranted it, he might be *telling* the patient what to do, *telling* the bystanders what to do, and even *telling* his partner exactly what to do. Do these telling/directive behaviors make him any less of a leader? We feel strongly the answer is "No," that both sets of behaviors are required by both leaders and supervisors at different times.

There is one significant difference between a leader and a manager that needs to be addressed. The one significant difference between a leader and a manager deals with where their power source is based.

Leadership, unlike management, is not a formal position. It is a relationship. Managers receive their power and authority from the organization. This is what we call legitimate or position power. Leaders may hold no position power. Their power base comes voluntarily from the followers. Ideally, we would like both of these power bases to be harvested by one person. That is, the manager is also the leader. In this scenario, the manager would have both the power of the organization and the power of the people. In the event that this is not the case, a leader potentially has more power. The reason is that the manager takes the power from the organization and then diffuses that power down through his or her employees. The opposite is true for the leader. The leader has the followers' power invested in him or her. This infusion of power from the followers creates an incredibly powerful source for action.

From time to time, managers say that with formal authority, they can always fire a negative informal leader. This is most definitely true. The only thing you can almost guarantee is that another informal leader will crop up and almost always have more power than the one who was fired.

The goal for all of us would be to perfect the skills and traits of both the leader and the manager. When we have the power sourced from both directions, we have the ultimate opportunity to create positive change for our organizations. The bottom line is that leadership and management are two distinctive and complementary systems of action. Both are necessary for success in our increasingly complex business environment.

Types of Power

There are four distinctly different types of power that a leader or manager may possess. Each type of power has different qualities and carries different weights in our efforts to lead people.

Type One: Power of Position

This is formal authority that gives you the sacred right to tell someone else to do something. There are times when we do not agree with our boss, and we may even state our disagreement to him or her. But then we go ahead and bow to our boss's demands. We may have responded to the power of the position. Most people respond to this power base because they practice a simple management concept called, "I want to keep my job!"

Type Two: Power of Competence

To be successful as a leader or manager, you need the competence to do the job. John P. Kotter, a Harvard Business School professor, states that effective leaders seem to have life experiences that demonstrate their competence.[7] These life experiences may consist of industry and organizational knowledge, relationships in the firm and industry, reputation and track record, and even formal schooling (although Kotter stated very little of these competence characteristics were developed by our educational system). According to Kotter, most of our competence is developed on the job as a part of our post-educational career. The more competent others perceive us, the more likely they will be to follow us.

Type Three: Power of Personality

If you have ever worked with someone who has rubbed you the wrong way, then you know the power of a personality. Personality defines the specific skills and behaviors you utilize to help build relationships. The easier it is for others to talk to you, listen to you, and work with you, the easier it will be for them to respond to your wishes.

Type Four: Power of Character

This component is your "credit rating." Do the people you interact with perceive you as trustworthy, credible, and honest? Do they perceive you as having high personal morals, being sincere, and possessing strong ethics? You acquire this power from the trail of promises you have kept and the expectations you have fulfilled or exceeded. To put this another way, you have done what you said you were going to do and therefore people trust you. What is interesting about this component is that you get no credit for being truthful when it costs you nothing to tell the truth, for being honest when it costs you nothing for being honest, for being dependable when it costs you nothing to be dependable. The measure other people use to determine your character is how far out you are willing to go to maintain your standards of honesty, dependability, trustworthiness, and credibility.

---

[7] Kotter, J. P. (March 18, 1999). *What Leaders Really Do.* Harvard Business Press.

As we look at these four bases of power, one is clearly managerial—the power of position. The other three fit under the realm of leadership. But these three components also need to be developed simultaneously by managers and supervisors. Of the four components, the power of character is the most powerful of all. If people do not trust you or do not perceive you as credible, it will affect every other aspect of your relationship.

Many people feel that the power of personality is equally powerful to that of character. They back this up with examples of "charismatic" personalities. One way to differentiate between the power of personality and the power of character is to ask the question, "Have you ever met a salesperson that you liked, but did not trust?" If you did not trust the salesperson, you probably did not buy his or her product or service. If his or her character was the most powerful factor, you probably would have made the purchase. You may even have some friends that you like, but do not trust. It is in these feelings where we find the difference between character and personality.

We have looked at the value of the four types of power and we have also discussed the importance of both managing and leading. Now, let's take a look at what we consider to be more "managerial-oriented" activities as well as activities considered to be more "leadership-oriented."

Managerial-Oriented Activities

Management, by definition, is getting things done through others. The science of management developed during the 20th century because organizations grew incredibly large. The goal was to be able to mass produce something in the most efficient way possible. Management practices and procedures were largely developed to cope with large, complex organizations. Without order and consistency, outputs such as quality, productivity, and profitability are adversely affected. To control these outputs, the following "managerial" functions are critical:

- **Planning.** Planning is the science of setting goals and targets for the future, and then deciding what steps you will take to achieve those goals. You can have the greatest dreams and goals in the world, but without the plan to turn the goals into a reality, you will not get far.

- **Budgeting.** Budgeting is the part of the planning process where finances are allocated to help achieve the plans.

- **Organizing.** Organizing means creating a formal structure that can accomplish the plans.

245

- **Staffing.** Once we have the plan and the organization in place to support the plan, the next managerial function would be to staff the jobs with qualified individuals, communicate the plan to those individuals, and delegate responsibility to carry out the plan.

- **Controlling and Problem Solving.** Controlling involves looking for variations from the plan. Managers look for the deviations, formally and informally, by means of reports, meetings, and other tools. Once deviations are identified, we then plan and organize to solve the problems.

Leadership-Oriented Activities

While management focuses on coping with complexity, leadership is about creating positive change. Part of the reason leadership has become such a needed quality in the past 20 years is because of the rapid changes and innovation we discussed in the first chapter. The net result of these changes is that doing what was done yesterday, or even doing it 15 percent better, is no longer a prescription for success. Major changes are necessary to survive and compete effectively in today's environment.

Steven Covey, author of *The Seven Habits of Highly Effective People,* says, "The leader is the one who climbs the tallest tree, surveys the entire situation, and yells, 'Wrong jungle!' But how do the busy, efficient producers and managers often respond? 'Shut up! We're making progress!'[8]" To help you focus on ways to ensure you have followers to lead, we have summarized aspects critical to your leadership development.

Developing a Vision. Leading an organization, whether it is a company or a small work unit, to positive change begins with developing a vision. A vision is a clear mental picture of a desired future outcome. If you have ever put together a large 1,000-piece jigsaw puzzle, the chances are you used the picture on the top of the puzzle box to guide the placement of the pieces. That picture on the top of the box is the end result or the vision of what you are trying to turn into a reality. It is much more difficult, if not impossible, to put the jigsaw puzzle together without ever looking at the picture. An organization without a vision is like a person trying to put together a jigsaw puzzle without ever seeing the picture on the box.

Effective leaders will create and articulate a clear vision for their organization or unit. A good vision is clear and compelling. It works like a magnet, pulling people toward it.

---

[8] Covey, S. (November 9, 2004). *The Seven Habits of Highly Effective People.* Free Press (revised).

Below are some benefits of a clear vision:

- **It ensures that all employees are moving in the same direction.** This means that all employees are working toward the same end result.

- **It helps overcome adversity.** Employees are more willing to tackle problems that get in the way of achieving the vision.

- **It helps create motivation.** If the leader is committed to and excited about his or her vision, the excitement is contagious. Employees will be more motivated to work toward the vision and will tend to focus on the positive rather than dwell on the negative.

- **It provides a guide for decision making.** A clear vision will help employees determine the right path when it comes to problem solving and decision making. For example, if the vision for your department includes providing superior customer service, employees will make decisions that support that vision. If an employee has to decide whether to return a customer's call now or wait until tomorrow, a vision of superior customer service tells the employee to make the call now.

Aligning People. In management, we staff the organization to fulfill certain functions. Leadership involves connecting and aligning people to the true purpose of the organization. This means communicating the vision and helping the employees see how they fit into the vision. The employee is a piece of the puzzle, and he or she helps create the overall picture. He or she needs to know how critical each piece is to the overall success of the organization. For example, a local health-care provider's mission statement says, "It is our mission to improve the health of those we serve with a commitment to excellence in all that we do." While the mission is apparent to a doctor or nurse, what does it mean to a housekeeper? Ideally, the housekeeper should be able to connect what she does—clean hospital rooms with a commitment to excellence—to helping improve the health of the patients in her rooms. To keep motivation and commitment up, each employee must be aware of the importance of the work he or she does, and how successful completion of the work helps the team and organization achieve its mission.

Motivating People. In a true management capacity, controls are in place to identify problems. At the end of the month, we have reports that tell us how we did on productivity, quality, and profitability. The problem of relying solely on the controls is that we find out we have problems at the end of the month when it is too late. The problem has most likely already done its damage. What we need is to have each individual inspired and motivated to do things right the first time. If we are solely using controls, we are pushing the employee to conform. Pushing employees does not satisfy basic human needs for achievement: a sense of belonging, recognition and self-esteem, and a feeling of control over one's life. Such feelings touch us deeply and create a powerful response.

Good leaders create a motivating environment. They articulate the vision and help align employees to the role they play in fulfilling the vision. They also give employees the power to be involved and make decisions that affect their work. Leaders solicit and value the feedback of their employees. And leaders help employees realize the vision by providing coaching, feedback, and role modeling. These activities help employees grow professionally and personally, which enhances their confidence and self-esteem.

Empowering People. By definition, empowerment means to give another person the authority and power to act. This means that the employees who work for you actually have the ability to get things done themselves. The opposite of empowerment is micromanagement. When we micromanage, we oversee every action and decision our employee makes.

What is important to note about empowerment is that it starts with *you*, not with someone above *you*. Before *you* can empower someone else, *you* have to feel that *you* have the power to change aspects of your own life and your area of influence. This is the feeling that *you* can control your own destiny. Developing a vision and then taking action will help *you* take a proactive stance in becoming empowered.

To empower your staff, you must also understand that power is not "zero-sum" based. Zero sum means that there is only a certain amount of power to go around, and if I give up power, I lose, and someone else gains. If I gain power, then you lose power. The problem with seeing power as a finite source is that you spend your time and energy protecting what power you do have. This is time that could be more productively spent, turning your vision into a reality or motivating your staff. The goal is to gain the confidence and understanding that when you empower others, you are taking a risk, developing trust, and creating an enlarged power base. In a sense, you are giving away power to gain power. The opposite is also true. If you do not trust your employees—if you do not give them the capacity to act—then they will most likely not invest their power in you or your vision. By not giving away power to your employees, you lose your own power.

Clarifying Values. The values that you carry with you are the basis for governing your decisions and behaviors. Values influence the relationships you enter into, the significant others you choose, the careers you develop, the family you raise, and millions of other decisions you are faced with each day. In many ways, values are like a moral compass that guides you through life. As a leader, it is important to clarify what values your organization or department is going to represent. What will you be known and remembered for?

One organizational value is being honest with your customers and employees. This sounds easy to live by until a decision comes up where, if you are honest, it costs you thousands of dollars. If you are true to your values, the values will be non-negotiable. When you have this value consistency, people will perceive you as having integrity. Without value consistency, you will be perceived as a hypocrite. Essentially, when you clarify values *and* you live by those values, you are "walking your talk." You are known as a leader who can be trusted. When espoused values (spoken words) and values in use (actions) meet and are consistent, you demonstrate integrity. If espoused values and actions do not meet or are in conflict, you demonstrate hypocrisy.

Building Trust. It sounds so simple: all you have to do is build trust with your employees. But, we know that this is no easy task. The following five points are some suggestions on how you can develop trust:

- **Do what you say you are going to do.** When you tell people you are going to do something, and then you either do not do it or you do something different, people begin to doubt your word. Consistently, do what you say you will do and you will gain credibility and trust.

- **Provide just a little more than expected.** Whether it is additional support and counseling for an employee, going the extra mile for a customer, or going a little out of your way to help a coworker or fellow supervisor, exceeding others' expectations builds trust and loyalty.

- **Be consistent.** If you are consistent, people can predict what actions you will take. When people are unsure of how you will act or react, they tend to proceed cautiously or not at all.

- **Increase responsibility.** One of the fastest ways to build trust with people is to increase their responsibility. By increasing someone's responsibility, you are taking a risk. When you take a risk and people fulfill or exceed your expectations, you develop trust in them. Your trust in them fosters their trust in you. It is a reciprocal relationship, and it is critical for good business and personal relationships.

- **Accept honest mistakes.** Supervisors and managers tend to forget that their value lies in their experience. Their experience comes from making mistakes and learning how to proceed so that the same mistakes do not happen again.

If we do not have the capacity to accept mistakes, then people in our area of influence will refuse to make decisions or take risks. Try not to see failure as failure, but only as a learning experience. Help people learn and grow from their mistakes. Ensure their self-esteem, and people will go out of their way to please you.

Mentoring. Mentoring is just a fancy word for coaching. The power of mentoring is two-fold. It not only builds up the esteem of the person being mentored, it also builds the esteem of the mentor. The reason this concept works so well is that most of us have a deep-seated need to help someone else. By helping someone else grow, we feel good in the process. And, to share something we know costs us very little except our time.

Being Willing to Learn. If leadership is about creating positive change in the organization, then being a leader is about continuous learning. As fast as things are changing, it is almost impossible to maintain any type of expertise. As long as we have a willingness and desire to learn, we have the ability to adapt to new environments.

Becoming an Even Stronger Leader

There are many practical reasons for becoming a better leader. After reading the following paragraphs, you will be able to cite additional ideas that are even more relevant to your work structure.

Recognize the world is rapidly changing. You can decide that you are going to help create change and learn from it, or you can try to resist change. Because of global competition and the rapid increase of information and technologies, many large organizations are eliminating layers of middle management and supervisors to be more responsive to change and to their customers. Knowing this, middle managers need to look forward and see how their talents and energies can be reapplied in the organization. As many managers in large organizations are finding, change is the one thing they can count on. Your ability to adapt to change will significantly impact your organizational success.

Develop a positive mental attitude. No one wants to follow someone with a rotten attitude. There are a lot of things in this crazy world that you cannot control, but the one thing you have complete control over is your attitude. Pick a positive one. Remember, your attitude, whether negative or positive, is contagious. People find it much easier and more personally rewarding to follow positive leaders.

Focus on what you can do, not on what you cannot change. Where are you going to spend your energy? Complaining about things you cannot change or creating the things you can? If you feel your destiny is in someone else's hands, you do not have to take responsibility for your actions. Focus on what you can do and take responsibility. There is power in responsibility.

Lead with your heart and head. We recently heard a manager say that he did not care about people's emotions. He went on to say, "We have a job to get done!" Unfortunately, people are the ones who are going to get that job done. And people have feelings. In fact, everything about motivation and the desire to do good work is based on a feeling. If we do not consider people's feelings, it is impossible to be an effective leader.

Reach out to people who have different perspectives. It is easy to communicate with people who think just like you. It is difficult to effectively communicate with someone who has a differing viewpoint. But if we only have the ability to communicate with people who think like us, we are limiting ourselves from learning new and valuable information.

Become comfortable with the unknown. One of the necessities to becoming empowered is to feel comfortable with the unknown. This is called having the ability to deal with ambiguity. As fast as our environment is changing, it is impossible to know all the facts or have all the answers all the time. If you think you know everything, you are obsolete.

Develop a leadership "tool kit." No one can have all the answers. What you can develop is a "tool kit" of resources that can help to solve problems. If you only have a hammer, you tend to see every problem as a nail. Collect information, and then learn and practice leadership and management techniques. Remember, good leaders never stop learning.

Look for multiple right answers. With information and the environment changing rapidly as it is, we can no longer afford to look unilaterally for one right answer. Become multilateral in your thinking. Search for additional possibilities, not just one solution.

Substitute effectiveness for perfectionism. If you wait until all the available information is in to make your decisions, the chances are you have waited too long. In today's environment, we no longer can afford the luxury of waiting until something is absolutely perfect. We need to ask the question, "What's the goal or purpose?" If we can satisfy the goal, then we are effective.

Develop the flexibility of a sapling. In San Diego, we have beautiful eucalyptus trees. Unfortunately, it seems like every time there is a rain or windstorm, some of the biggest trees blow over. Fortunately, eucalyptus trees are great at dropping seeds that start new saplings. What is amazing is that the wind and the rain do not bother the saplings. They are pliable and just blow with the wind. The large trees are not so adaptable. They snap because they are not able to sway with the changing wind. In today's environment, supervisors need to be like saplings.

In closing, true leaders understand that success does not depend on their titles, but on the values they uphold and the choices they make on a daily basis. True leaders know that leadership is not achieved through technical expertise, but rather is based on an emotional connection or relationship with followers. It is our hope that the insights we presented in the previous chapters will help you with both the technical expertise and "people smarts" you need to be not only a great supervisor, but an outstanding leader!

Finally, we would love to hear from you. If you have suggestions, stories to share, or questions about anything we have written, please contact either of us at peter@peterstark.com or jane@peterstark.com.

☛ Tips for Success

Leadership

1. Recognize that leadership is not a formal position, it is a relationship. If you want to be a leader, you need to earn followers.

2. To be effective, you need to have strong skills in both areas—leadership *and* management.

3. As a leader, your greatest source of power comes from your character. The more others trust you, the more power you will have.

4. Create a compelling, positive vision for yourself as a leader and for your work group. A vague vision is not motivating to you or to your people.

5. Help your employees see how they contribute to bringing the vision to reality.

6. Empower your employees. Give them the freedom to act and make decisions as necessary to get the job done.

7. Clarify the values you will use to guide you and your work group. Values are the basis for governing your decisions and behaviors.

8. Increase responsibilities for your employees. If you are doing your job, your employees should be growing by taking on added responsibilities.

9. Develop a willingness to learn. With the economy and environment rapidly changing, you need to be continuously learning and relearning.

10. Reach out to people who have different perspectives. If you surround yourself with people who think just like you do, eventually your work group's strengths will become their own weakness.

About the Authors

Peter Stark is a consultant, speaker, author, and principal for the past 20 years of the Peter Barron Stark Companies, a management consulting firm located in San Diego, California. His speaking repertoire includes an impressive lineup of programs in the areas of employee engagement, leadership, customer service, leading organizational change, and negotiation skills. His firm is also a leader in employee opinion surveys and leadership development assessments. Peter is one of only a handful of speakers to hold the prestigious dual designation of Accredited Speaker from Toastmasters International and the Certified Speaking Professional from the National Speakers Association.

Peter has been published worldwide in over 300 articles and coauthored six books with Jane Flaherty:

- *The Only Leadership Book You'll Ever Need*
- *Lifetime Leadership Leaving Your Legacy*
- *The Competent Leader*
- *The Manager's Pocket Guide to Leadership Skills*
- *The Only Guide to Employee Opinion Surveys You'll Ever Need*
- *The Only Negotiating Guide You'll Ever Need*

Peter's expertise has been featured by *The New York Times,* Inc.com, CNN, Bloomberg, and *USA Today.*

Peter's career takes him around the world as he helps leaders build organizations where employees *love* to come to work and customers *love* to do business.

Jane Flaherty is a noted consultant, speaker, and author who has worked with the Peter Barron Stark Companies for the past 17 years. Her speaking and training expertise covers a wide range of topics, including leadership, customer service, presentation skills, and negotiation. She also works closely with her clients, designing customized employee opinion surveys, leadership development surveys, and organizational team assessments.

Prior to joining Peter Barron Stark Companies, Jane worked around the world for 15 years as an educator and administrator for the Department of Defense, working in diverse locations such as the Philippines and Germany.